American Icons

AMERICAN ICONS

An Encyclopedia of the People, Places, and Things that Have Shaped Our Culture

VOLUME THREE

Edited by Dennis R. Hall
and Susan Grove Hall

GREENWOOD PRESS
Westport, Connecticut • London

Library of Congress Cataloging-in-Publication Data

American icons: an encyclopedia of the people, places, and things that have
shaped our culture/edited by Dennis R. Hall and Susan Grove Hall.
   p. cm.
  Includes bibliographical references and index.
  ISBN 0–275–98421–4 (set : alk. paper)—ISBN 0–275–98429–X (vol. 1 : alk. paper)—
ISBN 0–275–98430–3 (vol. 2 : alk. paper)—ISBN 0–275–98431–1 (vol. 3 : alk. paper)
  1. United States—Civilization—Encyclopedias. 2. Popular culture—United States—
Encyclopedias. 3. Americana—Encyclopedias. I. Hall, Dennis, 1942– II. Hall,
Susan G., 1941–
E169.1 .A472155 2006
306.0973'03—dc22   2006006170

British Library Cataloguing in Publication Data is available.

Library of Congress Catalog Card Number: 2006006170
ISBN: 0–275–98421–4 (set)
    0–275–98429–X (vol. 1)
    0–275–98430–3 (vol. 2)
    0–275–98431–1 (vol. 3)

First published in 2006

Greenwood Press, 88 Post Road West, Westport, CT 06881
An imprint of Greenwood Publishing Group, Inc.
www.greenwood.com

Printed in the United States of America

The paper used in this book complies with the
Permanent Paper Standard issued by the National
Information Standards Organization (Z39.48–1984).

10 9 8 7 6 5 4 3 2 1

Contents

VOLUME TWO

VOLUME THREE

CONTENTS

Guide to Related Topics

Art and Architecture

Art Fair
Capitol
Coney Island
Crayola Crayon
Dollar Bill
Golden Gate Bridge
MAD Magazine
Mickey Mouse
Mount Rushmore
Olmsted Park
Patchwork Quilt
Whistler's Mother

Commerce, Consumers, and Marketing

Art Fair
Barbie
Betty Crocker
Coney Island
Crayola Crayon
Dollar Bill
Flea Market
Ford Mustang
Halloween Costume
Hershey Bar
Kodak Camera
Las Vegas
Log Cabin
McDonald's

Polyester
Poster Child
Elvis Presley
Scrapbook
Tupperware
Wal-Mart

Community or Civic Identity

Amish
Courtroom Trial
Dollar Bill
Albert Einstein
Golden Gate Bridge
Billy Graham
Gun
Harley-Davidson Motorcycle
Hollywood
Martin Luther King, Jr.
Rush Limbaugh
List
Log Cabin
Mexican-American Border
Miami
Mickey Mouse
Mount Rushmore
Olmsted Park
One-Room Schoolhouse
Patchwork Quilt
Stonewall
Suburbia

Preface

We can best introduce you to these entries by giving you the same description we sent to their writers, when asking them to contribute to the collection. We invited them to interpret a cultural "icon" in an essay for a wide readership, from casual readers in public libraries, to investigating students, to scholars researching patterns in American culture and popular culture. We asked for the essay to make cultural scholarship accessible to the general reader, and also to add to critical understanding of the subject and of its "iconic" character.

The term "icon"—as we pointed out to the writers—is now used everywhere. It has mushroomed in popular usage, coinciding with the growth of interest in popular culture and of popular culture studies. What does it mean when we say some person, place, or thing is an icon? We have speculated about features of people, places, and things commonly characterized as iconic. We have also tested lists of "icons" with various age groups, looking for patterns of recognition, understanding, agreement, and disagreement. We have surveyed scholarly research, studied the programs of recent conferences on popular culture and other fields, and attended many presentations, attempting to identify the popular phenomena which are now commanding attention, and to locate the best understandings of this attention. In the process of these discussions and research, we realized that "icons" generate strong reactions.

We gave writers our hypothesis about features that we came to associate with an icon. These qualities include the following:

—An icon generates strong responses; people identify with it, or against it; and the differences often reflect generational distinctions. Marilyn Monroe, for instance, carries meanings distinctly different for people who are in their teens and twenties than for people in their sixties and older.

—An icon stands for a group of related things and values. John Wayne, for example, images the cowboy and traditional masculinity, among many other associations, including conservative politics.

—An icon has roots in historical sources, as various as folk culture, science, and commerce; it may supersede a prior icon; it reflects events or forces of its time. The log cabin has endured as an influential American icon, with meanings and associations evolving from our colonial past through the present.

—An icon can be reshaped within its own image, or extended in updated images by its adaptations or imitators. The railroads and trains, for instance, have shifted from carrying associations of high technology and the modern, to conveying ideas of nostalgia and a retreat from high technology.

—An icon moves or communicates widely, often showing the breakdown of former distinctions between popular culture and art or historic American culture. Icons like "Whistler's Mother" and the patchwork quilt are both revered as high art and widely accepted as popular art.

—An icon can be employed in a variety of ways, and used in visual art, music, film, and other media. For example, references in text or graphics to Ernest Hemingway or to Mount Rushmore or to the gun add meanings to every artistic text in which they appear.

—An icon is usually successful in commerce. Every advertising campaign, every corporation, hopes to become the next Mickey Mouse, the next Las Vegas, the next Golden Arches.

In our invitations to the writers, then, we suggested that the essays should reveal an icon's origins and changes, its influences, and the meaning of its enduring appeal—and repulsive reactions. When the articles began to arrive, though, we found we had underestimated either the subjects or the authors, or both; the essays were fascinating for many reasons we had not anticipated. We have been surprised by the insights they offer, and pleased to learn much that we had not envisioned having importance, complexity, or charm. And as their numbers mounted to over a hundred, we continued to be surprised by what we learned, and increasingly curious, as the entries touched on related topics from differing viewpoints, and added to the attractive qualities of icons—and to their dubious qualities as well.

These items we call icons hold a depth of significance we had not foreseen; it's fortunate we did not attempt or request any definition of an icon, or of its appeal, because neither would have held true. We sought, instead, the range of meanings an icon holds for people. As we see it still, this range of meanings, plus people's disagreements about an icon's meanings and value, reflect the cultural resonance it holds, and provide the best indication of its character. In other words, a contest of possible meanings and values makes up the drawing power of an icon, and makes it dynamic, rather than static, evolving, rather than securely definable.

There are more icons than any three volumes could address. In making a selection, we have aimed at a representation of various kinds of icons, so that the entries treat principles and modes of differing types. Our arrangement of the icons into alphabetical order illustrates our idea of the equal, or random, relationship among icons, and the curious fact that out-of-the-way places, and small items we take for granted, influence popular thinking as importantly as the hero or celebrity who is touted by media. The entries themselves illustrate a variety of approaches for understanding icons. Indeed, our basic purpose is to furnish useful demonstrations of how to "read" cultural artifacts, to make readers alert to such significant things around us, and to enable readers to interpret them.

Thus these writings should generate thought, not necessarily agreement. They are entries with lively variations in style and method, and often the writer rhetorically "animates" the subject. They present distinct viewpoints, but in ways that are thought-provoking and inviting of response. Icons may well be controversial in their very basis; these entries, separately, and much more in their convergences, should stir question and even dispute.

The entries provide a fund of themes and perspectives for study and scholarship. Among them are intriguing suggestions of possible patterns and modes among icons of differing types, related to such important concepts as identity, generational differences, and myths. Linking many of the essays are intersections of meaning, and webs of associations. To those who are or will be engaged in the study of icons, this collection will bring a wealth of resources, and make them accessible as subjects in the index.

Acknowledgments

We first thank the many people who shared their thoughts and opinions about icons with us as we developed our plans for this collection. These discussions—including the arguments—increased our understanding, stirred our curiosity, and encouraged our efforts to gather together the best voices for a worthwhile forum on the large but mysterious presence in our midst of those people, places, and things we call iconic.

We thank our writers for the help, encouragements, and pleasures they have given us. Some of the contributors we have known through many years of hearing their presentations at popular culture and literary conferences, and sharing critical discussions with them. Others we found as we searched for current writing, scholarship, and teaching on iconic subjects, or in the disciplines which study them; through subsequent conversations with them, we've enjoyed getting to know some very lively and original thinkers. We're appreciative that popular culture scholars ranging from the long-established to new contributors joined efforts with us, so the collection represents the flourishing vitality of popular culture studies. Our energy for this project has not flagged, because we kept hearing, from old associates and new, that they themselves looked forward to the finished volumes with great interest.

We are grateful to Eric Levy for asking us to consider editing a collection of essays on icons, whose suggestion started our thinking and investigation. Eric was then at Greenwood Press, where he was editor of *The Greenwood Guide to American Popular Culture*, essays on research and bibliography co-edited by M. Thomas Inge and Dennis Hall. Eric has moved to the Wesleyan University Press. Since then we have enjoyed having the attentive help of Lisa Pierce with the many questions and issues involved in bringing this collection to publication.

To the University of Louisville English Department and its chair, Susan M. Griffin, we are very grateful for the moral and material support they have given our efforts.

The University of Louisville Ekstrom Library and its librarians have provided help at every stage of our research on icons and preparation of this collection.

The Louisville Free Public Library has furnished many resources necessary for surveying and selecting popular icons, for finding books and articles with perspectives on them, and for fact-checking all kinds of matters from quotations to bibliographies. Their interlibrary loan and information services librarians have given us especially timely, needed help. Ruth Ellen Flint, information specialist at the Highlands–Shelby Park Branch, deserves our special thanks, because we took to her our problems of the most esoteric matters of fact, and she has never yet failed to devise a stratagem for finding the obscure detail which so often has seemed the key to correctness.

Railroad

Arthur H. Miller

The heyday of intercity rail passenger service has passed, eclipsed in the 1950s and 1960s by cars and federal highways as well as by inexpensive long-distance intercity jet air travel. Even so, the railroad lives on as an icon, embodied in powerful electric and diesel locomotives, ubiquitous commuter trains in population centers, great transcontinental freight trains serving global commerce, and even nostalgic preserved scenic and railfan short-line service, often with restored steam locomotives or trolley cars. Unlike other pervasive American images, perhaps, railroads reflect a continuity of contemporary vitality with a distinctive and long heritage tied to American industrial or economic and also geographic development.

By 1996, Americans' love of railroading was best expressed in popular culture, as George H. Douglas found in *All Aboard! The Railroad in American Life* (352). The power and centrality of the railroad image in American life recently was recognized in a 2004 conference entitled "Iron Icon: the Railroad in American Art," whose proceedings were published in 2005 as a special number (14) of *Railroad Heritage,* the periodical of the Center for Railroad Photography and Art.

OVERVIEW OF PERIODS

As railroads and locomotives burst on the American scene in the 1830s and 1840s, they were only one of a number of significant inventions of the time promising irrevocably to alter the character of life on the continent. The railroad's appearance in America was part of a cluster of changes that launched an epic of expansion, as the East Coast–focused United States spanned the North American continent between the 1830s and the 1890s. Through all this development, the railroad's image as a powerful force for change was a dominant national symbol.

European and British precedents led to a U.S. rail network by the 1850s, mostly in the industrial and relatively urban northeast. The unprecedented push into areas unsettled by European descendants by mid-century sparked a crisis of transatlantic consequences as the American union's regional rivalries descended into open civil war, in 1861–1865. This conflict was won by the industrial and rail-organized north, and it settled the hub of western expansion at Chicago—where eastern lines from the Atlantic shore terminated and the new lines west began. The first line of five thrown across the continent to the Pacific Ocean was completed in 1869, and by 1893 the by-then settled continent frontier was declared closed by historian Frederick J. Turner at the Chicago world's fair of that year.

As rail travel erased time and distance it introduced a new culture of standardization: time zones, standard track gauges, and combined or merged rail lines, which swept away local isolations and initiatives; rail terminals and depots recentering communities; new commuter and light-rail lines decentralizing the exploding new metropolises like Chicago and New York (while at the hub grew new skyscrapers); new wealth for (and from) rail builders, financiers, and wholesalers; and a new unified transatlantic, largely urban/suburban culture. The pervasiveness of the railroad in the nineteenth-century United States was signified, even often anthropomorphized, in the image of the locomotive, also an epochal culmination of machine age power and the pinnacle of industrial achievement. Controlled and channeled raw, elemental power—fire, steam, smoke, and iron—in motion, the locomotive sped across the landscape in the daylight, momentarily lit up the rural night, and reached far beyond its immediate visible area through the sound of its mighty, distinctive whistle.

The locomotive, its train, and the people who ran them were also powerfully iconic figures in popular American perception. They represented the best of the new industrial men, the engineers and the conductors asserting their authority over the lifelines of communities and regions and serving as stewards of the lives of passengers and customers. Synchronizing their watches in classic photographs, they appear as men ultimately integrated into the Machine Age—sovereign but subject to the higher, preordained rules of timetables and their subculture's strict social hierarchy. Richard Rhodes observes that for every country boy over four years old and into maturity, one ambition in life . . . was to be a locomotive engineer or, failing that, to ride with one (91).

As rail lines pressed inexorably westward, the locomotive pulling a train symbolized, as in the famous Currier & Ives print "Westward the Course of Empire," the wedge being driven by railroads between the exploding industrial, European-American culture and the retreating and shrinking hunter-gatherer Native American way of life, which was in harmony with nature. As recently as the 1990s this iconic image has been vividly portrayed in the Disney animated feature film *Spirit*, wherein a dark, menacing steam locomotive is the villain for this story, centered on wild horses and Native Americans in western America of the late mid-nineteenth century.

There was indeed a dark or sinister side of the locomotive in this period of its stretching out to encompass and settle the continent. It brought fire, noise, and soot into the heart of pristine nature and bucolic settings. If all the efficiency and standardization broke down, dramatic train wrecks also captured the popular imagination, and many memorable surviving photographic images record these fearsome and somehow wonderful iconic occurrences. In his novel, *The Octopus* (1901), Frank Norris creates in his title a highly visual image of the 1890s railroad, at its peak with the country settled, reaching out with its tentacles to strangle the by-now-subject farmers with confiscatory freight rates for their grain, after having given them easy access to the land. By the 1890s many railroad workers had organized to protect themselves against the monopoly power of the railroads. Labor organizer Eugene Debs arose as an icon of workers' dissent during the 1894 Chicago Pullman company strike, which quickly spread nationwide to the workers on lines that operated Pullman cars, due to the new unions. Distrust by workers and customers led to regulation of the rail lines in the early twentieth century.

Emerging in the 1890s, flourishing into the 1940s, and surviving into the 1960s and some beyond within Amtrak, the new elite high-speed, long-distance deluxe express trains incorporated the best of the sleeper, diner, and club car technology and luxury which had been introduced by George Pullman of Chicago in the years following the Civil War. As longer lines were consolidated from local ones, and as the new transcontinental lines west of Chicago developed, speedy and comfortable transit became a sought-after commodity for elite business and leisure travelers. The major east-west lines especially competed for passengers with their ever-better, faster trains—such

A group of railroad workers standing before a building and alongside locomotive wheels, 1904. Courtesy of the Library of Congress.

as the New York Central's "20th Century Limited" and the Pennsylvania Railroad's "Broadway Limited," which competed and even raced between Chicago and New York in less than a day, over their respective rail rights of way. High society, important businessmen, and, later, entertainers chose their favorite lines to their destinations. Photographers in Chicago stations snapped shots of film stars between trains, for example. Starting in the 1930s Lucius Beeby (later joined by photographer Charles Clegg) brought to the general reading public the beginning nostalgia for the era of great trains of the Gilded Age; soon after, he helped mold an image or icon of a great age of high-speed rail travel in books such as *High Iron*. The glamor and popularity of trains and celebrities were represented in Arthur D. Dubin's *Some Classic Trains* (1964) and *More Classic Trains* (1974), reproducing several hundred images of trains, cars, layouts, menus, celebrity travelers, and routes.

The era of the great trains between the 1890s and the 1940s was characterized by stiff competition which stimulated creative and innovative advertising, to distinguish one from the other among the various lines, which all ran Pullman standardized equipment. By 1948–1949 a change in rail promotion was signaled by the Chicago Railroad Fair, held for two summers on the site of the 1933–1934 Century of Progress exhibition on the lakefront near the Loop. The romance, simplicity, and comforts of long-distance modern rail passenger travel were touted, but without the need to contrast them to the post–World War II automobile boom already underway, or the increasing viability of air travel advanced by technical developments from wartime and new airfields, such as Chicago Midway.

Most major railroads gave up their intercity deluxe and regular passenger service by around 1968. To fill the vacuum, around 1970 the federally-funded Amtrak corporation was established to preserve, through subsidies, the essential and most viable intercity and long-distance trains. In the cities commuter service still carries hundred of thousands of travelers daily, but with a highly simplified service based on conductors to take tickets. This matrix of services provides an alternative to the car in an age of high gas prices, and the image of the railroad is on the rise as an efficient carrier, a modern civilized counterbalance to the age of the automobile since World War II. The train, no longer a monopolizing and controlling power squeezing the populace, offers a lifeline of alternative commuting for many.

At the same time as intercity trains changed, the world trade, especially with Pacific nations such as Japan and later southeast Asian countries, and by 2000 increasingly with China, led to a greatly increasing volume of trade from the West Coast. Thus, train watchers at Flagstaff, Arizona, can see an unbroken series of long Santa Fe freights heading east from southern California ports with goods from Chinese factories. The image of the train is still one of power and even speed, but more an icon of computer-controlled transport efficiency, essentially labor-free compared to the days of steam. A few fortunate men and now women staff the locomotive cabs to wave at youngsters as they pass by.

THE "IRON ICON" ACROSS THE MEDIA AND IN MATERIAL CULTURE

Popular stories about railroaders and their life were the staple of *Railroad Stories,* a periodical which flourished in the 1920s and 1930s—becoming in time *Railroad Magazine,* and later *Railroad* and *Railfan.* From the glory days, stories and articles on railroad subjects appealed to railroaders and to young men especially. Not surprisingly, these pulp stories highlighted the dangers and thrilling experiences of railroad life. In this period the railroad was a ubiquitous presence in American life, with all the romantic and escape images that offered to young people, especially those in small towns and on farms, promises of travel, interesting colleagues, and colorful escapades.

From before the first running of railroads in this country, they had become the subject of song. The first stage of the rail icon was the booster's rose-colored view. It began with the July 1, 1828, publication of the "Carrollton March"—looking forward to the opening of the Baltimore & Ohio Railroad that year (Douglas 353). Railroads were staple subjects of songwriters in the nineteenth century, who wrote tunes printed up as sheet music, to be played and sung at home. This era was the most participatory period for audiences of songs and music relating to trains. As radio came along in the 1920s and 1930s, when rural electrification was subsidized, the rural and Southern audiences for country music identified with the subjects of rail-riding hobo songs by Vernon Dalhart, including his "Big Rock Candy Mountain," which by the 1940s and 1950s was in elementary school song books. By the 1940s, of interest to elite travelers and workers both were the train songs from films and musicals, such as "The Atchison, Topeka and the Santa Fe" from the Judy Garland film *The Harvey Girls.*

As movies, with sound after 1930, evolved and matured, trains provided good settings for action, due to the limits imposed by the compact, fast-moving, standardized and well-known settings. Also, trains continuously have provided the dangerous settings for action films, as in the recent *Mission Impossible*, utilizing the subway train and the added constraint of a tunnel overhead. Fast freights and subways are modes of railroading known to a wide, popular audience and, thus, they reflect the image of the rail icon today. On the other hand, by the 1980s Amtrak had so much become the butt of jokes in John Candy and Steve Martin's *Trains, Planes, and Automobiles* that the company would not let any reference to the organization be shown.

For the specialist railfan there have been 8mm home movies since World War II by amateur train-watchers. Preservation and conversion of these to videotape by the 1980s has provided a major advance in access to railroad sites for a wide popular audience. In the last decade again these videos and photographs have been converted to CDs and DVDs, increasing the likelihood of their ultimate preservation, as well as wide distribution at low cost. The Internet has been a major new distributor of railfan information and of

A photograph showing Union Pacific's 291-ton locomotive, 1930. Courtesy of the Library of Congress.

associated community building, promoting preservation of the railroad as icon.

Making model trains and also toys goes back to the nineteenth century, but this hobby reached a high point in the era of radio, from the late 1920s to about 1950, when listeners' ears were occupied but their eyes and hands were not. After World War II many youngsters were able to own H or HO small scale model train outfits from Lionel and American, archetypically first set up in an oval under a Christmas tree. As with other 1950s images and icons, the model train, with its idealized microcosm of ordered suburban or ex-urban living served by handsome trains, suggests a postwar/Cold War yearning for an idealized, uncomplicated world. The young, mostly male, model railroaders, with their fathers and grandfathers, worked together to create little utopias centered on trains, with all the iconic power and dominance implied, which they could manage, grow, and ultimately control.

On a larger scale have been the preserved railroads and rail museums, of the last forty years especially. These now are in every corner of America and offer a nostalgic, preserved sample of railroad life or glimpse at railroad history. Notable examples include the still-running narrow-gauge Durango and Silverton line in southwest Colorado, since before 1960 a tourist mecca; the Baltimore & Ohio Museum in Baltimore, with its significant collection of early locomotives; and the California Railroad Museum in Sacramento, which includes the collections of the Railway & Locomotive Historical Society and also the Beeby and Clegg photo archive. Smaller, more informal museums are located across the country and are run largely with amateur volunteer efforts.

As in many other popular hobby areas, various collectibles are sub-icons, if you will, of the larger whole. Antique and recovered signal lanterns recall a pre-electronic era of standardized, ingenious labor-intensive communications. Dining china, linens, and servers' uniforms recall and represent the elegant era of the great trains. Posters, brochures, and timetables incorporate increasingly treasured railroad commercial art, as seen for example in Michael Zega's "Iron Icon" conference paper (24). One of Zega's examples is *The Burlington Number One*, with an engineer in the middle of the illustration and flanked by locomotive views and high Rockies scenery, highlighting a new fast locomotive employed by the line. The engineer, the new locomotive, and the scenery reflect in one view the icon the advertisers sought to convey to their would-be passengers, bringing them speed, reliability, and exotic mountain views: the new America of the Machine Age.

WORKS CITED AND RECOMMENDED

Beeby, Lucius. *High Iron: A Book of Trains*. New York: Appleton-Century, 1938.

Douglas, George H. *All Aboard! The Railroad in American Life*. New York: Smithmark, 1996.

Dubins, Arthur D. *More Classic Trains*. Milwaukee: Kalmbach Publishing, 1974.

———. *Some Classic Trains*. Milwaukee: Kalmbach Publishing, 1964.

Iron Icon: The Railroad in American Art, April 22–23, 2004, special number (14, 2005) of *Railroad Heritage*. Madison, WI: Center for Railroad Photography and Art <www.railphoto-art.org>.

Norris, Frank. *The Octopus: A Story of California*. Garden City, NY: Doubleday, Doran, 1928.

Rhodes, Richard. *The Inland Ground: An Evocation of the American Middle West*. Rev. ed. Lawrence: UP of Kansas, 1991.

Zega, Michael. "The American Railroad Advertising Booklet, 1870–1950." *Iron Icon: The Railroad in American Art* 20–25.

Robot

Ira Wells

Robots are our assembly-line workers, space and ocean explorers, household vacuum cleaners, and toy companion pets; they reflect us, and serve our needs and desires. It can also be said that we resemble them, for in our ever-increasing hours connected to electronic systems, whether of robots, computers, cellphones, or Internet, we are under cybernetic controls and leading "cyborg lives"; the cyborg is "an icon of contemporary labor" (Hicks 95, 91).

Since Mary Shelley's fictional scientist Frankenstein jolted to life a hybrid creature in *Frankenstein; or, The Modern Prometheus* (1818), science fiction has explored the hopes and fears of a synthetic android superior to human nature. Shelley's hybrid was a male monster who punished his creator's ambition with horror. In recent years, however, women science fiction writers have projected female cyborgs and robots who liberate women from domination and empower them. In such works as Marge Piercy's *He, She and It* (1991), women's cyberfiction takes up the possibilities raised in Donna Haraway's 1985 essay "A Cyborg Manifesto: Science, Technology, and Socialist Feminism in the Late Twentieth Century," that cyborgs are "potentially utopian" figures for women (Hicks 86). As Brian Attebery explains in *Decoding Gender in Science Fiction*, "according to Haraway, the story of a cyborg assumes no original wholeness, no fortunate fall, no natural order of things that always, somehow, ends up elevating the signs of masculinity at the expense of the feminine" (95). Haraway synthesizes the artificial as a means of liberating the female subject from patriarchal myth and signification.

Haraway's theory points to a related question, though: why is it that, in the popular conceptualizing of the cyborg figure in speculative fiction, the cyborg is coded predominantly as male? The robotic hardware itself—used for radical resignification by Haraway—seems to have been preemptively claimed for the masculine by popular culture. This trend is evidenced not only in the countless examples of male robots and cyborgs in recent science fiction articulations, but also on a more basic grammatical level. English speakers refer to most inanimate entities, from boats to nations, by the female pronoun; technology, however, is different. Linguist David Crystal writes, "The only consistently male trend in personification which the author has heard in recent years is in computing, where word processors and other devices are widely given male pet names and pronouns" (209). Crystal cites the apparently male super-computer Deep Thought as an example. A great majority of science fiction's robots—technically, as sexless as cars and screwdrivers—are popularly understood as "male." Why is it that robots are almost always men, and what, in turn, does that say about men? Moreover, why do robots (generally) so perfectly embody their manliness? Through a pair of popular examples, we can trace the relationship that exists between the masculine and the robotic.

Cinematic representations of the robotic have existed for almost the entirety of the medium's short life—consider Fritz Lang's *Metropolis* (1927)— and robots and cyborgs continue to populate the silver screen with some frequency. While Isaac Asimov's *I, Robot* (1950)—itself given the blockbuster movie treatment in 2004—did much to popularize the anthropomorphized robot character in the popular mind, the prolific Asimov invented neither the term, nor the concept. The word "robot" was first used in the modern sense in a 1920 play by Karel Capek, *R.U.R.* (*Rossum's Universal Robots*); the word corresponds to an old Greek word meaning "forced labor." The origins of the robotic concept—that is, of an invented agent contrived to operate in place of a living being—are, of course, more ambiguous, although Mary Shelley's *Frankenstein* presents one obvious precedent. Like Haraway's cyborg, the Frankenstein monster is not of woman born (indeed, he may not be "human" in any sense—animal parts were used to an uncertain extent in the composition of the monster), and yet his manhood is patent: the monster demands a female counterpart, a wife, for the procreation of children (and for the satisfaction of those manly urges implied therein). Robots were somehow masculine, therefore, before they were even "robots"—or at least Frankenstein's and Pinocchio (who so desperately wanted to be a "real boy") seem to suggest as much.

The qualities of scientific deduction and analytical reasoning are highly valued in science fiction's male icons. The various masculine heroes of *Star Trek* (1966), for example, are frequently able to save themselves (and thus all of civilization) from certain galactic destruction due to a highly developed capacity for scientific analysis. This dispassionate positivism enables the heroes of *Star Trek* to devise weapons that are more effective, and strategies that are more cunning, than those of their (often animalistic) enemies. Examples proliferate; consider the original series episode "Arena," in which Captain Kirk, stranded in a desert environment and locked in mortal combat with an immense green lizard, harvests the planet's natural resources to fashion a diamond-shooting bazooka. Importantly, it is not Kirk's *physical* prowess that saves him (although admittedly, much of the episode's considerable excitement comes from watching William Shatner wallop on the terrible hulk). The episode ends with a revelation: the encounter between Kirk and the Gorn creature was staged by some vastly more powerful species;

Kirk, as the representative of humanity, is allowed to live because he didn't kill his opponent, even when he had the chance. In other words, "Arena" underlines that, in science fiction, the passions are subservient to the intellect. In *Star Trek*, it is science that allows humanity's journey to the stars in the first place, and it is science, ultimately, that saves the men and women of the Federation from the malevolent, and often barbarous, forces of the universe; the animal logic of tooth-and-fist violence is more at home in the jungle than in the stars. In short, science seems masculine, and led by men.

In the *Star Trek* universe, then, who could be more masculine than Data, the synthetic crewmember aboard the *Enterprise* D? Data, an android, is capable of nothing less than perfect logic (and is, therefore, the "science officer"); his "positronic neural network" (his brain) is incapable, in the television series, of the stereotypically feminine quality of emotion. (Apparently, this stereotype still roars in the twenty-fourth century: it is Deanna Troi, after all, who is ship's counselor aboard the *Enterprise*.) Moreover, Data demonstrates other, more traditional codes of hegemonic masculinity. He possesses immense, superhuman strength. Despite his modest frame, Data is the ship's most physically powerful crewmember—often to the chagrin of the Worf character. Furthermore, Data is also the first *Enterprise* male (we know of) to engage in sexual intercourse with a woman. In "The Naked Now"—only the third episode of *The Next Generation*—the sultry Tasha Yar entertains a lingering technofetish, and propositions the android. He seems more than willing to oblige, announcing, "I am programmed in multiple techniques and a broad variety of pleasuring." Thankfully, the steamy specifics of the "robot-on-woman" sex are left to the viewer's imagination.

In *Star Trek: The Next Generation* (1987–1994) the android Data, as played by actor Brent Spiner, embodied such stereotypically masculine traits as reason unencumbered by the "feminine" quality of emotion, superhuman physical strength, and apparent sexual prowess. Courtesy of Photofest.

It would seem that Data's stoic, masculine aspect attracts more than just twenty-fourth-century females. Women in our own century have also taken a liking to the pasty, Pinocchioic robot. There is, apparently, an entire subculture of women in the United States dedicated to worshiping the emotionless super-robot as a love-object. The "Spiner-Femmes"—named in honor of Brent Spiner, the actor who portrays Data—demonstrate a fanatical devotion to all things Data, from attending *Star Trek* conventions, to creating elaborate Web pages detailing their intimate fantasies involving the character, to stalking Spiner himself. While the "Femmes" take their name from Spiner, the actor is in fact not their principal focus; rather, it is Data, Spiner's android alter ego, on whom these women project their fanatical energies. "Fan fiction" (or "fan *friction*" as it is sometimes called) constitutes a primary activity of the Spiner-Femmes. While Data's sex-life aboard the *Enterprise* is restricted by the standards of decency imposed by prime-time television, the peculiar writings of the Spiner-Femmes liberate Data from the draconian impositions of the FCC, and allow him to fully explore his robot sexuality. One Spiner-Femme, known online as "Rosie," authored what proves to be a fairly typical example of the Femmes' fan friction—a work of short fiction entitled "Losing Control: A Data Story." In the climactic scene, Data operates upon Laira, a character unfamiliar to *Star Trek*:

> Data moved his mouth from her thighs to the thin fabric covering her soul and began to warm her even further with his mouth. . . . She had orgasm after orgasm, leaving her dizzy with sensations she'd never felt before. . . . He then executed his voluntary erection, but he was afraid that, being so well endowed, he would hurt her. All he wanted was to make her happy. (http://www .geocities.com/Area51/Nebula/5525)

In this passage, the technofetish surfaces as the central metaphor: as a mechanical and electrical device covered by a skin-like membrane, Data is, essentially, a man-sized vibrator.

In *Star Trek*, then, as with other science fiction articulations, the android figure proves to be deeply masculine—perhaps more masculine than men themselves. Data is physically stronger, more logical, and more sexually virile than his fleshy counterparts. Women, in both the twenty-fourth century and our own, affirm his robot masculinity through sexual desire.

Star Trek, in its plethoric incarnations, amounts to only a fraction of contemporary science fiction; but a similar argument applies to a great number of recent science fiction articulations, which often equate technology with phallic power. Indeed, when James Cameron cast his menacing cyborg assassin in *The Terminator* (1986), only a former Mr. Universe, Arnold Schwarzenegger, could properly embody the machine's hyper-masculinity. Powerful machines are not necessarily gigantic; in fact, history has shown the reverse: through successive generations of technology, machines grow proportionately more powerful and more compact. Nevertheless, to dramatize the fetishized, phallic power of the Terminator, it took the biggest of all men. The "meaning" of the Terminator's bulk, therefore, resides in metaphorical and psychological levels of interpretation, rather than in the literal and technological.

The Terminator, like Data, possesses astonishing strength. Unlike his pasty counterpart, however, the Terminator is not completely bereft of emotion: he does, after all, develop a sense of humour. Consider one of the final scenes in *Terminator 2: Judgment Day* (1991), in which the battered cyborg, who has finally dispatched the homocidal T-1000, hobbles on-screen, limping and one-armed, and moans, "Ah need a va-*ca*-shun." The Terminator, it would seem, is incapable only of stereotypically feminine emotions, such as empathy and sadness. Indeed, during one early conversation with John Connor, the cyborg's teenage charge, the Terminator tells us that he is incapable of tears.

The Terminator, as the sequel goes, arrives from the year 2029, sent by human survivors of an apocalyptic war against machines. The cyborg's mission is not only that of the messenger, to warn John, but also to protect him from an imminent attack. The Terminator's mission, in short, is to provide John with a father, and in the end, the machine proves to be a better father than a man ever could—he keeps the boy alive when all others have failed. In the process, the Terminator also becomes a surrogate husband to Sarah Connor, and satisfies her needs for security, protection, and companionship. In his twin roles of father and husband, the Terminator shows that, in the realm of science fiction, the robot comes to inherit the role of its male creators.

Popular culture has long associated masculinity with robots. According to the logic of Western dream narratives—that of comic books, graphic novels, fantasy, and science fiction—masculine men, or super-men, are quite literally men of steel. When we explore the connection between robots and masculinity, we find that, in science fiction, the robot comes to embody a masculine perfection unattainable by biological men. In *Star Trek*, robots are more logical thinkers than men are; they are more powerful and, it is sometimes implied, they are better lovers. In *Terminator 2*, robots are better killers, and better fathers. Of course, robots lack an embodied soul, but perhaps that's appropriate. For men, flesh has always been a liability—science fiction shows us that in the future, there will be more perfect men, for whom the phallus will be made of steel.

WORKS CITED AND RECOMMENDED

Attebery, Brian. *Decoding Gender in Science Fiction*. New York: Routledge, 2002.

Crystal, David. *The Cambridge Encyclopedia of the English Language*. 2nd ed. Cambridge: Cambridge UP, 2003.

Haraway, Donna J. "A Cyborg Manifesto: Science, Technology, and Socialist Feminism in the Late Twentieth Century." *Simians, Cyborgs, and Women: The Reinvention of Nature*. Ed. Donna J. Haraway. New York: Routledge, 1991. 149–81.

Hicks, Heather. "Striking Cyborgs: Reworking the 'Human' in Marge Piercy's *He, She and It*." *Reload: Rethinking Women + Cyberculture*. Ed. Mary Flanagan and Austin Booth. Cambridge, MA: MIT P, 2002. 85–106.

Star Trek: The Next Generation. Paramount Pictures, 1986–1994. Created by Gene Roddenberry.

Terminator 2: Judgment Day. Dir. James Cameron. Pacific Western/TriStar Pictures, 1991.

Eleanor Roosevelt

Maurine H. Beasley

Every four years a U.S. presidential election foregrounds the roles likely to be played by the candidates' spouses—will a potential first lady be "another Eleanor Roosevelt," journalists ask, meaning will she be a political activist in her own right like Roosevelt's best-known successor, Hillary Rodham Clinton? Or will she follow a more traditional White House model of a wife, supporting her husband and being cautious in airing her own views like Barbara Bush and her daughter-in-law, Laura? According to reports in *Newsweek* and other news media, Roosevelt's influence on Rodham Clinton was so great that she held imaginary conversations in the Clinton White House with her famous predecessor. Rodham Clinton apparently was endeavoring to determine whether Roosevelt's example could provide guidance in coping with her own personal difficulties as a first lady criticized for allegedly being too powerful. It would be unlikely to find any more telling example of Roosevelt's iconic status.

Eleanor Roosevelt (1884–1962) occupied an unparalleled place in the history of the twentieth century. Acclaim peaked at the time of her death on November 7, 1962. In a cartoon titled simply "It's Her," published on November 13, 1962 in the *St. Louis Post-Dispatch* and widely reprinted elsewhere, Bill Mauldin pictured a group of angels peeking out from heavenly clouds to get a glimpse of a new arrival. There was no doubt to whom the cartoon referred. After years of being in the public eye, Eleanor Roosevelt had become a symbol of humanitarian concern for the downtrodden everywhere, acquiring the status of an icon known all over the globe.

Tributes flowed to her family from world leaders including President John F. Kennedy, Soviet premier Nikita Khrushchev, Secretary-General of the United Nations U Thant, Indian Prime Minister Jawaharlal Nehru, and Queen Elizabeth of England. At the United Nations, U.S. Ambassador Adlai Stevenson eulogized her in a memorable quotation. It was circulated throughout the world in Associated Press and United Press International dispatches of November 9, 1962: "She would rather light candles than curse the darkness." The *New York Times* of November 11, 1962 praised her devotion to duty along with "thirst for life and insatiable curiosity" that brought her stature "far beyond her position as a President's wife and widow."

As first lady from 1933 to 1945, Eleanor Roosevelt established a precedent for the wife of the United States to involve herself in good works on behalf of the nation. For years, both before and after her death, public opinion polls ranked her as the most admired American woman. Betty Winfield, a journalism historian, pointed out that she was the first president's wife to play an important role in public, raising expectations in the political realm that her successors would (or should) do likewise. Lewis L. Gould, a scholar of first ladies, called attention to the use Roosevelt made of publicity to spotlight her activities.

Through lectures, press conferences for women journalists, radio and television broadcasts, magazine articles, a daily newspaper column, and some two dozen books, Roosevelt endeavored to communicate her ideas on political and social issues to a wide audience. She stood for racial justice, religious tolerance, government aid to the disadvantaged, and a host of causes linked to the liberal agenda of her day. A political partner to her husband and the mother of six children, one of whom died in infancy, she personified a gracious, motherly figure, nurturing those around her.

Even more importantly, when she left the White House after the unexpected death of her husband, President Franklin D. Roosevelt, on April 12, 1945, she emerged as a powerful diplomatic force. Appointed U.S. delegate to the United Nations from 1946 to 1953, she led the successful effort to draft the Universal Declaration of Human Rights. A half-century later, Mary Ann Glendon, Learned Hand Professor of Law at Harvard University, praised the declaration as the foundation for the contemporary human rights movement and referred to it as Eleanor Roosevelt's preeminent achievement.

Yet, her iconic status has not obscured the controversy that marked her career and continues to color reappraisals of her life by contemporary writers. Even in the midst of their profuse adjectives, Roosevelt's obituaries, like some recent studies, were not altogether worshipful in tone. Writers commented on her personal appearance, noting that she had described herself as plain, and that she had experienced difficulties for many years with her mother-in-law, Sara Delano Roosevelt. For example Cynthia Lowry, an Associated Press feature writer who knew Roosevelt personally wrote in 1962 that "She was a curious mixture of kindly, deep concern for people and impersonality" who became interested "in individuals only when they had problems." An Associated Press report from New York the previous day referred to her as being "as controversial as she was prominent," adding, "loved or despised, she was a woman too vital ever to be ignored."

Despite her iconic status today, historians still are trying to assess her influence as first lady, disagreeing on the extent of her impact on public policy. Gould, for instance, contended that she did not always focus her efforts productively. The extent of her feminism was argued based chiefly on her opposition for many years to the proposed equal rights amendment on grounds it would wipe out protective legislation for women and children. Her sexuality and family relationships were hotly debated in the wake of the opening of correspondence between her and Lorena Hickok, a newspaper reporter and intimate friend. The nature of the correspondence, released to the public in 1978 by the Franklin D. Roosevelt Library at Hyde Park, New York, suggested, but did not offer conclusive proof, of a lesbian relationship between the two women. The Roosevelt family denied such a relationship existed. Also, her attachment to Earl Miller, a highway patrolman who was her bodyguard in the pre–

Eleanor Roosevelt, 1945. Courtesy of the Library of Congress.

White House era, was scrutinized as a possible romance, although letters between the two have been lost and the exact nature of their friendship is unknown. Somewhat similarly, her friendships with Joseph P. Lash, who later became her biographer, and David Gurewitsch, her doctor, testified to her intense personal involvement with a few individuals who occupied an extraordinary place in her life.

Blanche Cook, who is writing a multivolumed biography of Roosevelt, contended at a centennial celebration of her life, "The truth is that a full understanding of her life requires an appreciation of its great complexity" (209–10). Roosevelt was a deep personality whose life took on many dimensions. Viewing her as an icon of sainthood masks the facts of her life. They reveal a woman who willingly described how she coped with adversity on several fronts, but kept other parts of her life separate from public scrutiny.

In her extensive career as a writer and speaker, Roosevelt referred to her own perception of herself as far less attractive than her beautiful mother, and gave details of a sad childhood in which she was orphaned by the time she was ten years old. She told of her insecurities as a young wife and mother and her resentment of what she saw as the domineering role of her mother-in-law. Relating how her interest in politics developed after her husband was stricken with infantile paralysis in 1921, Roosevelt called attention to a network of influential feminist associates. She pictured herself as a woman who emancipated herself from the conventional life of an upper-class matron, personified by her mother-in-law, while still fulfilling the role of a wife helping her husband. "I was one of those who served his purposes," she wrote in assessing her husband's presidential legacy.

At the same time there was much that Roosevelt did not say. She did not reveal her emotional devastation in 1918 when she discovered her husband was having an affair with her social secretary, Lucy Mercer, and agreed to stay with him for the sake of the children and his political career. She made little reference to her own needs for understanding and affection, which she found with a select number of persons who were outside, rather than within, her own family. By no means did she touch on issues of her own sexuality. She did not deal with what appeared to be growing estrangement between her and her husband during World War II that led her to spend much time away from the White House. Neither did she reveal conflicts with and among her children. Nor did she delve deeply into her relationship with her mother-in-law, whom she may have depicted somewhat unfairly, according to a recent study by Jan Pottker.

No doubt, it is well for Roosevelt's iconic status that she did not. Factual data, which still is coming to light, may eventually result in a more realistic interpretation of her life. At present she is enshrined in American collective memory as a woman of superhuman devotion to others with little thought for herself.

WORKS CITED AND RECOMMENDED

Cook, Blanche W. "Eleanor Roosevelt, Power and Politics: A Feminist Perspective." *Eleanor Roosevelt: An American Journey*. Ed. Jess Flemion and Colleen M. O'Connor. San Diego: San Diego State UP, 1987.

Glendon, Mary Ann. *A World Made New: Eleanor Roosevelt and the Declaration of Human Rights*. New York: Random House, 2001.

Gould, Lewis L. "The Historical Legacy of Modern First Ladies." Afterword. *Modern First Ladies: Their Documentary Legacy*. Comp. and ed. Nancy Kegan Smith and Mary C. Ryan. Washington, DC: National Archives and Records Administration, 1989. 167–75.

Lowry, Cynthia. "Only as a Widow Did Mrs. FDR Have Own Home." *Los Angeles Herald-Examiner* 9 Nov. 1962: A12.

"People, Opinion and Polls: 'Most Admired' Man and Woman." *The Public Perspective* Feb./Mar. 1995: 33.

Pottker, Jan. *Sara and Eleanor: The Story of Sara Delano Roosevelt and Her Daughter-in-Law, Eleanor Roosevelt*. New York: St. Martin's, 2004.

Roosevelt, Anna Eleanor. *The Autobiography of Eleanor Roosevelt*. New York: Harper, 1961.

Thomas, Evan. "Hillary's Other Side." *Newsweek* 1 July 1996: 20–23.

Van Thoor, Mieke. "Death of Eleanor Roosevelt." *Eleanor Roosevelt Encyclopedia*. Ed. Maurine H. Beasley, Holly C. Shulman, and Henry R. Beasley. Westport, CT: Greenwood, 2001.

Winfield, Betty H. "The Legacy of Eleanor Roosevelt." *Presidential Studies Quarterly* 20 (Fall 1990): 699–706.

Rosie the Riveter

Kathleen L. Endres

When Westinghouse artist J. Howard Miller created a poster during World War II that featured an unnamed woman factory worker in overalls and bandanna, flexing her muscles and asserting "We Can Do It!" no one predicted the power that image would convey. Here was an image that captured the spunk, determination, and confidence of millions of American women who "enlisted" for war production. This image—Rosie the Riveter—also came to represent female empowerment for another generation of American women. Rosie the Riveter—as she appeared in that poster that debuted in Pittsburgh for the Westinghouse War Production Coordinating Committee in 1942—has been reproduced on millions of t-shirts, mugs, buttons, stickers, post-it notes, and Web sites as a sign of a strong woman—a feminist—who can accomplish anything.

A closer look at the Rosie the Riveter image of that poster—along with the World War II advertising and editorial content employing its appeal—suggests that feminists might be better served with another icon. There is a duality of meaning packed in the self-assured cultural icon named Rosie. During World War II, she embraced all the traditional values of the day—home, family, motherhood, and apple pie—even as she packed her lunchbox and headed out for the work that promised to speed victory. That Rosie looked forward to giving up her job, marrying her favorite GI, buying a house, and settling down for the *really* important work, raising a family. In contrast, the Rosie icon of the feminist movement promised much more. She took the slogan "We Can Do It!" literally. The feminist Rosie is strong enough to break traditional bonds and accomplish anything she wants. The feminist Rosie is one empowered babe.

It was inevitable that World War II Rosie would be a conservative lass, who embraced all the traditional values that had made America a great, powerful, affluent land (Honey 28–47; Lewis and Nevill 222–24). After all, she was at the very heart of a publicity campaign designed to bring millions of women into the workforce during the war. Developed within the War Advertising Council in 1942 and 1943, the Women in War Jobs/Industry campaign, which continued until 1945, culminated in approximately 125 million advertisements in the major magazines in the nation. But this was not just an advertising campaign. Rosie the Riveter, the personification of this campaign, was a personality in motion pictures, radio programs, newspaper stories, magazine covers, and in-store displays. The Women in War Jobs/Industry campaign has been called one of the most successful recruitment campaigns in American history ("Women in War Jobs").

Few advertising executives could have predicted such enormous success. Creating a personable image of a woman factory worker ran counter to accepted advertising practices of the time. As late as March 1942, an advertising executive bemoaned the fact that the only women featured in advertising were white-collar workers or housewives (Karp 26). But how do you portray a personable female factory worker, one that would be appealing to middle-class American women who clung to traditional values? One woman writer for *Advertising and Selling Magazine* thought she had the answer—develop an image of a female factory woman that reflected the values American women treasured. Advertisers needed to "appeal to women's basic instincts—mother's love, self-preservation, the search for happiness, the desire to improve their lot in life . . .—that is the starting point of powerful advertising to which women will react," the writer observed. Advertisers needed to make a "heroine" of the "lady on the assembly line" (Carewe 23).

The Rosie the Riveter of World War II was the "heroine" on the assembly line. With few exceptions, Rosie was an attractive miss. Her hair might be tucked beneath a bandanna, but a curl always seemed to peek from beneath. Rosie might work a long, hard eight-hour shift, but her makeup remained perfect—arched eyebrows, a touch of mascara, a fresh application of lipstick, and, of course, the perfectly manicured, painted finger nails ("Announcing the New Grit"; "Tale of Lucy and Polly"; "Don't Shirk War Work . . . Still, Don't Let It Harm Your Charm"; "2,000,000 Girls with Paychecks Are Learning to Buy"). One "Trousered Angel" featured in the *Saturday Evening Post* had "lips like rose petals" (Lynch 84). The tiny miss who handled the heavy press had "spun-gold hair" ("Woman-power"). And one boss observed that the "Rosie" from the Pond's advertisement had " 'as pretty a pair of hands as ever monkeyed a wrench' " ("Hints for Hands"). It was Rosie's duty to keep up her appearance. As one advertisement for Formfit undergarments asserted, "everyone agrees that preserving feminine charm is a big factor in maintaining morale" ("Don't Shirk War Work"). As another advertisement—for Tangee Lipstick—claimed, "It's a reflection of the free democratic way of life that you [women workers] have succeeded in keeping your feminity—even though you are doing man's work" ("War, Women and Lipstick").

Moreover, Rosie never challenged gender-specific roles. She merely *transferred* her traditional responsibilities from the home to the workplace. Her sewing ability gave her an edge in everything from riveting airplanes to welding ships—or as a writer for the *Women's Home Companion* emphasized, "Any woman who can run a sewing machine can run almost any factory machine" (McNutt 41). One advertiser in the *Saturday Evening Post* boasted, "Give them [women workers] a rivet gun for a needle, sheets of metal for material, and these war workers will stitch you an airplane wing in half the time it used to take" ("Now, They're Sewing Metal Twice as Fast"). "Joan of Arc," a fictional character working in the shipyards, stitched "steel for fighting ships," another advertiser asserted ("Joan of Arc Is Stitching Steel for Fighting Ships").

Even Rosie's experience in child rearing could be transferred to the workplace. Mothers had patience and that was an ideal trait for women working in a factory. The patient Rosie could easily deal with the endless routine of factory work. "Repetition, monotonous tasks fail to break down this care taking attitude," observed one writer for *Advertising and Selling Magazine* (Gray 70). And was the kitchen all that different from a factory? One

Norman Rockwell's cover illustration of "Rosie the Riveter" for the *Saturday Evening Post*, 1943. Courtesy of the Library of Congress.

advertisement for GE Mazda Lamps emphasized the similarities. A woman worker, writing to her husband away at war, explained that she had started at the war plant as a drill press operator. The factory, she assured her husband, was "bright and cheery as our own kitchen" (GE Mazda Lamps).

Rosie was retaining her feminine charms and keeping up her traditional skills—in the home or in the factory—because she was planning to return to the family after the war. According to advertisements and stories during World War II, Rosie never saw herself as a permanent employee in the factories. She was just "helping out" during a wartime crisis, showing her patriotic stripes, so to speak. But this was Rosie's decision.

So inculcated with traditional values, Rosie looked forward to giving up her job and going home where her true responsibilities rested. As early as 1942, editors and advertisers were emphasizing this message. Two writers for the *Ladies' Home Journal* insisted that young women working in war plants, "when the war's over, will probably go home again and wash dishes" (Matthews and Hannah 30). As the war ground to a halt, a *Ladies' Home Journal* survey asserted that the women looked forward to leaving their jobs, having families, and caring for their homes (Gilles 22–23). Even if some women wanted to keep their jobs, they were greatly influenced by popular opinion—and a real fear of being termed an "old maid" ("Woman's New Independence").

Rosie the Riveter of World War II accomplished much with her "We Can Do It" attitude. She encouraged women of wartime America to work outside the home in war-related industries—and thereby speed victory to the Allies. She accomplished this by emphasizing that women who worked outside the home during the war need not surrender any of their traditional values. Wartime working women could retain their femininity. They were not challenging traditional gender roles. They were merely *transferring* their traditional responsibilities from home to the workplace; and, at the end of the hostilities, they continued those same responsibilities from within the home.

What happened to the demure little miss with the "We Can Do It" attitude of World War II? She was introduced into a new cultural milieu. Stripped of her advertising and editorial context, Rosie the Riveter found herself smack dab in the middle of the feminist movement—and she was quite comfortable there.

When the women who were employed outside the home during World War II—the real-life Rosie the Riveters—went home, they married and raised a whole new generation of daughters. Those daughters were brought up with stories of how their mothers—and, in some cases, grandmothers—worked in munition plants and factories to help win the war. They had been, the mothers and grandmothers insisted, real-life Rosie the Riveters.

These daughters, who had been born in the first decade of the baby-boomer era, came of age in the 1960s and 1970s, a time when the feminist movement was flourishing. Betty Friedan had identified the "problem with no name"— the dissatisfaction of middle-class housewives with their narrow role in society—in *The Feminine Mystique* (Friedan 15); Congress had passed Title VII of the Civil Rights Act barring discrimination in employment on the basis of race and sex and the Equal Pay Act; the Supreme Court struck down state laws prohibiting the use of contraceptives by married couples in *Griswold v. Connecticut*; feminists (including Friedan) had started the National Organization for Women, pledged to end sexual discrimination, especially in the work force; *Ms.* and a host of smaller periodicals had debuted to give voice to the feminist movement. Not all was well in feminism, however. Younger, radical feminists feuded with their more conservative sisters, over goals and strategies. Young feminists took to the streets—and were greatly lampooned by the press of the day. Meanwhile, the more conservative feminists pushed hard for a constitutional amendment. Finally in 1972, Congress passed the Equal Rights Amendment (ERA) and sent it to the states for ratification. As the feminist movement seemed to be on the brink of unparalleled success, hopes were dashed when the ERA fell just three states short of ratification. (Felder 243–51, 265–74).

The feminist movement seemed fractured, stalled.

What American feminism needed was a new icon, one that would be non-threatening but empowering, one that would bring middle-class women into the fold and galvanize the next generation of feminists.

Into this breach came a pleasant little miss with a "We Can Do It!" attitude. Rosie the Riveter was the ideal icon for feminism for several reasons. She appealed to the baby-boomer generation, many of whom were active in the feminist movement. These women had grown up hearing the stories of how their mothers and grandmothers had speeded victory for the Allies by working in factories. These women realized that no one ever doubted Rosie the Riveter's patriotism. No one ever lampooned Rosie's strategies or motives.

Moreover, much of Rosie the Riveter's editorial baggage had long been forgotten. The stories and advertisements—that told how Rosie needed to be ever attractive, how she did not break the bonds of her traditional roles, and how she needed to return to the home after winning a war—had long been filed away, seldom consulted.

But there was also a more practical reason why Rosie the Riveter was the ideal new icon for feminism. When she was created in Pittsburgh in 1942, neither the artist, J. Howard Miller, nor Westinghouse ever got around to copyrighting the image of the girl with the "We Can Do It!" attitude. That meant that the Pittsburgh-born miss could be reproduced in publications, t-shirts, stationary, post-it notes, and anything else without fear of copyright infringement or paying royalties.

And, thus, the feminist Rosie the Riveter emerged. Stripped of her editorial and advertising bondage, Rosie emerged with a new identity. She could do anything. She could accomplish anything. She was one empowered babe.

WORKS CITED AND RECOMMENDED

"Announcing the New Grit." *Advertising and Selling Magazine* Dec. 1943: 85.

Carewe, Sylvia. "Where's the Woman's Angle in This War?" *Advertising and Selling Magazine* Aug. 1942: 23.

"Don't Shirk War Work . . . Still, Don't Let It Harm Your Charm." *Saturday Evening Post* 20 Feb. 1943: 53.

Felder, Deborah. *A Century of Women: The Most Influential Events in Twentieth-Century Women's History.* Secaucus, NJ: Birch Lane P, 1999.

Friedan, Betty. *The Feminine Mystique.* New York: Norton, 1997.

GE Mazda Lamps. *Saturday Evening Post* 30 Jan. 1943: 7.

Gilles, Nell. "What About the Women?" *Ladies' Home Journal* June 1944: 22–23, 157–59, 161.

Gray, Albert. "America's Womanpower." *Advertising and Selling Magazine* May 1943: 69, 70.

"Hints for Hands." *Women's Home Companion* Feb. 1943: 37.

Honey, Maureen. *Creating Rosie the Riveter: Class, Gender and Propaganda during World War II.* Amherst: U of Massachusetts P, 1984.

"Joan of Arc Is Stitching Steel for Fighting Ships." *Saturday Evening Post* 7 Aug. 1943: 60.

Karp, A. Lawrence. "Selling the Female Industrial Group." *Advertising and Selling Magazine* Mar. 1942: 26.

Lewis, Charles, and John Nevill. "Images of Rosie: A Content Analysis of Women Workers in American Magazine Advertising, 1940–1946." *Journalism and Mass Communication Quarterly* 72.1 (1994): 216–27.

Lynch, James C. "Trousered Angel." *Saturday Evening Post* 10 Apr. 1943: 23, 84, 87.

Matthews, Ruth, and Betty Hannah. "The Changing World for Women." *Ladies' Home Journal* Aug. 1942: 27–30.

McNutt, Paul V. "Wake Up and Work." *Women's Home Companion* May 1943: 40–41, 85.

"Now, They're Sewing Metal Twice as Fast." *Saturday Evening Post* 26 June 1943: 99.

"Tale of Lucy and Polly." *Saturday Evening Post* 2 Jan. 1943: 2.

"2,000,000 Girls with Paychecks Are Learning to Buy." *Advertising and Selling Magazine* Mar. 1944: 133.

"War, Women and Lipstick." *Ladies' Home Journal* Aug. 1943: 73.

Wharton, Don. "The Story Back of the War Ads." *Advertising and Selling Magazine* June 1944: 49.

"Woman-power." *Saturday Evening Post* 13 June 1943: 55.

"Woman's New Independence." *Advertising and Selling Magazine* 3 July 1943: 92.

"Women in War Jobs—Rosie the Riveter (1942–1945)." Advertising Educational Foundation Museum. 16 Feb. 2005 <http://www.aef.com/02/ ad_council/2150/ :pf_>.

Route 66

Thomas A. Greenfield

Aristotle got it right. Tragedy stays put. Epic and romance move around. As America enters a third century of defining its cultural identity, the genres of mobility—epic adventure and romantic journey—have emerged as the national narrative forms of choice. From Lewis and Clark, to the Underground Railroad, to the California Gold Rush, to Huck Finn, to *Easy Rider*, the quintessential American story (whether literary, historical, or cinematic) tells the tale of the willful, restless optimist heading out from the oppression of Who-Needs-This to the undefined promise of God-Knows-Where.

Remarkable in its persistence, the American journey as rite of passage and consecration of cultural citizenship has changed little in two hundred fifty years of post-colonial history. Making adaptations in logistics as necessitated by the passage of time, the American pilgrimage evolved in the twentieth century from a pioneering quest onto uncharted waterways and newly-blazed wagon trails to a modern automobile journey along America's byways and back roads. In the literature and folklore of such journeys, the one road that came to symbolize the spirit of every automotive quest and the adventures that it held was U.S. Route 66, stretching 2,400 miles from Chicago to Los Angeles.

At various times in its history and various locations along its path, Route 66 was at once a smoothly paved highway, a foreboding desert trail, a country back road, and the chain that linked together countless small town main streets across the Midwest and South. In the late 1930s Route 66 embodied all the promise of America's ascendance to international power as it supported newly emerging truck commerce and pre-war military preparations running east and west. Only a few years earlier it was the primary roadway for desperate families fleeing the Oklahoma Dust Bowl for California, aided, abetted, and often rescued by the "mom and pop" gas stations, diners, and auto campgrounds that lined its path. And as the one highway in America's first nationally planned public road system specifically designed to link small towns together, Route 66 gave shape and form to the still resilient, mythical idea of Small Town, USA.

Form followed function and so did fable. By the time it was decommissioned as a U.S. highway in 1985, Route 66 had come to represent, as one anonymous traveler noted, "a multitude of ideas: freedom, migration west, and the loneliness of the American heartland." Often adulated through personification, Route 66's "resumé" rivals that of an A-list celebrity. It is the subject of over 100 books and documentaries, and it "Googles" over 1 million Web references. It has its own national museum. It inspired a popular hit song that has been recorded over 100 times (at least once in each of the past seven decades) as well as a solid-selling tribute CD album of eleven different songs devoted exclusively to it. It commands its own chapter in one of the greatest American novels ever written, *The Grapes of Wrath*, and as a long-running, golden-age-of-television weekly series it in turn, fire-glazed the myth of the Chevrolet Corvette convertible, an American cultural icon in its own right.

The free-spirited independence and solitude commonly associated with Route 66 belie the highly political and bureaucratic nature of its creation. From the Civil War era to the end of the nineteenth century, road transportation was a local matter. Federal interest in transportation was confined to trains and shipping. The early 1890s saw a shift in public attitude toward a definitive government role in road-building, owing to the popularity of the bicycle and a growing awareness that the automobile was looming on the

Route 66 gave shape and form to the still-resilient, mythical idea of Small Town, USA. Courtesy of Shutterstock.

horizon. In 1893 the federal government took its first baby step into roadway development, creating an Office of Road Inquiry to provide states and local communities with roadway engineering advice and other consultant services (Weingroff). With the advent of the automobile in the mid-1890s, public demand for better roads developed in earnest. Travel advocacy groups (more or less early political action committees, including the now ubiquitous AAA founded in 1902) sprang up all across the country. Their efforts came to be known collectively as the Good Roads Movement, which pressed for improved roads (constructed with the newest technology: pavement), durable automobiles, and accurate maps.

Events leading to a national road system moved rapidly thereafter. The first transcontinental automobile trip on record occurred in 1903 with much ballyhoo and fanfare. In 1907 the Supreme Court ruled that federal funding and management of roadways were legitimate, constitutional exercises of government authority. By 1908, Henry Ford had introduced the Model T, making automobile ownership affordable for the middle class. The idea of widespread individual automotive ownership and road travel over long distances, only fifteen years earlier a remote fantasy, was now a vision coming quickly into focus and a dream clamoring to come true. To its credit, the federal government was paying attention.

The 1910s saw a flurry of federal legislative lobbying efforts as farmers, arguing for rural farm-to-market roads, contested with motorists' associations advocating for national highways. The Federal-Aid Highway Act of 1916, the first major congressional legislation to fund road planning, supported the farmers over the motorists groups. However, the fact that Congress had appropriated funds for road construction at all catalyzed political efforts to create a national highway system.

A journey of inestimable significance occurred in 1919, when the army conducted its first successful cross-country troop convoy. This accomplishment might have amounted to little more than a footnote in American highway history but for the fact that along for the ride was 28-year-old Lt. Colonel Dwight D. Eisenhower, whose excitement about the journey made of him a lifelong advocate for progressive road travel. Twenty years later, as general of the U.S. army preparing for America's entry into World War II, Eisenhower would send convoys of troops west on Route 66 for assignment and training. As President in the 1950s, he would place what would become today's interstate highway system at the top of his administration's agenda (D'este 143).

A 1921 revision of the original Federal-Aid Highway Act called on states to identify local roads for possible inclusion in a forthcoming national highway system. A federally-supported national roadway system was finally "on the table" in Washington, and ensuing lobbying efforts for competing master plans and route locations became intense.

A Chicago-to-Los Angeles route was an early "no-brainer" priority floating in Washington during the lobbying period. However, the idea of having that route dip south into Arkansas, Oklahoma, and Texas, linking town main streets along the way, was the result of local visionary thinking and hardball public relations. Many of the national highways were being planned as direct-route, high-speed roadways for commerce, which would necessitate bypassing population centers. Small town businesses and politicians felt threatened by this concept and pressed for compromises on behalf of local communities. The idea of designating a national roadway running through small towns, rather than away from them, linking "Main Streets Across America" is generally attributed to Cyrus Avery, an Oklahoma oil and coal entrepreneur. Avery and his supporters "sold" the federal government on the idea of running the Chicago-to-Los Angeles route diagonally through towns and cities of the southwest red-clay region, including Avery's hometown of Tulsa.

The year of consecration was 1926. Congress formally approved a national highway system, appropriating funds and developing national policies for highway paving and maintenance. A newly-created Federal Highway Commission formally numbered and mapped out the designated national highways, conferring upon Avery's Chicago to Los Angeles diagonal "red line" across America's heartland the seemingly innocuous name "U.S. Route 66." That same year Henry Ford, America's leading automobile manufacturer, lowered the price of some of his models and increased production, anticipating correctly that the next phase of his good fortunes lay in expanded volume and the rising expectation of the average American family that they could and should own a car (Weingroff). By 1927 credit purchases of automobiles would exceed cash purchases. One year later, Herbert Hoover would be elected to office on a campaign of prosperity that promised famously a chicken in every pot and a car in every garage.

By the time the Great Depression hit in 1929, Hoover's prophecy on automobile ownership may have been more accurate than his prophecy on chickens. By then Ford had sold 15 million Model T's alone and total automobile sales had reached approximately 30 million since the 1890s. Ownership rates from the outset were higher in small towns and rural areas than cities, because rural economy and culture had long-since depended upon individual transportation afforded by horse and wagon. Many small town and rural families who had not been prosperous even during the 1920s boom nonetheless owned a family car at the start of the Depression. For many of them, that car and U.S Route 66 would be their salvation as the economy and the weather turned against them in the Dust Bowl of the 1930s.

The flight of "Dust Bowl Okies" was a well-known social phenomenon before Steinbeck immortalized it in his 1939 novel *The Grapes of Wrath*. But Steinbeck is duly credited with initiating the cultural mythology of Route 66 by making that road the focus and symbol of all automotive flights from Depression-era poverty. The novel's immortal Chapter 12, devoted entirely to the particulars of life on 66 during the Depression, conferred upon Route 66 two of its most enduring appellations, "The Mother Road" and "The road of flight," and immortalized the highway with apocalyptic solemnity:

66 is the path of people in flight, refugees from dust and shrinking land, from
the thunder of tractors and shrinking ownership, from the desert's slow
northern invasion, from the twisting winds that howl up out of Texas, from the
floods that bring no richness to the land and steal what little richness is there.
From all of these, the people are in flight. (118)

Its federal highway designation notwithstanding, pavement of U.S. Route
66 was not completed until the end of the decade, and the journey of
Steinbeck's minions was often long, difficult, and hazardous. Steinbeck's
migrant families are eerily reminiscent of eighteenth-century American pioneer covered-wagon parties, with flat rubber tube tires replacing broken
wagon wheels and gasping engines replacing dying horses. Gas was as precious as the early settlers' water . . . and in summer so was water. The kindness
of strangers and the camaraderie of the shared journey intersected with lar-
ceny and even violence spawned by the pressures of limited supplies, fuel,
time, and patience.

In a curious way Steinbeck's stark portrait of life along Route 66 validated
Cyrus Avery's wide-eyed vision of a single American main street. Steinbeck's
narrative names towns along the way, in many cases immortalizing places
heretofore unheralded outside of their own regions: "66 across the Panhandle
of Texas, Shamrock and McClean, Conway and Amarillo . . . then the high
mountains, Holbrook and Winslow and Flagstaff . . . and then the great pla-
teau rolling like a groundswell. Ashfork and Kingman" (118–19). Thereafter,
the naming of towns became essential to chronicling the Route 66 journey—a
theme picked up in song, story, and a weekly television series.

By the 1950s America's economy and morale had progressed from the
grimness of the Depression and World War II to a new era of prosperity.
Young war veterans and their families excitedly set out by car for new lives in
the burgeoning suburbs of America's cities and the flowering economy of the
West Coast. As the fortunes of this new car-driving, car-driven middle class
grew, so did the legend of Route 66, now a major route for westbound
emigration to the tan-lined promised land of Southern California. Motorists
on this far more pleasant journey than the trip Steinbeck chronicled still
celebrated the adventure of discovering America along 66's main streets just
as they had a generation earlier. No single artifact of popular culture embraced the post-war Route 66 adventure so richly as did the hit song by which
most people probably yet know its lore and legend, Bobby Troup's "Get Your
Kicks on Route 66."

The genesis of the song embodies postwar optimism as powerfully as does
the song itself. In 1946 Troup, a young pianist, songwriter, and newly dis-
charged war veteran, set out from Pennsylvania toward Route 66, hoping
eventually to make it in the Los Angeles music scene. Troup claims, credibly
enough, he wrote most of the song on a motor trip west, and used Steinbeck's
naming devices from St. Louis, Missouri; through Amarillo, Gallup,
and Flagstaff; to Ponoma, California. Troup's turn of fortunes bore out the

The Cadillac Ranch in Amarillo, Texas, on Route 66. Courtesy of Shutterstock.

joyous, youthful swagger of his verse. Promptly upon his arrival in Los Angeles, he got the song into the hands of music executives and within a few weeks he joined all America in listening to Nat King Cole snappin' out his hit tune on radios across the nation.

The broad, sustained appeal of the song's upbeat, man-on-the-move message is reflected in the astonishing array of artists who have recorded it in the sixty years since its initial release: 1940s pop icons Bing Crosby and the Andrews Sisters; 1950s jazzmen Oscar Peterson and Mel Torme; then rock superstars Chuck Berry, the Rolling Stones, and Van Morrison; 1980s British electro-pop's Depeche Mode; country crooner Michael Martin Murphy and honkytonkers Asleep at the Wheel, among some 100 others. In the twenty-first century, the song found new life, perhaps even immortality, by way of regular inclusion in "song packs" for Karaoke machines.

The legend of Route 66 received yet another boost from popular culture in the early 1960s with a four-year run of a CBS weekly television series of the same name. While not great television, *Route 66* added well-drawn characters and filmed-on-location adventures to the folklore of its namesake. Debuting only five years after publication of Jack Kerouac's classic Beat novel *On the Road*, the *Route 66* television series charmed with well-written road stories, amiable young stars (Martin Milner and George Maharis), a hot convertible car, and a nimble instrumental theme by soundtrack maestro Nelson Riddle. (Urban legend to the contrary, Kerouac's *On the Road* has very little connection to Route 66. Kerouac traveled on and around U.S. Route 6, a northern, lesser known numeric first cousin of 66.)

Even as the television series was making its mark on Route 66's cultural legacy, the federal government was well on its way to orchestrating the demise of the original national highway system—and Route 66 along with it. The end of the road for Route 66 came in the form of today's interstate highway system, a federal approach to roadway planning that was different from the original U.S. route system in both degree and kind. While the original U.S. routes were so many disconnected strands of cross country roadway, the emerging interstate highway system laid out interconnected regionally-based roadways to form a true, national network. Moreover, nationwide access to "superhighways," with more and wider lanes, upgraded pavement, roadside amenities, direct routes, and high speed limits (at all costs bypassing residential areas that would slow down traffic) had by the mid-1950s taken on the status of an inalienable human right. Eisenhower made the new interstate highway system a top priority of his presidency and Congress went along with him. In 1956 a new Federal-Aid Highway Act gave birth to "the Interstate," signaling the end of the U.S. route as the motorist's road of choice.

Over time the original U.S. routes were formally decommissioned, losing their status as federal projects and eligibility for highway funds. Route 66 was decommissioned in 1985 but, having already been subsumed by several Interstate routes, had long since ceased to be a heavily traveled thoroughfare. Lack of federal funding and motorist adoration of the Interstate resulted in physical deterioration of many of the original U.S. routes. Today several stretches of Route 66 are no longer traversable or do not even exist.

Nevertheless, Route 66 as a vivid image of the restless modern American spirit survives in the legacy of Steinbeck's novel, along with Troup's song, countless academic and trade publications, auto museums, numerous Route 66 preservation and revival societies, the memories and tall tales of old timers, and the surviving roadside gas stations and diners that still cater to the off-road traveler embarked upon the definitive twentieth-century American journey.

For many Americans, perhaps for America itself, Route 66 will always be *the* way west.

WORKS CITED AND RECOMMENDED

D'este, Carlo. *Eisenhower: A Soldier's Life*. New York: Holt, 2002.

"Route 66." Unattributed entry article in Wikepedia. 1 July 2005 <http://en.wikipedia.org/wiki/Route_66>.

Steinbeck, John. *The Grapes of Wrath*. New York: Vantage, 1939.

Troup, Bobby. "Get Your Kicks on Route 66." ASCAP, 1946.

Weingroff, Richard F. "Building the Foundation: Federal Aid Road Act of 1916." *Public Roads On-line*. U.S. Department of Transportation: Federal Highway Administration, 1996. 1 July 2005 <http://www.tfhrc.gov/pubrds/summer96/p96su2.htm>.

Babe Ruth

J. Peter Williams

You know, I saw it happen, from beginning to end. But sometimes I still can't believe what I saw: this nineteen-year-old kid, crude, poorly educated, only lightly brushed by the veneer we call civilization, gradually transformed into the idol of American youth and the symbol of baseball the world over—a man loved by more people and with an intensity of feeling that perhaps has never been equaled before or since. I saw a man transformed from a human being into something pretty close to a god.
—Harry Hooper, Babe Ruth's teammate on the 1918–1919 Red Sox

The point of departure in approaching any iconic figure is always this: public figures lead two distinct and separate lives. One, of course, is the natural life of the individual, a progress through time, shared by everyone, from birth through life and, ultimately, to death. The other is a mythical life unintentionally contrived by a usually adoring public, a public comprised of people who, with few exceptions, have no personal connection with or knowledge of the icon. When Red Smith said that George Herman Ruth had an "uncanny sense of the theater," he had it backwards; the epic drama in which Ruth starred was really written by the fans.

As Harry Hooper suggests, the popular construction of a mythical figure is no different from deification, and the icon that results will usually have qualities we associate with gods. Here is a partial checklist: (1) great strength, even as a child or an old man; (2) magical powers and the ability to work miracles; (3) a Dionysiac, Olympian appetite; (4) immortality, and (5) eventual martyrdom. If an individual who is prominent in the public eye can possess one or some of these qualities, that person is likely to become an icon.

Babe Ruth had all of them.

One of the obvious proofs of Ruth's rank at the very top of the iconic pantheon is that his name has become a standard of excellence against which anyone, in any field, might be measured. Robert Creamer gives a few examples: Willie Sutton was "the Babe Ruth of bank robbers," Franco Correlli was "the Babe Ruth of operatic tenors," Alfred A. Knopf was "the Babe Ruth of copy editors" (16). Creamer's book is thirty years old, but the analogies persist: on Mia Hamm's retirement from women's soccer in 2004, the headline in the sports section of the December 8 *New York Times* emphasized that she would have a place in sports history "LIKE RUTH."

In most cases, a hero's iconic life is measured in stages, years or decades in his career which call him most to mind: think of Sinatra the teen idol, Sinatra the failure and, finally, Sinatra the jazz singer and leader of the Rat Pack, or of Cassius Clay the loudmouth morphing into the international hero Ali. Babe Ruth's mythical history is different in that it is best measured less in temporal periods than in isolated (and very dramatic) moments. True, he hit 714 home runs during his career, but the one he hit in September 1927, his sixtieth of the season, is much better remembered. For that matter, can all of us remember the very recent year Barry Bonds set the new record? Or what it is? And, yes, Ruth was a Catholic Democrat who allowed his name to be used in support of Al Smith over Herbert Hoover in the presidential election of 1928, but all we recall is one comment: when, just after the stock market crash, he was asked why he made more money than the Republican incumbent, Ruth pointed out that he should have, because he'd had a much better year.

Still, isolated moments can define an iconic trajectory as well as chronological periods and, in Ruth's case, they clearly do. In 1914, for example, the young hero (he was not nicknamed "Babe" for his good looks) was poorly treated by Red Sox veterans and stars Tris Speaker and "Smokey" Joe Wood. Rather than sit still, Ruth got the Boston manager, Bill Carrigan, to call a team meeting for him. In that meeting Ruth said that if Speaker and Wood did not agree to stop their hazing, he wanted to fight them then and there, in the locker room. Speaker and Wood said nothing. The hazing stopped. Ruth was 20 years old.

Ruth's strength, of course, is legendary. Maris, Aaron, McGwire, and Bonds never hit home runs as long as the ones Ruth stopped hitting in 1935. Often Ruth seems to be the figure Bernard Malamud modelled on him in *The Natural,* or one based on the earlier legend of Arthur and *Excalibur.* Descriptions of Ruth's bat—Malamud's *Wonderboy* or Arthur's sword—underscore that power.

It weighed fifty-four ounces, and, as he told F. C. Lane, "I have enough strength to swing it...when I meet the ball, I want to feel that I have something in my hands that will make it travel." Jim Bottomley, a pitcher, said his hand was sore for three days after fielding one of Ruth's drives (Wallace 59, 198–200). Damon Runyon was relieved that Babe hit few line drives through the infield, because "he would kill or dangerously injure any man who got in front of one of his powerful punches at short distance" (Reisler 107). In *Headin' Home,* the 1921 silent film in which Ruth starred (and in which he looks remarkably youthful, even thin), he whittles his own bat from a large tree limb and immediately starts hitting more home runs than anyone else. As "Bugs" Baer, who wrote the film subtitles, put it, "he made

Babe Ruth crossing the plate after hitting his first home run of the season, 1924. Courtesy of the Library of Congress.

the nation of leagues forget the League of Nations." Or as the *New York Times* said in the year the film came out (1921 was one year after the non-fictional Babe's first great season, the year he hit one home run for every ounce in his bat), "Sir Isaac Newton would have found out much about the laws of gravitation if he had seen Ruth bang baseballs. He probably would have decided that there weren't any" (Reisler 201). Finally, of course, there was 1927, when he used his version of Excalibur or Wonderboy to hit sixty.

Ruth's strength seemed, if not supernatural, at least superhuman—or possibly even atavistic, the strength of a neanderthal. The *Times* said that "with no weapon but a primitive club" he made "the famed clubbers of the Stone Age" look as if they were playing badminton. His teammate Joe Dugan, wondering where on earth Ruth had come from, said he couldn't simply have been born. "The sonofabitch fell from a tree," he said. In fact, Ruth was himself the standard against which he was measured. "You can't compare him with anybody else," said his first Yankee manager, Miller Huggins. "He's Babe Ruth" (Reisler 230, 109, 129).

Nor did Ruth lose his legendary strength even as an old player. On May 25, 1935, he hit his last major league home run, number 714, in Forbes Field. His legs were so shot the pitcher who threw him that ball said Babe could only hobble around the bases. That last home run was Babe's third of the day, the first ever hit over the right field grandstand and the longest ever hit in Forbes Field, a very spacious park. The pitcher who watched Ruth limp around the bases was Guy Bush, the same man who had needled Ruth from the Cubs' dugout just before Babe's "called shot" in the 1932 World Series.

Ruth's final home run in Pittsburgh was unusual in that, although it became part of the iconic legend, it was also a tremendous effort by a real man. That was not the case with the "called shot." The "called shot," possibly still the most famous home run in baseball history (with due apologies to Messrs. Thomson, Mazeroski, Fisk, and Dent), provides a clear example of the individual diverging from the icon. Virtually all serious authority agrees that the Babe never pointed to center field, to the exact spot in the bleachers where his drive would land, before he hit that pitch. The myth, however, was both too good to be true and too good to pass up. Ruth *was* gesturing angrily, and he *did* point, but probably either to Guy Bush on the Cubs' bench or at Charlie Root on the mound. Still, and as is always the case with icons, the myth is what we remember. Ruth, in his role as magician and miracle-worker, promised something only divinity can achieve, and he delivered. Even eyewitnesses who clearly knew better consciously chose denial. Here is sportswriter Joe Williams on his preference for fable over fact:

> This much I do know. Even if Ruth didn't mean it, the thunderous drama still lives in my memory. And no amount of testimony to the contrary is ever going to change it in the slightest. I always was a pushover for wonderful fairy tales, anyway. (Williams 64)

The other memorable miracle in Ruth's iconic life also involves promising a home run and then hitting one (this moment remains vivid enough to have inspired a *Seinfeld* episode involving Kramer and latter-day Yankee Paul O'Neill). In 1926, just before the World Series, 11-year-old Johnny Sylvester was in hospital after being thrown by a horse. A friend of his father with a clubhouse "in" brought Johnny a bunch of autographed baseballs along with Ruth's promise to hit a home run in the Series. The Series went a full seven games, and Babe, with twenty at-bats, hit four homers, later visiting a delighted Johnny in his sick room. Not a bad performance for an individual ballplayer, but not good enough for an icon. The legend insists that Johnny was dying, that Babe picked the game and at-bat for a single home run, and that it saved Johnny's life.

Ruth had great strength, then, both as a youth and as a has-been; and he had (or, rather, was assigned by his adoring public) a magical capacity to work miracles. Given what we already knew, how could his appetites be moderate, even human? It's hard to imagine where to start in this category. He was a notorious womanizer who often entertained a plural number of women a night and who, according to Creamer, "was very noisy in bed, visceral grunts and gasps and whoops." He had, according to the same source, by far the foulest mouth in the Yankee clubhouse. And he ate and drank enough for half a dozen men, with predictable results. "He belched magnificently," says Creamer, "and, I was told, could fart at will." Among Ruth's numerous trophies, in fact, was one of which he was inordinately proud. "I won first place in a farting contest," he said, pointing it out to a friend. "Honest. Read the writing on it. Boy, I had to down a lot of beer and limburger to win that one" (Creamer 321, 329, 320, 326).

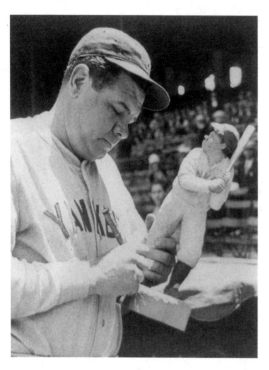

Babe Ruth autographing a wooden statue of himself made by Carl Hallsthammar, 1930. Courtesy of the Library of Congress.

The single moment that best illustrates the Babe's Dionysiac propensities is given an entire chapter by Creamer: "The Disaster: The Bellyache Heard Round the World." Once again, there is a gulf between icon and individual. According to the Ruth myth, one of two cardinal sins put him in the hospital, either gluttony or lust. W. O. McGeehan circulated the story that it was gluttony, that, trying to match his season record for home runs (in 1925, when the Babe got sick, it was fifty-nine), he had tried to eat the equivalent number of hot dogs. The other version, spread *sotto voce* among those who thought the sin was lust, was that McGeehan's hot dog tale was just a ruse, a cover-up to prevent Mrs. Ruth from discovering that her husband was really being treated for a severe venereal infection. The truth, if less flamboyant, was far more dangerous, too much of an early reminder that, however iconic, Babe Ruth was still a very vulnerable and mortal human individual: he had diverticulitis, a frequently fatal condition, and only immediate surgery saved him.

Because the operation on the human was a complete success, the public could return to considering Ruth as the unshakable divinity he had always seemed, the man virtually every biographer calls a "legend," an "immortal," a "god" who "transcended sport," a hero who added the word "Ruthian"— roughly synonymous with "Jovian" or "Jehovan"—to the dictionary. Ruth the god was not so much above the law as beyond it: once, driving the wrong way down a one-way street, he was pulled over by an angry cop who immediately softened when he recognized the Babe, even apologizing for slowing him down. Another time, in training camp in Shreveport in 1921, the locals gave Apollo a chariot, a brand-new luxury car with no plates, only "Babe Ruth's Essex" painted on the spare, and he was, of course, never stopped.

When the god finally proved himself only an exceptional individual by having the temerity to die, it was hard if not impossible to accept. At the funeral, one of Ruth's pallbearers, Joe Dugan, turned to another, Waite Hoyt, and said, "I'd give a hundred bucks for an ice-cold beer." "So would the Babe," Hoyt said (Ritter and Rucker 289). A pitching coach frustrated by his staff's reluctance to challenge hitters wanted to remind them that they would never have to face the greatest hitter in history, so he had a T-shirt made. "Babe Ruth Is Dead," it read: "Throw Strikes!" (Rubin 69). Red Smith marvelled at the god's lasting power, how—even long after the individual's death—he seemed "insistently alive," and Creamer, the best of the biographers, said as much, pointing out the essential difference between indomitable icon and fragile man: "Ruth lives, all around us," he said, adding that, even though he had the historian's obligation to be objective, "Ruth is alive for me, too" (Creamer 17, 18).

But George Herman Ruth is not alive. He has been dead for more than half a century. In 1947 he grew very sick, and in June 1948 attended the celebration of the twenty-fifth anniversary of Yankee Stadium, "The House That Ruth Built." He had been given two earlier "Babe Ruth Days," both in 1947, but this is the one we remember, if only for the famous photograph of a thin and ravaged Babe using his bat as a cane. George Herman Ruth died of the cancer he probably didn't know he had on the morning of August 17, 1948, at age 53. In doing so he achieved one more quality of the icon, martyrdom. Had he lived beyond middle age, like his rival Ty Cobb and most of the other stars of his era, some of the mythical luster might have been tarnished, but when the individual exits not long after the icon stops playing, the public has more reason to preserve the heroic image of a man denied old age.

There is one more iconic quality that can conveniently be attributed to Babe Ruth: that he was the emblem of the culture of his time. Ruth was as perfectly suited as any public figure to the free-wheeling, high-living atmosphere of the 1920s and early 1930s—as, for example, his polite and Columbia-educated teammate Lou Gehrig was not. Babe drank with Bix Beiderbecke, asked Marshal Foch if he had been in World War I, and, in the Second, got fan mail *from* Betty Grable. His name was even used by the enemy in an attempt to dishearten our troops: Japanese soldiers in the Pacific theater would shout "To hell with Babe Ruth!" before they attacked. But his real era was the period between the wars. One historian put it succinctly: "Ruth's heyday, 1921 to 1933, was in relation to the American era of which his incredible home run performance was so spectacular a part if not, indeed, symbol.... He was *the* American success story of the 1920's" (Meany 162).

Just as Frank Sinatra epitomized the urban "cool" of the fifties and Muhammad Ali served to represent the rebellious sixties and seventies, so did the Dionysiac Ruth personify the melodrama and colorful hedonism of his era. In looking over his twin careers—his progress through life as both individual and popular icon—it's hard to resist a bit of wistful melancholy, a sadness in knowing we can't attend a Dempsey fight, or watch Walter Hagen play golf in the tux he was still wearing from last night's party, or find a speakeasy with a password like "swordfish," or sit down at a table in the Stork and share a martini with Nick and Nora Charles.

WORKS CITED AND RECOMMENDED

Creamer, Robert. *Babe: The Legend Comes to Life*. New York: Simon and Schuster, 1974.

Meany, Tom. *Baseball's Greatest Hitters*. New York: A. S. Barnes, 1950.

Reisler, Jim. *Babe Ruth: Launching the Legend*. New York: McGraw-Hill, 2004.

Ritter, Lawrence S., and Mark Rucker. *The Babe: A Life in Pictures*. New York: Ticknor and Fields, 1988.

Rubin, Louis D., Jr., ed. *The Quotable Baseball Fanatic*. New York: Lyons P, 2000.

Wallace, Joseph. *The Autobiography of Baseball*. New York: Abradale P, 2000.

Williams, Peter. "Did Babe Call the Shot?" *The Baseball Research Journal* 16 (1987): 62–64.

Scrapbook

Patricia Prandini Buckler

The enthusiasm for scrapbooking today is massive—by some estimates one in every four American households makes and keeps scrapbooks—and lucrative, estimated at $2.5 billion per year. The magnitude of this pastime and the mass production of supplies and materials would seem to indicate that scrapbook-making is a phenomenon of the late twentieth and early twenty-first centuries. In reality, today's scrapbook makers ("scrapbookers" in their jargon) are engaged in a practice with long and deep connections in American culture.

Teresa Viewegh of Greenwood, Indiana, typifies modern scrapbookers. Shortly after the birth of her first child, Viewegh and her mother-in-law, Brenda, attended a scrapbooking party sponsored by the giant scrapbook materials supplier, Creative Memories. Teresa wanted to begin a scrapbook of photographs to record her son's growth and development, along with their family and friends. She also hoped a common hobby would cultivate a closer relationship with her mother-in-law. The two women have been scrapbooking now for six years—they have strengthened their friendship and produced numerous decorated pages of photos and other memorabilia marking events in their lives.

Teresa explained in an interview on June 3, 2005, that although she started the hobby in order to save and display photos, she continues it for many other reasons. Once a month she gets together with a group of friends to work on their scrapbooks, usually for six or seven hours on a Friday night. These gatherings allow them, mostly busy mothers, to visit and catch up with one another's news, while providing a scheduled time for them to update their scrapbooks. They enjoy socializing as much as they enjoy crafting their pages. At other times, Teresa and Brenda get together at one of their homes to crop, cut, and paste. Once a year, the group goes on a weekend scrapbooking retreat at some vacation cottages. The purpose is to "crop 'til you drop." They also take classes from Creative Memories consultants that introduce new methods or materials for enhancing their pages, such as the use of die cuts, stickers, rubber stamps, eyelets, and stencils.

From sources such as Creative Memories, *Creating Keepsakes Magazine*, and *Better Homes and Gardens*, they have learned to follow several basic principles: tell a story, identify everybody, record the dates and the ages of the kids, and explain the activity or event portrayed. Additional "journaling" includes writing thoughts that others might enjoy reading later. For Teresa, describing her feelings about her son at different stages is as important as recording his facial expressions, his first steps, and his first words.

Teresa Viewegh proudly displays her scrapbook. Courtesy of Patricia Buckler.

In fact, Teresa and Brenda and their millions of co-hobbyists are participating in an American practice pursued for nearly 250 years. The Library of Congress's online catalog cites a "Scrapbook of poetry, newspaper clippings, etc., ca. 1760" (LC Control Number mm 83093096); and another "Scrapbook of newspaper clippings, etc. . . . : commonplace book, 1770–1846" (LC Control Number mm 82075671).

Over the years, the form and materials have changed along with the tastes and technology of the times. Yet for individuals and institutions alike, the scrapbook (also referred to as "album," "friendship book," and "self book") has persisted as a focal point for compiling and organizing information, preserving memories, exploring identity, and expressing creativity. Scrapbooks also served as repositories for collections of color advertising cards, clippings on specific topics, or educational materials, and even as herbaria.

The scrapbook evolved from the commonplace book, a type of school book used for copying exercises. Usually the child would copy excerpts of classical works and their translations, quotations of wisdom and virtue from the Scriptures, famous authors, or preachers, poems, and other bits of literature or "scraps." (One American commonplace book in the Perkins Library Special Collections at Duke University is dated 1720. However, the practice of the commonplace book in Europe can be traced as far back as the Middle Ages.) Besides learning the languages, practicing penmanship, and internalizing wisdom and virtue, the student was expected to keep the commonplace book as a lifelong repository of quotations for use in everyday life. Compiling books for storing all types of information was a natural extension of the schoolroom practice. When paper and printing became inexpensive early in the 1800s, people clipped interesting or important passages. Many pasted over the writing in their commonplace books, and others thriftily recycled business or domestic account books in this manner. While the making of copy and commonplace books continued, the scrapbook genre began to go in its own direction.

For many, the making of scrapbooks, albums, or friendship books combined an impulse to preserve memories with the urge to record, examine, and appraise the bits and pieces of an individual's daily life. These personal memento volumes included singular, hand-created items such as autographs, handwritten poems or prose pieces, drawings, and theorem paintings (paintings made from an arrangement of stencils on paper or cloth), as well as objects with emotional associations, such as ornaments, fanciwork, locks of hair and jewelry (Motz 75). Items were arranged in a manner that made sense of personal experience by systematizing it. Handwritten comments often complemented the pasted-in items, indicating their personal or historical significance (Allen and Hoverstadt 16).

In the nineteenth century, girls and young women used their leisure time to compile friendship albums (a type of scrapbook with a specific focus). The blank books, made by hand or purchased from a local printer, were passed among friends who hand-inscribed verses, quotations, pictures, or glued in cuttings from mass-produced sources. Judging by diary entries, letters, and domestic advice books of the day, composing albums was considered a leisure activity but not a frivolous one. Order, symmetry, and system were valued qualities. Family members discussed the appropriateness of various submissions, and contributors frequently practiced their drawings, paintings, and penmanship elsewhere beforehand, so that the actual entry would be flawless. It was customary for individuals to collect scraps on a variety of subjects so that a suitable contribution could be made (Smith 66–69).

Advances in color printing technologies made printed colored images available for use in albums early in the nineteenth century. These "scraps" or "chromos" were the leftover pieces from larger printing jobs, sold to collectors who preserved them in books or scrapbooks. Other printing inventions and improvements contributed even more paper collectibles, until printed paper artifacts became common.

In 1825 a serial called *The Scrapbook* described the hobby of scrapbooks as the keeping of a blank book in which pictures, newspaper cuttings, and the like were pasted for safe-keeping. Cheap printing and the invention of photography tapped into the collecting urge of an increasingly capitalistic society, and people hoarded mass-produced paper items such as newspaper and magazine clippings, valentines and other greeting cards, invitations and programs, trade cards and printed scraps. Although colored scraps were added to personal memento scrapbooks, they also became the focus of collections, resulting in albums dedicated to preserving and displaying them. In true American fashion, advances in technology and increased prosperity fostered a hobby available to all. By the mid-nineteenth century, scrapbooks had become icons of American culture.

Nineteenth-century entrepreneurs recognized the commercial potential of scrapbooks. Besides scraps and other ephemera especially produced and marketed for scrapbooks, the blank volumes themselves became customized.

Some were preprinted with headings, picture frames, and quotations that suggested organizational patterns; some had pages of different colors for different sections; some had star connections such as the Jenny Lind scrapbook featuring a frontispiece portrait of the glamorous opera singer. The Mark Twain Scrapbook, patented in 1873, came with pages precoated with mucilage—one moistened the glue and applied the scraps.

Scrapbooks signify both the individual maker and the culture in which they are created. Although many are autobiographical statements, many more reflect the particular interests or obsessions of their compilers. Scrapbooks were created with single subjects or with single types of materials—they focused on a particular individual, historical event, stage or opera star, disaster, or world's fair. An extremely popular subject for collectors was the theater. These scrapbooks, found today in almost all library special collections, can be single format—devoted to playbills, photographs, drawings, or ticket stubs—or they can concentrate on a single performer, theater, company, or genre.

Scrapbooks were made to mourn lost loved ones. These books held death and funeral announcements, obituaries, personal writings about the deceased, condolence notes, prayers, religious poems, locks of the deceased's hair, sentimental verses and, after the advent of photography, photos of those who had passed away. Photographs and paintings of dead infants and of mourners grouped around an open casket were common.

In the last quarter of the nineteenth century, a popular collectible for scrapbooks was the trade card, an advertising card that usually had a printed color image and the merchant's name and address. Millions of the cards were distributed inside product packages, door-to-door, in the mail, and at national expositions and local fairs.

Scrapbooks in library archival collections are often anonymous and without reliable provenance; however, enough are identifiable to suggest that members of both genders and all ages practiced the hobby (Smith 66–69).

Nineteenth and twentieth century scrapbook keeping is generally associated with girls and women, who found that through their scrapbooks they could articulate who they were in a society that did not privilege female voices. Furthermore, scrapbook-making was linked with the nursery and the education of children, endorsed by educational and child-rearing experts: scrapbooks fostered artistic values, neatness, dexterity, attention to detail, and organizational skills. They were inexpensive, easy-to-make, valuable resources for information on any subject ranging from history through science, art or biography. Teachers compiled information about their subjects as resources or textbooks for their students, while housekeepers relied on scrapbooks for recipes and hints on housekeeping and the toilette. Scrapbooks even became the sources for published books of household hints.

Men and boys also composed scrapbooks; however, they had different purposes and audiences in mind. Most notably, men kept scrapbooks that tracked their careers or compiled a knowledge base to which they could refer professionally. Successful men, especially, had secretaries or assistants, or wives or daughters, who did the actual compiling. In these cases, the scrapbooks may have been about personal subjects—themselves—but were not exactly personal. For instance, physicians at the turn of the twentieth century assiduously compiled scrapbooks of new knowledge and practices in their field.

Individuals kept (and keep) scrapbooks, but communal or collaborative scrapbooks were also popular. For instance, Mary Baker Eddy, the founder of Christian Science, kept her own personal memento scrapbooks as a young woman, but later her clippings and collections focused on her religious movement and its institution, and they were organized and placed into scrapbooks by her assistants. In New Orleans, a communal scrapbook was kept at the Ursuline Convent and School (Tulane University Library). In Rhode Island, the Perry Davis and Son pharmaceutical business kept a scrapbook that included their patent for a vegetable pain killer, and the Gorham Manufacturing Company kept a scrapbook of its silver patterns. In Boston, members of the Utopian Club, "a popular Hebrew organization," kept an organizational scrapbook that included newspaper clippings, invitations, programs, tickets, and small posters. (The Davis, Gorham, and Utopian Club scrapbooks are in the John Hay Library at Brown University.)

The universality of scrapbooks in the United States can be measured both by the volume of trade in blank books and scraps, and by the variety of individuals who compiled them. Besides Christian Scientists, Roman Catholics, Jews, silversmiths, and pharmacists, people from many other segments of American society assembled scrapbooks. Monte Grover, a prostitute in nineteenth century Wyoming, kept a scrapbook, as did author Willa Cather. Cather made her scrapbook by sewing pieces of cotton cloth and binding them with a fabric cover. This scrapbook reappears in her American classic novel *My Antonia* as the picture book Jim Burden makes for Yulka and Antonia. (See Ott, Tucker, and Buckler for accounts of both these scrapbooks.)

African Americans likewise documented themselves and their relationships in scrapbooks. Besides personal scrapbooks, they compiled historical clippings, photo albums, and collection scrapbooks. African American leader W.E.B. Du Bois created photo albums for the 1900 Paris Exposition to show African Americans as "not different than whites in terms of religion, politics, language, and daily life, yet as members, also, of another 'vast historic race.'" Japanese-American children held in American internment camps during World War II were encouraged to make scrapbooks about their experiences to be shared with chapters of the American Junior Red Cross (Ott, Tucker, and Buckler).

Scrapbook materials are highly corruptible, especially those from former times, and their irregularity and fragility make them difficult to preserve, to categorize, and to use. However, in recent years, archivists and scholars have gradually recognized scrapbooks' value for studying not only the material cultures that produced them, but also as repositories of information neglected by history books. Because of this combination of brittleness and significance, modern scrapbook makers look for materials that are acid-free and lignin-free, an important marketing point made by manufacturers of scrapbook supplies.

By the 1930s, the most popular type of scrapbook in the United States was the photo album, not surprisingly, since cameras had become more and more portable and less and less expensive to own and use. Kodak had a folding, pocket camera on the market in 1902, and the first Brownie in 1907; Kodak models targeted at females included the Girl Scout in 1929; the Camp Fire Girls' in 1831; the Coquette, a Petite Camera with matching lipstick holder and compact; and the Ensemble, a Petite Camera in a suede case, with lipstick compact, and mirror, that came in beige, rose, or green, with cosmetics by the House of Tre Jur.

Large bound blank books provided the canvas for photo artists to show off their creative accomplishments. As the times changed, the albums were re-designed to appeal to different social groups and consumer markets. In the 1950s, for example, books with symbols of the youth culture aimed at the large teenage market.

One of these teenagers was Lyndel Petry Trissell of Piqua, Ohio, who received her first camera for her sixteenth birthday in 1956. The camera took black-and-white photos using 127 film. Lyndel began her scrapbooking hobby at that time, using the "Pony Tail Photo Scrapbook." In the years since, she has consistently collected, mounted, and labeled photos of friends, family, co-workers, special occasions, ordinary occasions, and anything else that she thought worth capturing and preserving. Lyndel carries on a custom that she learned from her parents, themselves passionate photographers who taught her to carefully label and organize her collection. Today she has se-venty-nine, and is still collecting and compiling.

Lyndel's procedure is different from scrapbook makers like Teresa and Brenda; her work is usually solitary, and she does not use commercial pro-ducts to embellish her pages. She labels her photos by hand and cuts out her own paper trimming when needed. She prefers plain pages without plastic leaves and uses old-fashioned photo-corners—simple but thorough. Although she usually works by herself, she does enjoy sharing her collection and was very generous during our interview on June 11, 2005. When asked why she has continued this hobby for nearly fifty years, she explained that she has a strong sense of history and family tradition. Scrapbooking keeps her con-nected with family and friends, and helps her stay in touch with herself and with people now departed.

The scrapbook has endured as a primary repository for information, memorabilia, photos, and other artifacts for centuries. People like Teresa, Brenda, and Lyndel carry on the practice rooted so deeply in the American past, but still growing new branches and leaves. If anything, the late twentieth and early twenty-first centuries have stolen the nineteenth's reputation as the "golden age of scrapbooks." The hobby continues to expand to new social groups that do not come from a scrapbook-rich culture, while the spreading popularity of digital cameras and computers makes picture-taking more accessible than ever. Retirement parties, weddings, birthday parties, and even funerals often project digital photo albums for the guests.

In fact, many modern scrapbook-makers create their pages wholly on computers. Digital scrapbooking has grown rapidly as Web sites become available from which hobbyists can download images, embellishments, and even special effects that make computer pages look three-dimensional. "Digi-scrappers" and "paper-scrappers" share the same demographics, however— women between thirty and fifty years of age. Furthermore, the digital scrapbook pages are often printed and bound into an album to be shared with family and friends (Balint).

Scrapbooks adapt remarkably well to changes in technology and culture, a fact that may explain their longevity in American society. Whether using advanced digital methods or plain old-fashioned paper, scissors, and glue, the essential human impulse to keep and share memories remains a driving force in the creation of self-made books. For it is this mixture of creativity, self-representation, and sharing that comprises the most enduring and pleasurable quality of the scrapbook hobby. Until these elements disappear, scrapbooks will remain a significant part of American life.

WORKS CITED AND RECOMMENDED

Allen, Alistar, and Joan Hoverstadt. *The History of Printed Scraps.* London: New Cavendish Books, 1983.

Balint, Kathryn. "Keepsakes by Computer; Digital Scrapbooks Now Rival Paper Version." *San Diego Union-Tribune* 12 July 2004, sec. C: 1. *LexisNexis Academic.* Purdue University North Central Lib., Westville, IN. 16 Aug. 2005 <http://lib-proxy.pnc.edu:2137/universe/printdoc>.

Motz, Marilyn. "Visual Autobiography: Photograph Albums of Turn of the Century Midwestern Women." *American Quarterly* 41.1 (1989): 63–92.

Ott, Katherine, Susan Tucker, and Patricia Buckler. *The Scrapbook in American Life.* Philadelphia: Temple UP, 2006.

Smith, Deborah A. "Consuming Passions: Scrapbooks and American Play." *The Ephemera Journal* 6 (1993): 63–76.

Tupac Shakur

Mickey Hess

The first time I heard Tupac's voice was on Digital Underground's 1991 single "Same Song." I was 15, and Tupac was four years older. His rhyme style was more restrained than it would become in his later releases, and his lyrics hadn't shifted to the social themes they would become known for, but already he was a dynamic presence. A decade later, I watched Digital Underground play a show in Louisville, Kentucky. Tupac had left Digital Underground for a solo career in 1991, and was murdered five years later, so I was surprised when the group launched into "Same Song." I wanted to believe the conspiracy theories that Tupac had faked his own death, and I hoped that Tupac would make his reappearance that night. But when the song came to his verse, Digital Underground held their microphones to the crowd and we shouted Tupac's lyrics. This tribute was followed by Digital Underground vocalist Shock-G's performing a cover of Tupac's "Hail Mary," a dark song from a posthumously released album. Shock-G asked at the end of the song for a moment of silence in remembrance of his friend, then asked us to follow the silence with "a moment of motherfuckin noise," which is exactly how Tupac lived his life. His performance treaded a line between optimism and fatalism, and caught him between his belief that he would influence his listeners to change their world and his belief in the inevitability of his living, and ultimately dying for, what he called a Thug Life.

It is fitting that the 2003 MTV Films release *Tupac: Resurrection* is narrated by Tupac Shakur himself. While Tupac was murdered in 1996, he had talked extensively in interviews about his birth, life, and death, and from these interviews the film's directors created voiceovers which frame the film as an autobiography in which Tupac narrates the story of his life, from his *in utero* stage during his mother's incarceration in 1971, to his murder at age 25 in a drive-by shooting in Las Vegas. Tupac's music shared this autobiographical focus, chronicling his impoverished childhood and often contextualizing his own message and actions as a legacy of his mother's involvement with the Black Panthers. Tupac most directly explored his connection with his mother in "Dear Mama," a song that chronicles his troubled youth with a mother who was often absent in his early childhood because of her activist involvement, and during his teenage years because of her addiction to crack cocaine. Afeni Shakur appeared in the video for "Dear Mama," which reenacts her reconciliation with Tupac. Afeni's place in her son's music works to establish two key facets of his credibility with listeners. First, Tupac connects himself to black radical history through his mother's affiliation with the Black Panthers. Second, her appearance in his music and videos confirms Tupac's music as autobiography and confirms that his life and performance form an organic whole, as she proves to the audience that 2Pac the artist is one and the same with Tupac the performer, and that the two share a common history and identity.

In both *Tupac: Resurrection*, and the "Dear Mama" video, Tupac calls the viewer's attention to the fact that Afeni actually spent time in prison while pregnant with her son. These images of Tupac's origins contrast with the death imagery which became a central focus in his music after a first, unsuccessful attempt on his life in front of a New York studio. In his music, his birth and death form a continuum; and as his career progressed, his lyrics became increasingly concerned with his own mortality, with the afterlife, and with resurrection. Tupac's artistic attention to his origins and to his mortality creates an organic performance that makes him vitally real to his audience. Tupac has sold more records worldwide than any other artist in hip hop, a music form that values authenticity and is concerned with the real. Tupac's lyrical skill and delivery find him ranked consistently among the best MCs of all time, but he is most iconic in the autobiographical nature of his lyrics. He connected with his audience by making himself authentic, organic, and vulnerable through his themes of birth and death, and by bringing together his life onstage as 2Pac with his life offstage as Tupac Amaru Shakur. His work included several albums, films, and a volume of poetry, but essentially his life became his performance, and his art stands as a legacy to his message. His murder in many ways works to validate this message through his own vulnerability to the issues about which he spoke.

Emerging at a historical moment when popular music listeners had become very mistrusting of the digitized and the simulated, Tupac made himself both authentic and organic. Tupac released his first solo album *2pacAlypse Now* in 1991, in the wake of hip hop's second, and furthest-reaching, wave of mass commercialization. MC Hammer and Vanilla Ice had crossed over to the *Billboard* pop charts, outselling any rap artists to date; but these artists each saw a backlash as listeners accused them of removing hip hop from its roots in the black urban community and watering it down for a mainstream audience. This backlash was heightened through two specific scandals. Within pop music, in 1990 the group Milli Vanilli was stripped of its Grammy award for Best New Artist after the group's record label admitted that Rob and Fab, who performed on stage and in videos as Milli Vanilli, had not recorded the vocals on their album and did not perform live vocals in concert. A few months later, Vanilla Ice plummeted from rap's biggest selling artist to its most discredited when a story from Ken Parish Perkins in the *Dallas Morning News* revealed several pieces of misinformation in the official artist biography Ice's record label had released to the press. The SBK Records bio claimed a connection to black urban experience, but the article's research revealed a very different and more middle-class upbringing.

Tupac Shakur as Ezekiel "Spoon" Whitmore in the 1997 movie *Gridlock'd*. Courtesy of Photofest.

With such scandals weighing on the minds of music fans, Tupac seemed to embody the real. Through his autobiographical lyrics he sought to remove the distance between 2Pac the artist and Tupac the performer, and his albums stood as a testament to his experience. Although he was involved in the music chart dominance of crossover pop rap as a dancer and vocalist for Digital Underground, Tupac as a solo artist worked to strip away the comedic showmanship and costumes that brought that group to pop listeners with their hit single "The Humpty Dance." Tupac's first solo video, for the song "Trapped," is filmed mostly in black and white, features him performing behind bars, and depicts him as the victim of police brutality. Tupac would soon experience such brutality off-screen, and in 1992 brought charges of abuse against the Oakland (California) Police Department. In an incident stemming from an original citation for jaywalking, Tupac was physically assaulted by two police officers and charged with resisting arrest. The case was settled out of court, with the Oakland Police Department paying Tupac over $40,000 in damages. In this case, his lyrics preceded his lived experience.

While Tupac's lyrics often narrated his own childhood and young adulthood, songs like "Brenda's Got a Baby" and "Keep Your Head Up" spoke about women's issues in the poor black neighborhoods in which he had grown up. Tupac's dedication to women's issues in his lyrics complicates his performance of hypermasculinity, and creates a complex picture of him as a young black male. His lyrics acknowledge his mother's sacrifices and urge young women to stand up and take charge of their lives. He tells women they don't have to rely on men to make their lives better, but then he objectifies them in a song like "I Get Around," or brags about having sex with the wife of rap artist Notorious B.I.G. on "Hit Em Up." It was this side of Tupac's lyrics that brought criticism from figures like Dionne Warwick and C. Delores Tucker, who blamed Tupac and other male rap artists for the perpetuation of violence and disrespect against black women. But nothing complicates Tupac's performance further than his 1995 conviction for the sexual abuse of a fan. Tupac spent eleven months in prison, and although he claimed he was not guilty of the charges of sexual abuse, he acknowledged that he was not innocent in his personal interaction with the 20-year-old woman who brought the charges against him.

In the weeks before the jury had made their decision in this case, Tupac was robbed and attacked by an unknown assailant who shot him five times. Only hours after surgery, Tupac checked himself out of the hospital, and days later went to trial in bandages and a wheelchair. In interviews included in *Tupac: Resurrection,* Tupac makes clear that he suspected rap artist Notorious B.I.G. and his producer Sean "Puff Daddy" Combs of being involved in the attack. The pair had been recording at a studio in the same building Tupac was shot in front of, and he never believed their innocence. This suspicion formed the basis for the "East Coast versus West Coast" rivalry that would end with both Tupac and Biggie dead in shootings that will be forever linked in the public mind, although police investigators claim there is no connection between the crimes. The murders of Tupac in 1996 and Notorious B.I.G. in 1997 will be remembered as markers of the end of gangsta rap's most violent and commercially viable period. The two stars became icons, then martyrs, of the rivalry between Los Angeles's Death Row Records and New York's Bad Boy label. The gangsta posturing from both camps during the 1996 MTV Music Awards became all too real only days later when Tupac died in a Las Vegas hospital one week after he sustained five bullet wounds in a drive-by shooting. His death sparked numerous conspiracy theories among his fans; and his killer, like Biggie's, has never been found. While the death imagery on *Me Against the World* forms the basis for many theories about his murder, some fans believe lyrics on Tupac's posthumously-released album *Makaveli— The Don Killuminati: The Seven Day Theory* seem to allude directly to his plans to fake his own death.

After the first attempt on his life in New York, Tupac's music became further concerned with death, resurrection, and the afterlife. He left behind the more overt political themes of his early songs like "Panther Power" and "Trapped" for more directly autobiographical treatment of his own mortality. A look at the track listing for his album *Me Against the World* reveals song titles like "If I Die 2 Nite" and "Death Around the Corner." To fans, these songs became prophecy after Tupac's murder. Most haunting is his video for "I Ain't Mad at Cha." The video, released only weeks after Tupac's death, depicts his being shot and fatally wounded after leaving a movie theater with a friend. Tupac performs in heaven, dressed in all white. The timing of the release of this video, only weeks after Tupac's murder, lends itself to conspiracy theories that either he faked his own death, or that his record label murdered him. The storyline of the "I Ain't Mad at Cha" video may be alternatively explained in that it was the last video he released under the name Tupac before his *Makaveli* album would hit stores.

Tupac was obsessed with the idea of resurrection, leading many fans as well as critic Michael Eric Dyson, in his book *Holler If You Hear Me: Searching for Tupac Shakur*, to position him as a Jesus figure. The *Makaveli* cover art supports this reading. Tupac's first posthumous album was released under the artist name Makaveli rather than 2Pac. Death Row Records released Makaveli's *Don Killuminati: The Seven-Day Theory* with cover art that featured a crucified Tupac with five bullet holes in his body. The Makaveli album's title and design sparked conspiracy theories among fans. Many of the theories center on numbers. Most obvious is the fact that the five bullet wounds of the cover art match the exact number of wounds Tupac sustained during the shooting that took his life. However, he had also taken five bullets when he was robbed in New York, and more likely the *Makaveli* cover was created in reference to that incident. Further theories are built from Tupac's Makaveli alias and the album's subtitle *The Seven-Day Theory*. Tupac was a fan of Niccolo Machiavelli's *The Prince*, which advocates faking one's death in order to gain power, and the number seven resounds in many statistics surrounding Pac's death. 2Pac died seven days after he was shot. He was 25, and two and five added together equal seven. Similarly, Tupac's time of death was 4:03, which again adds to seven.

Tupac's productivity during the last months of his life spurs more conspiracy theories from fans. Tupac certainly had a sense that he was not long for this earth, and after Death Row CEO Suge Knight bailed him out of prison, he began working furiously on recording new tracks. His mother won a court case for control of his unreleased work, and in 1997, she released *R U Still Down*, the first of several albums of material collected and produced after her son's death. While some fans still believe Tupac is alive and recording music in hiding, his resurrection is more likely achieved through these posthumous releases, including *The Rose That Grew from Concrete*, a collection of Tupac's poetry that his mother released in 1999 with a foreword from Nikki Giovanni. In one poem, "In the Event of My Demise" Tupac voices his urge to die for something he believes in. *Tupac: Resurrection* echoes this sentiment with Tupac's statement that while he may not change the world himself, he is certain he will influence the person who will. His influence stands today through such forums as the University of Washington course "The Textual Appeal of Tupac Shakur," a University of California—Berkeley course on his poetry, and in English classes in schools like Los Angeles' Crenshaw High. Along with such courses, Afeni Shakur has established a scholarship in her son's name, and oversees his legacy through her control over Tupac's unreleased recordings.

Through *Tupac: Resurrection* and the songs, albums, and compilations still being released more than seven years after his death, Tupac continues to speak to his fans. His untimely death, as with other American icons like Marilyn Monroe or James Dean, has furthered his cult of celebrity, yet Tupac's celebrity is perhaps more intensely linked to his death through the death imagery of his music. His lyrics anticipated his murder, so his murder seems to complete the narrative of his lyrics. The reality of his death authenticates his work in a music form where artist authenticity remains a shifting and debated issue.

WORKS CITED AND RECOMMENDED

Dyson, Michael Eric. *Holler If You Hear Me: Searching for Tupac Shakur*. Philadelphia: Basic Civitas, 2002.
Machiavelli, Niccòlo. *The Prince*. New York: Bantam, 1984.
Perkins, Ken Parish. "Under Raps: Hot Pop Vocalist Vanilla Ice Shrugs off Conflicting Versions of His Background." *Dallas Morning News* 18 Nov. 1990: 1A.
Shakur, Tupac. *The Rose That Grew from Concrete*. New York: MTV Books, 1999.

Spaceship

Angela Hague

The appearance of the spaceship in modern American culture dates from June 24, 1947, when private pilot Kenneth Arnold, who was searching for a crashed C-46 Marine transport plane, reported seeing nine crescent-shaped objects flying in formation at approximately 1,200 miles per hour over Mount Rainier, Washington. His sighting is the origin of all mythic narratives that feature the spaceship as cultural icon, and his description of the objects as moving "like a saucer would if you skipped it across the water" to William Bequette, a reporter for the *East Oregonian*, led to the phrase "flying saucer," a term that early on created a less-than-serious context for the spaceship that would continue long after flying saucers were renamed "unidentified flying objects" (Arnold 11). Arnold's claim generated a huge amount of publicity, but it was not the first time Americans had been riveted by stories of strange objects in the sky. From November 1896 to May 1897 what became known as the Great Airship Controversy captured the imagination of the public and newspapers when reports of "airships"—typically metallic, cigar-shaped vehicles with wings or propellers and high-intensity searchlights or colored lights—occurred first in California and later spread to Nebraska, Kansas, Michigan, Texas, Tennessee, Arkansas, West Virginia, Illinois, Iowa, South Dakota, Missouri, and Wisconsin.

When unexplained aerial phenomena reappeared fifty years later, their hold on the public imagination would persist until the present day and become an important reflection of the fears, desires, and fascinations of postwar American culture. The spaceship has proven to be a protean signifier of our cultural needs that develops and changes as our world evolves, functioning as a warning of government and military vulnerability, conspiracy, and cover-up; as an indicator of our ambiguous relationship with science, technology, and medicine; as a reminder of the limits of human power and autonomy; and, finally, as an image of the ultimately mysterious and inaccessible nature of the world we inhabit.

There had been other reports outside the United States of strange objects seen in the sky during and immediately after World War II. What became known as "foo fighters," small balls of variously colored lights that appeared to follow bombers in the European and Pacific war theaters, were reported by Allied and Axis pilots, and both military forces speculated that they were the secret weapons of the other side. A military explanation was also offered for the "ghost rockets" that were seen in the Scandinavian countries in 1946. But Kenneth Arnold's sighting initiated a very different attitude in the American public. Large numbers of people quickly claimed to have seen flying saucers, overwhelming the Army Air Force with reports, and the flying saucer phenomenon almost immediately became inextricably linked with Cold War paranoia. Flying saucers allowed the public effectively to displace fears of Soviet invasion and nuclear attack with the possibility of watchful and ubiquitous aliens traveling in spaceships around the planet: a force much more frightening and fascinating than the Russians was making incursions into our skies.

Two films released in 1951 set the model for two very different ways that aliens and their technology would be perceived in the future. Robert Wise's *The Day the Earth Stood Still* established the alien as benefactor: "Klaatu" comes to earth to warn against war and atomic weapons and to give a brief show of superior alien technology. He is rewarded by being shot, for the film depicts human beings as woefully primitive in their violent emotional responses and ignorance of the consequences of their actions. Just as *The Day the Earth Stood Still* reflected Cold War fears about the atomic bomb, Howard Hawks's *The Thing from Another World* spoke to contemporary anxieties about communist invasion and takeover. When a spaceship crashes at the North Pole and its frozen occupant thaws out, the monstrous creature turns out to be an alien vegetable life form that reproduces asexually and—like H. G. Wells's Martians in *The War of the Worlds* (1898)—needs human blood to survive. Like many of the aliens of the future, he lacks an emotional and sexual dimension and is uninterested in the fate of his intended prey. *The Day the Earth Stood Still* and *The Thing from Another World* early on provided the blueprint for two divergent ways of portraying the alien presence: beneficent or predatory, vastly superior or inferior to human consciousness and morality, human-like in appearance or akin to the monsters that roared and stormed through the horror movies of the time.

Aliens and their spacecraft were at the center of another movement in popular culture in the 1950s, a group of people who became known as "contactees" who claimed encounters with individuals from planets in our solar system and beyond. These "space brothers" and their female counterparts were described as physically flawless, human-appearing entities who, like Klaatu in *The Day the Earth Stood Still*, had come to earth to save it from nuclear devastation and to preach a doctrine of peace, love, and spirituality. The most famous of the contactees, "Professor" George Adamski, wrote several books documenting his relationships with aliens and trips to other planets, as did the other contactees, who included Harold Menger, Truman Bethurum, "Doctor" Daniel Frye, and Orfeo Angelucci. Another well-known contactee, George Van Tassel, founded the Giant Rock Space Convention in 1954, which until the 1970s brought together contactees and individuals interested in aliens and space travel. The contactee movement, more than any other single event in the history of the public's perception of the spaceship, made the issue of alien visitation the butt of jokes by undermining the necessity for scientific enquiry into the phenomenon and by characterizing people who believed in the reality of unidentified flying objects (UFOs) and aliens as crackpots and eccentrics.

But while many people, including scientific and military critics of UFO believers, were laughing at the absurd claims of the contactees, UFOs were gaining national attention and inciting some citizens to join civilian UFO research groups which challenged the official pronouncements of the Air Force about the reality of UFO phenomena. From the 1950s onwards the spaceship came to represent conspiracy and cover-up, by a government and military that consistently lied to the public about its knowledge—or lack of knowledge—about UFOs and aliens. These attitudes were intensified when it came to light that in September 1948 the Project Sign team, the first organized military group to investigate UFOs, had produced a top-secret "Estimate of the Situation" that determined that spacecraft seen in the skies were probably extraterrestrial. The Air Force's response was a significant event in the history of UFOs as images of governmental conspiracy and cover-up: it claimed that the report hadn't proven its case, declassified it, and ordered all copies burned.

Events, however, kept spaceships in the public sphere, particularly the July 1952 "Invasion of Washington," when during two consecutive weekends (July 10–26) unidentifiable objects were reported flying over the capital by Air Force and commercial pilots. Seen also by ground observers, the objects were picked up on radarscopes at Washington National Airport and Andrews Air Force Base. The Air Force's explanation, that temperature inversions were responsible for the phenomena, was generally accepted by the public. But the publicity surrounding the event and the intervention of the CIA into the controversy resulted in the formation of the Robertson Panel, whose recommendations issued in January 1953 increased the suspicions of a growing number of UFO believers. The Robertson Panel concluded that UFOs posed no physical threat to the United States, but that belief in and publicity about them created a glut of reports that could compromise the military's ability to protect the country from real threats of invasion. As a result, the panel recommended training citizens to recognize natural objects in the sky and, in a more controversial move, suggested that a program of debunking should begin that would make use of the media to reduce public interest in UFOs. In addition, civilian UFO research groups should be "watched" because of their influence on mass thinking.

The Robertson Panel's recommendations firmly established the profound suspicion with which many UFO believers and researchers viewed the U.S. government's attitudes and actions, a suspicion that continues today and has become an important dimension of many mythic narratives that involve spaceships and aliens. Chris Carter, the creator of the Fox Network's *The X-Files* (1993–2002), calls the show's "mythology" its continuing narrative of alien intrusion into earthly matters, including abduction of citizens and hybridization of human-alien beings; and this "mythology" has as its basis the government's knowledge of and collusion with aliens and its long-term deception of the American people. Carter's plots drew on the real-life "Dark Side" theories of John Lear, Paul Bennewitz, and William Cooper, just as he made use of the conspiracy theories that surrounded the stories of a crashed spaceship and alien bodies near Roswell, New Mexico, in July 1947.

The spaceship narrative continued to grow and develop more complex associations after the 1950s. When in January 1969 the University of Colorado published its study of UFOs commissioned by the Air Force, it concluded that "nothing has come from the study of UFOs in the past 21 years that has added to scientific knowledge. . . . further extensive study of UFOs

The depiction of the immense spaceships and nearly invincible warrior aliens in *Independence Day* (1996) is an example of the darker side of popular culture's fascination with spaceships and their inhabitants. Courtesy of Photofest.

probably cannot be justified by the expectation that science will be advanced thereby" (Condon 1); and the Air Force used the report to eliminate Project Blue Book in December 1969. However, as sightings of landings and occupants were increasingly reported in the 1960s, the UFO ceased being imagined simply as a mysterious machine and became imagined more as the environment of the beings who piloted it. Alien creatures were first reported near landed spacecraft taking samples of soil or plant life; and, as the narrative developed, human-alien interaction became more complex, culminating in stories of humans abducted for the purposes of physical and reproductive examination. The first reported abduction in the United States, which allegedly took place in the White Mountains of New Hampshire on September 19–20, 1961, involved Barney and Betty Hill, and their abduction, like Kenneth Arnold's 1947 sighting over Mount Ranier, is the founding event for the series of mythic narratives that derive from it. Abduction accounts increased dramatically during the 1970s and 1980s, accounts that depicted the spaceship as housing entities vastly more scientifically and technologically advanced than human beings.

The spaceship became the locus for events that positioned earthlings as both ignorant and powerless, the victims of alien research, experimentation, and genetic hybridization with alien creatures. In this scenario human beings, rather than functioning as empowered individuals who colonize, manipulate, and harvest other places and peoples, become the invaded and the colonized. The spaceship becomes a sign of a complete reversal of the power relations between the human and nonhuman, an image of the diminution of human achievement and knowledge, and of the dangers of the consequences of science and technology in the hands of an alien power. And at the same time, the alien "doctors" who examine and implant humans with monitoring devices and hybridized fetuses embody our own troubled attitudes toward medical technology and personnel, particularly their lack of concern with the individuals whom they serve and the increasing anonymity of medical procedures and relationships.

The spaceship has always had a close relationship with modern conceptions of science and technology; and the connection has elicited a variety of strong responses from both the scientific and UFO communities. For scientists such as Donald Menzel, Carl Sagan, and Phil Klass, belief in UFOs and aliens is part of a rising tide of irrational belief systems, and they view these "pseudo-sciences" with alarm and irritation. For many UFO believers, scientific rejection of their beliefs is an indication of the narrow-minded paradigms that science forces on phenomena that it refuses to investigate. UFOs and aliens, which have increasingly become an important aspect of New Age beliefs and practices, have also become associated with other popular anomalous phenomena such as crop circles, animal mutilations, "men in black" visitations, and sightings of black helicopters. The spaceship continues to be an icon of all that is mysterious, unexplainable, and unavailable to scientific enquiry, an image of an alternative world that interfaces with our own but refuses to reveal itself or to become assimilated into our mundane existence. At the same time, the narrative of alien visitation in popular culture helps provide an explanation for the confusion and irrationality of postwar American culture: television shows such as the short-lived *Dark Skies* (1996–1997), Steven Spielberg's ten-part miniseries *Taken* (2002), and *The X-Files* use UFOs and human-alien relationships as a prism through which to comprehend the complexities of postwar events.

Popular culture's long love affair with the spaceship and its inhabitants began in the 1950s and still shows no sign of tiring with its content; aliens both friendly, as in the cases of Steven Spielberg's *E.T.: The Extra-Terrestrial* (1982) and Jeff Bridges's alien character in John Carpenter's *Starman* (1984), and monstrously dangerous, as in Ridley Scott's *Alien* (1979) and Roland Emmerich's *Independence Day* (1996), continue to flourish. Throughout its history as an icon, the spaceship has both created and derived its meanings from its manifestations in film and television. Radio has made other important contributions to its development: Orson Welles's 1938 *War of the Worlds* broadcast preceded the first sighting of a flying saucer but clearly revealed the power of the spacecraft to mesmerize and terrify, and, in the 1950s, Long John Nebel's late-night talk show provided a forum for the contactees to publicize their experiences. In the 1990s talk radio programs such as Art Bell's *Coast to Coast AM* and shows hosted by Jeff Rense and Laura Lee provided more evidence of radio's close relationship with UFOs by offering stories of sightings of spacecraft and encounters with alien beings to their listeners.

The spaceship has continued to evolve as a cultural icon, developing a narrative that has increasingly brought alien beings to the foreground. As abduction stories proliferated in the 1980s and 1990s, beginning with the publication of UFO researcher Budd Hopkins's *Missing Time* (1981) and horror novelist Whitley Strieber's first-person account of his abduction in the best-selling *Communion* (1987), the spaceship has become less important as a narrative element, sometimes disappearing altogether; in many abduction stories no "ship" is ever referenced. Instead, the spaceship has become a visual correlative of the alien experience, functioning as an image that evokes a powerful response to the notion of a universe that exists beyond what human beings can comprehend, and as a cynosure for other anomalous phenomena that connote the mysteriousness of the world we inhabit.

Like most influential cultural images, the spaceship signals profoundly ambiguous and diametrically opposed meanings. The aliens are here to save us from ourselves and also to exploit and destroy us, just as the spaceship represents both our reverence for and suspicion of scientific technology and achievement. Alien spacecraft suggest the ignorance and failure of our government and military to protect us, and, simultaneously, their collusion with alien invaders; they also assert the primitive nature of human knowledge and achievement while placing the importance of human beings and their DNA at the center of the abduction narrative. The spaceship is an icon that has remained remarkably accessible to a wide variety of meanings from its beginnings as a "nuts and bolts" flying saucer in the 1940s and 1950s to its emergence as the referent of the abduction narrative, which continues to evolve in the direction of supernatural, mystical, and even quasi-religious experiences. The hazy, dreamlike image of a flying saucer that began the credits to *The X-Files* is particularly indicative of the spaceship's iconic status: protean, mysterious, imprecise, and ambiguous, its vagueness provides a blank slate upon which any number of cultural narratives can be written.

WORKS CITED AND RECOMMENDED

Arnold, Kenneth, and Ray Palmer. *The Coming of the Saucers.* Amherst, WI: Amherst P, 1955.

Bartholomew, Robert E., and George S. Howard. *UFOs and Contact: Two Centuries of Mystery.* Amherst, NY: Prometheus Books, 1998.

Bryan, C.D.B. *Close Encounters of the Fourth Kind: A Reporter's Notebook on Alien Abduction, UFOs, and the Conference at M.I.T.* New York: Penguin, 1996.

Cohen, Daniel. *The Great Airship Mystery: A UFO of the 1890s.* New York: Dodd, Mead, and Company, 1981.

Condon, Edward U. *Final Report of the Scientific Study of Unidentified Flying Objects.* New York: E. P. Dutton and Company, 1969.

Hopkins, Budd. *Missing Time.* New York: Ballantine Books, 1981.

Jacobs, David M. *The Threat: Revealing the Secret Alien Agenda.* New York: Simon and Schuster, 1992.

———, ed. *UFOs and Abductions: Challenging the Borders of Knowledge.* Lawrence: UP of Kansas, 2000.

Mack, John. *Abduction: Human Encounters with Aliens.* New York: Scribner's, 1994.

Peebles, Curtis. *Watch the Skies! A Chronicle of the Flying Sauce Myth.* New York: Berkley Publishing Group, 1995.

Story, Ronald D., ed. *The Encyclopedia of Extraterrestrial Encounters.* New York: New American Library, 2001.

Thompson, Keith. *Angels and Aliens: UFOs and the Mythic Imagination.* New York: Fawcett Columbine, 1991.

Vallee, Jacques. *Passport to Magonia: On UFOs, Folklore, and Parallel Worlds.* 1969. Chicago: Contemporary Books, 1993.

Sports Bar

William R. Klink

"Let's get another. Unnh. I just can't get down the line as quick as I used to."

"Yeah, well, look at Sosa, he can't either."

"He's in a slump again."

"Maybe we should go to a game."

"Nachos? Waitress!"

A conversation like this could occur in any place that serves food and drink. But it is the kind of conversation that is the signature of the sports bar: two men talking about sports, a little about themselves, referencing current professional sports, and making plans to do something, all while eating and drinking. There is no direct mention of feelings, no personal disclosure, no linearity; action, group identity, and pastiche is what there is, all supported by the iconic meanings of the sports-bar space.

The history of sports bars is a history of evolution rather than revolution; the English medieval publican dispensing local knowledge to a crowd is now supplanted by the television. The Victorian era's three-sectioned space—tap room, saloon, and lounge—has given way to bar, tables, and video game areas. The earlier division of interior space to reflect social distinctions is paralleled in America by bars separately catering to different classes, race, and genders. Sports bars, which morphed from originally male working-class neighborhood bars, bring together, arguably, the two most prominent leisure-time activities of the working class—drinking and television watching. Clearly, they are a distinct social space, differing from other male niche bars, such as strip clubs, which feature feigned intimate relations between patrons and employees; singles bars, where the supposedly unmarried go to attain new partners; and the Hooters-type bar which tries to span the differences between the two. In patriarchal America, there can be no female sports bars. By definition these spaces would be lesbian bars; the closest to the niche would be the "dykes on bikes" bar.

As a social third place, situated between work and home, sports bars have important cultural intersections of even deeper meaning. The shriveling of open public spaces for adults (parks in the cities and suburbs), the decline of the church, and the amorphous quality of communities all create social and political pressures that are resisted by sports bars. One may argue that neighborhood bars perform the same service, but there is a difference. Neighborhood bars feature a discourse that replicates the other side of masculine culture, the side that values self-control, efficiency, and a work ethic. The discourse is frequently directly about these topics or about intimate feelings and admiration for, and about social consequences of, certain valued behaviors. Most of these concerns, by contrast, are directly devalued in sports bars by the technology of alcohol consumption and without the moral agency of female influence. To illustrate, consider if the essence of the conversation cited above were to remain the same but be spoken in a neighborhood bar:

> "Can I get you another drink? Unnh. It bothers me I can't move the way I used to."
>   "Oh, what's wrong? Have you gone to the doctor? Stuff happens at our age."
>   "I'm just putting it off for now. I don't notice it at work."
>   "If it's bothering you now, we can leave."

Here the discourse models male behavior in its self-control, shown through caring for each others' feelings and the linearity of topics; efficiency, through concern about time usage; and economic value, the judgment that anything that does not affect job performance is trivial.

The value of sports bars in part for the working class is in their democratic aspect: they are places where leisure behavior is self-selected and therefore contests prescribed behavior in employment. Sports bars also contest other hierarchies in society; they are, for example, by choice of their patrons usually, places of no particular race or ethnicity, especially if they are destination sports bars.

Sports bars sell or commodify for sale traditional masculine values in three specific iterations: the site-specific sports bar, the franchised sports bar, and the independent sports bar. Murphy's Bleachers, for example, which occupies its space just outside the bleachers at Wrigley Field, home of the lamentable losers the Chicago Cubs, and which

Waitresses at Hooters strike a pose as Charlie's Angels. Courtesy of Shutterstock.

started as a hot dog stand, is a site-specific sports bar. Its patrons are upscale office workers. The expensive beers and the rail drinks reflect the economic power of their consumers, who cheer with usually restrained enthusiasm for their Cubbies. Site-specific sports bars are especially found around college campuses and other locations where there are nearby sports teams that charge admission. These sports bars exist because they are close to sporting events, in the same way the Murphy's Bleachers is a sports bar taking advantage of its location close to a major sporting venue. One other such near-stadium sports bar is Bob Baumhower's Wings Sports Grille in Birmingham, Alabama. He is a former football hero at the University of Alabama, a hotbed of college football, and a great player for the professional Miami Dolphins. There, before, during, and after Alabama football games, pitchers of beer, loud shouting, and broad gesturing are the norm, reflecting the down-home values of the fans of southeastern college football.

Some sports bars, in contrast to the site-specific sports-bar model of Murphy's, are born whole. Major sports-bar chains Legends, Champs, Champions, and ESPN Zone are well established, though challenged by the fastest growing restaurant franchise, Darden's Smokey Bones Sports Bar and BBQ. Of all of these franchises the most spectacular is ESPN Zone. Interestingly, it replicates the segregation within its space that existed in the early English tavern three-section set-up. There is the bar space and soft-chair area right in front of a giant television with little televisions and electronic tickers surrounding it as the bar space. There is a parlor area with tables, chairs, and televisions farther away from the big screen in rooms that nevertheless provide some access to the bar view. There is an arcade area, with its many athletic electronic games and other machines where patrons may try their hand at shooting basketballs, among other skill tests. Rather than by age or gender, the segregation is by level of attention deficit to the television(s).

Another kind of sports bar is the one located in no particular proximity to any sports venue and not a franchise operation. Among these is Willie and Reed's in Bethesda, Maryland, notable for its sleek, modern, chrome look, and for its efforts to broaden appeal to women's tastes by acquiring cable packages that feature television shows favored by women—such as *Sex and the City*—available in slack times of sports television viewing.

Models for independent sports bars are so ubiquitous that "the bars and pubs with and without food in the U.S. are normally distinguished only by the degree of their sports orientation," say Krotz and Eastman (18). Sports bars are a genus with limitless species.

There are then two physical requirements of a sports bar that differentiate it from any other kind of bar. The first is that the television tuned to sports must be prominent, and the attention of the clientele must be on that sports event or one that is aligned with it. There may be one television; there may be twenty; there may be one twenty feet wide with twenty flatscreen televisions surrounding it, and others over every urinal. The second physical requirement is that the television focus is abetted by decoration of the interior space with sports memorabilia that directs attention to history in the making on the television and suggests that patrons have a place in the unfolding of that history. For example, a locked transparent case (one that might otherwise be found housing a Grecian urn in a museum) containing hundreds of baseballs autographed by all members of the last twenty Major League Baseball All-Star teams creates a backdrop to set the customer in a place that shares its history and that of its patrons with the history to be made on the television. All things are commodified as sports history, a history that is about and written by men for men.

The main requirement of a sports bar is not its things however, but the behavior that the things lead to within the space. The prevalence of bars with televisions and memorabilia not only works as a model for those attempting to start one, but also provides models for the behavior of those who enter one seeking peak experiences of consumption at a relatively low cost. In a sports bar, both men and women produce behaviors that fit gender perceptions of male behavior and support gendered roles in the networks of social relationships that they establish and maintain. Behavior is not a function of freedom in a sports bar, but instead a matter of conformity to the expected behavior of such a public house, whose eye is the television and whose other senses are the sports memorabilia, both of which, along with other patrons, provide estimable models to follow. Television and memorabilia reflect manly images that are so effective at controlling behavior that these athletic images are themselves therefore iconic, making acolytes of sports-bar patrons and those with whom they interact both inside and outside the bar.

To some, going to a sports bar is better than going to a neighborhood bar because sports-bar behavior is mediated and altered to conform to the behavior of being at the live sports event on the television. Thus, the bar chooses what is on television and that in turn influences the behavior of patrons. To that end then, managers of sports bars use television to attract customers for food and drink sales by providing entertainment, decoration, and atmosphere that construct sports-bar behavior.

Going to watch television in a public space is to watch television in a male area—the public space traditionally controlled by men. The visual cues at the public sports bar enable sports-bar patrons to pursue what researchers call typical male friendships, begun in a place of socially constructed sexual segregation and then built on behaviors that share less than intimate emotional experiences. To some sports bar patrons, these behaviors are liberating and nostalgic. Sports bars provide the perfect setting for developing male friendships in the way that team sports do. The combination of cooperative and antagonistic competition, central to team sports, as Steven J. Harvey notes, is encouraged by the sports-bar space, the simulacrum of a team-sports setting. The television itself manages and is managed by the cooperative and antagonistic behavior of the male viewers speaking and directing activity both toward and away from the television. In turn, this behavior dramatizes the patrons as performers in the making of their own self-images as men who go to sports bars and who are constructed from the range of social interactions that take place there as real sports-loving men.

During big games on television that monopolize the attention of the patrons, men huddle in groups like a football team, and respond to the television together with shouts and curses, many specific to the teams, "Wa-Hoo-Wa," for example, for a University of Virginia team. When there is no big game on and the multiple screens show a wide selection of sports events, the behavior is less unified. Men and the few women huddle in basketball team–sized groups to cajole and tease each other with sex and sport jokes. The conversation points to its analog, the sports talk radio show. In both scenarios, the overriding sound emits such phrases as "Sosa sucks," "They're all on steroids anyway," "f***ing ump is blind," "Stewart is a mean bastard," "She's got a nice leg," "The wings are better at Smoky's," "I was totally wasted," repeating the nonlinear discourse that could be heard on a team bench during that very game on the television or televisions, while speakers are reminded of such patter by the memorabilia that surrounds them. Meanwhile, some patrons may rebel, asserting their American individualism by talking quietly about their sports preferences or sexual objects or even discussing matters as if they were at a neighborhood bar.

The individual is destabilized by the mirroring effect of self-reflexivity demanded by sports bars, even while amplifying the small differences in behavior that he is allowed within behavior rules in sports bars, whether by dress, gesture, or speech. Sometimes these differences themselves are picked up by others and replicated so that small differences become first imitated and then dominant when taken up by everyone. The most obvious of these behaviors is the impromptu cheer that gets adopted and then reused constantly. Its successful progenitor becomes a heroic icon himself. His behavior is replicated because it suggests the totality of the experience.

In that way, highly controlled physical and verbal behavior produces a social order that mimics that of a team. Though patrons are well aware of the contextual and behavioral knowledge of sports bars that contributes to their behavior (for example, that movement is encouraged, as is yelling at the television, and crude, aggressive joking), such knowledge is never part of the actual conversation. As a kind of subtext, the discourse at sports bars is competitive about teams and individuals, both those provided by the cues and those in attendance. The topics range from food, particularly beer, to women's roles in a male-dominated culture, to talk about group behavior and distinctions. Power flows away from those with little to say and those who display little energy to say it, to those who have lots to say and lots of energy to say it. The discourse as a microproduction reproduces the macrorelations of the sports bar itself, representing the opinions and favored topics of discourse of its clientele, who choose it specifically for that reason. Other discourses are resisted—what happened today on "Days of Our Lives"—and some discourses are contested as marginal, for example, talk about high school experiences, as skewered in "Glory Days" by Bruce Springsteen.

Power circulates unevenly among all on the "team" as if everyone is allowed a turn at bat. Though some may decline and some may be forcibly pinch hit for, others will swing and miss and strikeout, others will draw a walk by uttering apt but unpointed remarks (the glue that holds discourse communities together), and others will get their hits. In the end, language is institutionalized as sports-bar language which becomes a normative behavior furthering its own hegemony, marginalizing or extinguishing all other discourses.

So while the patrons are legally free to say what they want, they are quite controlled by forces that construct the discourse to its own preexisting rules, an approximation of those governing a team as well, having limited themes, modes of thought, ideas, values, actions, interactions, and technologies.

Drinking, watching, and talking create consumption that in turn constructs socially-situated identity and its icons by customizing behavior that differs with behavior at a neighborhood bar and with behavior attendant to television watching at home. The sports-bar customization does away with individuation altogether, deferring individuation for just those other sites, the neighborhood bar and at-home television. The at-home experience features just a few pre-chosen others who already know the personal items that are avoided in the sports bar and who will refer to them in the most off handed way. "Just like you, the way he dropped that pass," is a phrase from the at-home sports watcher who is just as likely to drink in the same pattern as if he were at a sports bar, but who is just as unlikely to gesture, to move, and to shout at length in a neighborhood bar or at home as he would in a sports bar.

Sports bars, thus, despite regulating customers' practices, work against rather than for social homogenization because they encourage temporary behavior based on illusory or virtual realities which do not have to be lived in the day-to-day existence but which, precisely because they are an escape from day-to-day life, present an opportunity for a peak experience. That peak experience is the dramatization of the self to a roomful of like-minded people, encouraged and supported by the technology present in the sports bar in the form of television and memorabilia.

WORKS CITED AND RECOMMENDED

Baird, Courtney. "Simple Biology Explains the History of the True Sports Fan." *New U* 13 Dec. 2005 <http://www.newu.uci.edu/article.php?id=1990>.

Bonabeau, Eric. "The Perils of the Imitation Age." *The Harvard Business Review* June 2004: 45–54.

Harvey, Steven J. "Hegemonic Masculinity, Friendship, and Group Formation in an Athletic Subculture." *The Journal of Men's Studies* 8 (1999). 13 Dec. 2005 <http://www.questia.com/PM.qst?a=o&d=5001833122>.

Krotz, Friedrich, and Susan Tyler Eastman. "Orientations Toward Television Outside the Home." *Journal of Communication* 49 (Winter 1999). 13 Dec. 2005 <http://www.questia.com/PM.qst?a=o&d=96498164>.

Salinger, Sharon V. *Taverns and Drinking in Early America*. Baltimore: Johns Hopkins UP, 2004.

Sherry, John F., Robert V. Kozinets, Adam Duhaceck, and Benet Deberry-Spence. "Gendered Behavior in a Male Preserve: Role Playing at ESPN Zone Chicago." *Journal of Consumer Psychology* 14.1–2 (2004): 151–59.

West, Lois A. "Negotiating Masculinities in American Drinking Subcultures." *The Journal of Men's Studies* 9 (2001). 13 Dec. 2005 <http://www.questia.com/PM.qst?a=o&d=5000997969>.

Stadium

Sylvester Frazier, Jr.

It is almost a daily occurrence. Thousands of people congregate at an indoor arena or a stadium to watch a sporting event. Many of the people come because they love the sports, others because of the social activities surrounding the event. Outside of the venue, the stadium provides needed work and income for some, but brings others annoyances. In short, for different people a sports stadium can be anything from a Mecca to a massive inconvenience.

Sports stadiums maintain a complex relationship between the cities in which they are located and the residents of those metropolitan communities. To the residents, the stadium can play opposite roles: a hostile interruption of their daily routine, a mere eyesore, a generator of income, a centerpiece monument of the city. Burdensome issues of financing the stadium through tax dollars, providing public transportation to the venue, or improving the infrastructure to and from the stadium complicate the citizens' situation more. The types and manner of relationships to the stadium apparently are equivalent to the number of communities or even individuals located in the city that houses the sports facility. If one regards the idea of stadium as a text, then it becomes possible to apply textual analysis to the multitude of interpretations that communities or individuals have of a sports venue.

Stanley Fish set forth the idea of interpretive communities in his larger work "Interpreting the Variorum" (1976). Literary scholars use Fish's ideas to analyze why certain persons read the same text in certain ways. He presents two central principles: "(1) The same reader will perform differently when reading two 'different' (the word is in quotation marks because its status is precisely what is at issue) texts; and (2) different readers will perform similarly when reading the 'same' text" (217). Again, replacing the idea of "stadium" with the idea of "text" and considering two stadiums in two different locations, one can look at how a person views a stadium built across town or in another city in a different manner from one built near his home. In *It's Hardly Sportin': Stadiums, Neighborhoods, and the New Chicago*, Costas Spirou and Larry Bennett describe the widespread reverence for Chicago's

Wrigley Field: "For those who take the history and lore of baseball very seriously, Wrigley Field is, quite simply, a pilgrimage site" (108). However, Wrigley Field, especially its post lights, provides a different view and meaning for those who live near the stadium: "But for the local residents the ballpark, which itself is usually viewed as an amenity, represents a threat to peace and local stability as the atmosphere of revelry spreads to adjoining areas" (138). For a baseball fan and resident of the Lake View on Chicago's north side, Wrigley Field can be viewed as essentially two texts, first as a historic sports stadium, a type of sports Mecca, and second, a nuisance that interferes with his or her daily life. The person belongs to two interpretive communities, baseball fans and local residents. His relationship to Wrigley Field will then be determined by the standards of which community he deems more important. This discrepancy often produces a sports fan who votes against improvements of a stadium or even the construction of a park that is located in his neighborhood, but would have no qualms about voting for improvements or construction in another part of town. Fish explains this phenomenon: "a single reader will employ different interpretive strategies and thus make different texts [because] (he belongs to different communities)" (219–20).

Fish's second notion is that different readers will read a text the same way. In regard to stadiums, varied individuals can view the same text in the same manner. Looking at the community mentioned above that considers Wrigley Field a pilgrimage site, one can think of two baseball fans, one who lives near the stadium in Chicago and another who lives in Dallas. If both have the same idea of Wrigley Field, it is because they are interpreting the stadium for its value to baseball. The actions of the individuals will correspond to their reading of value. The fan living in Chicago will cherish the fact that he can spend multiple afternoons in the stadium, while the Dallas fan, viewing Wrigley Field as a prized destination, may take a summer vacation to Chicago in order to experience a game in the bleachers, possibly sitting a row below the Chicago fan.

Like people, cities also view stadiums in different manners depending on the beliefs of their community, as represented by their government officials. Many cities, for example, value stadiums as economic-generating entities even when there is no real proof that the stadiums are. Spirou and Bennett point out, "Most of America's older industrial metropolises are presently attempting to redevelop their physical spaces and redefine their national and international identities through sports- and culture-driven growth initiatives" (13). Later, however, the authors question the true economic benefits: "there remains considerable uncertainty concerning the utility of sports construction projects as tools for economic development and urban regeneration" (19). In such instances, individual cities view stadiums as necessary entities. The city and those involved in urban planning read the idea of the sports stadium in the same manner, as an economic and social must for their particular city. In situations such as this, Fish writes, "it has always been possible to put into action interpretive strategies designed to make all texts one, or to put it more

Franklin D. Roosevelt seated in the presidential box at Griffith Stadium preparing to toss a
baseball onto the field, 1933. Courtesy of the Library of Congress.

accurately, to be forever making the same text" (218). The cities all read their
needs as the same; so one city will have the same relationship to a stadium as
its so-called rival city. In this sense, all cities then make the same text of
meaning, with, in Fish's terms, "a set of directions for finding it, which of
course is a set of directions—of interpretive strategies—for making, that is,
for the endless reproduction of the same text" (219). The city official who
finds justification for building new stadiums, despite evidence that contradicts
the economic benefits, then becomes no different from the literary critic who
forces a novel into a certain genre even when the work only has one or two
characteristics in common with the genre.

When building a stadium is proposed, the community's reaction to the project is often problematic. Different members of what appears to be the same
community employ different strategies of interpretation, which are constantly
in flux. Communication and cooperation often become difficult to achieve
between the government and members of the community, on crucial issues
such as location, funding, economic value, and audience attraction. In such
cases, Fish observes, "the only stability, then, inheres in the fact that interpretive strategies are always being deployed, and this means that the communication is a much more chancy affair than we are accustomed to think it"

(220). Understanding the divergent texts of the responses is difficult because one can never be sure of the relationship that an individual community member has to the stadium. Judging a response to be more or less representative or authentic cannot be objective: as Fish concludes, "the only 'proof' of membership is fellowship, the nod of recognition from someone in the same community" (221).

To highlight the differences in the reaction of the same group to a similar stadium project, two recent projects in the city of Arlington, Texas, just west of Dallas, can serve as examples. The first involves a new stadium for the Dallas Cowboys. The other proposes a new stadium and football program at the University of Texas at Arlington (UTA).

In the first case, Texas Stadium, located in Irving, Texas, has been what many view as a classic stadium. It has been the home of a successful sports franchise. The stadium has a unique feature—the hole in the roof—and has been the site of historic games; the stadium is also aging in disrepair. Despite its physical decline, Texas Stadium is an icon. The city of Arlington already has the Ballpark at Arlington, the home of the Texas Rangers. Moreover, Six Flags Over Texas Amusement Park viewed the opportunity for a new Cowboys stadium as adding another piece to Arlington's collection of leisure destinations. The cost to the city involved raising sales tax and kicking some of its residents out of the lower-cost areas of the city. Arlington, which is a middle to upper-middle-class city of around 300,000, does not have a particularly large or intense crime problem in its poorer side of town; however, despite that fact, proponents of the stadium marketed the plan with that implication. The pro-stadium marketing was aggressive, high-cost, and professionally done. The anti-stadium campaign, on the other hand, came from the grassroots, with homemade handbills. The stadium referendum passed easily. With the tradition of the Dallas Cowboys and the economics of entertainment prevalent in the city already, that anti-stadium interpretation had little chance.

With the proposed stadium at the UTA, the same city used a different strategy in order to come to its conclusion. The stadium project at UTA was analyzed using economic logic and common sense. The university has not had a football team in twenty years. When there was a football team, it was poorly supported and only moderately successful. After consideration, the university tabled the idea of bringing back football and building a new stadium for five years. Unlike the Dallas Cowboys, the university did not have widespread intangible goodwill to bank on. In parallel, a new Cowboys stadium was nearly a slam-dunk to win, but the UTA proposal was nearly a guaranteed loser. In central differences, there existed a positive relationship between the community and the professional team proposing the stadium. The Cowboys maintained a relationship of goodwill and fellowship within the community. In Arlington, the same group of people read similar texts of stadiums in different ways.

Aerial view of Busch Stadium in St. Louis. Courtesy of Corbis.

In regard to a stadium, the fellowship that builds "membership" arrives in the form of people congregating to view a sports event. The nod of recognition then comes from votes cast by the constituency during a referendum to build or not build a stadium. Outside that, the community seems to play a guessing game as to whether or not everyone is in agreement regarding having a stadium. Each group, even each person, has his own interpretation of the importance of a particular stadium or the idea of a stadium.

In sponsoring fellowship, stadiums function as a gathering places for the fans to be participants as well as viewers. One activity that has grown is tailgating. Tailgating entails ticket holders coming early to an event and congregating in the parking lot to eat, drink, and socialize prior to the event. Joe Cahn, the self-proclaimed "commissioner of tailgating" explains its offer of "membership": "Tailgating. The last great American neighborhood. . . . In today's society, people yearn for socialization and the parking lot provides the perfect place for everyone to come together." At first, many stadiums fought the idea of tailgating because it potentially cut into profits on concessions, but now tailgating is not only allowed, but also encouraged as part of the game-day experience. Contests are held as to who has the best food or most energetic group. The previously mentioned commissioner of tailgating rides from stadium to stadium attempting to determine which stadium has the best tailgating atmosphere.

Also, the game-day experience is enhanced by other attractions surrounding the stadium. The owners of the stadium directly sponsor some of these activities. These types of events include mini-fairs which have skill contests mimicking the sport which is being attended. Besides that there are dancing girls, t-shirts being shot out a cannon, half-time contests, and myriad other distractions for the casual fan. In fact, to a large extent sports no longer market to or develop hardcore, long-term fans; instead, they attempt to market to the casual fan who does not want to learn the complexities of the particular sport. All of these activities that invite casual fans occur within the confines and jurisdiction of the stadium, contributing to its iconic stature, making it superior to the game inside.

The modern sports stadium of services is a centerpiece to an economy based on leisure. Arlington, Texas, exemplifies cities where the major industry is not a productive plant, but rather where the center of the economy is leisure-time entertainment. As stated earlier, the city is home to an amusement park, a baseball stadium, and soon a football stadium. The venues are all within five minutes' drive of each other. The area has restaurants and hotels in the general vicinity. The appealing text that has been sold to the sponsoring city residents is that after the games, fans frequent eateries and bars near the stadium. Arlington, though, unlike other cities, has not used the stadium as the center of a specific entertainment district; but the economic welfare and more importantly the cultural identity of the city are centered on the three large entertainment venues. While the economic benefits of a specific building are probably overstated, the cumulative effect of how a city portrays itself remains vital. Andrew Zimbalist contrasts the economic importance with the cultural importance of a city's sports team: "It is a common perception that sports teams have an economic impact on a city that is tantamount to their cultural impact.... In most circumstances, sports teams have a small positive economic effect, similar perhaps to the influence of a new department store" (58).

While marketed as a place of fun and games, the modern stadium is anything but just a place to go and take in a ballgame. Once a person drives or walks near the grounds, the ballgame is now an experience involving the consumption of products and services surrounding the venue. Not all of the stadium's features serve merely entertainment, but all play for the goals of cultural and economic benefits for the city involved in hosting the team. Stadiums are about much more than just the game.

WORKS CITED AND RECOMMENDED

Cahn, Joe C. "The State of Tailgating." *A Study of Food, Fans, and Football.* 15 Mar. 2005 <http://www.tailgating.com/StateofTailgatingReport.htm>.

Fish, Stanley. "Interpretive Communities." *Literary Theory: An Anthology.* Ed. Julie Rivkin and Michael Ryan. 2nd ed. Malden, MA: Blackwell, 2004. 217–21.

Spirou, Costas, and Larry Bennett. *It's Hardly Sportin': Stadiums, Neighborhoods, and the New Chicago.* Dekalb: North Illinois UP, 2003.

Zimbalist, Andrew. "The Economics of Stadiums, Teams, and Cities." *The Economics and Politics of Sports Facilities.* Ed. Wilbur C. Rich. Westport, CT: Quorum Books, 2000. 57–69.

Stonewall

Thomas Piontek

The Stonewall Inn, a gay bar located at 53 Christopher Street, just off Sheridan Square in Greenwich Village, New York, gave its name to what has become arguably the most emblematic event in American gay and lesbian history: the Stonewall Riots that took place at this site starting on June 27, 1969. As it happened, this was also the day that Judy Garland, the tragic actress, singer, and gay male icon in her own right was buried in New York City—an event that, some have argued, may have in part precipitated the riots. In any event, the Stonewall Riots have long been considered to mark the beginning of the contemporary gay and lesbian political movement; for many, the term "Stonewall" itself has become synonymous with the struggle for gay rights.

Gay writers, historians, and politicians have compared the significance of Stonewall to a wide variety of other highly symbolic historical events, including the tearing down of the Berlin Wall (Carter), the effect of the Six Day War on Jews around the world (Kaiser), Rosa Parks's taking a "Whites Only" seat on a bus, and even the Boston Tea Party. For more than three decades, the Riots have been memorialized with annual Gay Pride marches and festivals in the month of June throughout this country and around the world. In Germany and several other countries these commemorative celebrations are more commonly known as Christopher Street Day (CSD), celebrating the Stonewall Inn's location and what post-Stonewall was considered "the gayest street in the U.S." In spite of its indisputable status as an important and enduring sign in gay history and gay politics alike, the precise meaning of "Stonewall" remains a bone of contention even today, more than thirty-five years after the riots that were the raw material out of which the icon has been fashioned.

The Greenwich Village neighborhood of New York City had been known as a bohemian community of artists and intellectuals since the early twentieth century. A homosexual subculture became visible in "the Village" as early as the 1920s, and in later decades it developed a reputation as a center of gay and lesbian life. In the 1960s, however, the situation of gay men and lesbians was significantly different from what it is today, and tolerance of homosexuals was severely limited. For one thing, in the course of the decade the New York City police systematically closed all gay bars by revoking their licenses. Thus, far from being gay-owned and operated, the only gay bars at the time tended to be run by the Mafia, who paid off the local police, so that they would turn a blind eye to what were basically illegal operations. In this climate the patrons of gay bars were used to police harassment and routine raids, and it is commonly assumed that it was a failure to pay off the police that led to the raid on the Stonewall Inn in late June 1969. However, as one historian remarks, "it turned out not to be routine at all. Instead of cowering—the usual reaction to a police raid—the patrons inside Stonewall and the crowd that gathered outside the bar fought back against the police" (Duberman, dust jacket). During the five days of rioting that followed, patrons of the bar and other protesters resisted arrest, threw bottles and cobblestones at the police and Tactical Patrol Force reinforcements, and even used an uprooted parking meter to ram the door when the officers retreated into the bar to regroup.

Gay activists who organized in the wake of Stonewall, for example by establishing the Gay Liberation Front, capitalized on the implausible fact that, "for once, cops, not gays, had been routed" when they coined the phrase gay power, to describe a novel force to be reckoned with (Duberman 202). For the new generation of gay liberationists, the Stonewall Riots signified a point of rupture, a radical break with the past, that suggested that there was a qualitative difference between the time period on either side of the divide— before and after Stonewall. The most extreme version of this before-and-after model of gay history has found expression in the notion that Stonewall marks the *beginning* of the modern gay and lesbian movement. This definition of Stonewall as an absolute beginning trivializes—or altogether ignores—gay and lesbian organizing and community building in previous decades. For example, the exclusive focus on Stonewall disregards the fact that the political efforts of gay men and lesbians in the 1970s were preceded by a generation of activists in the 1950s and 1960s who composed the Homophile Movement, comprised of such organizations as the Mattachine Society and the Daughters of Bilitis.

According to several historical accounts, homophile organizers and gay activists, in spite of their differences, did work side-by-side in organizations such as the Gay Liberation Front (Jay and Young). Nonetheless, gay activists portrayed the discord between the two groups as a generational conflict between the old homophile organizations, which they disqualified as assimilationist, and the younger group of gay radicals. In a way, this rhetorical strategy, which recalls the 1960s maxim "Don't trust anyone over 30," allowed the young activists to save the Stonewall Riots "from being simply 'an event.' They fleshed out the implications of the Riots, and ensured that they would become the symbol of a new militancy" (D'Emilio 245). In order to claim an identity of their own, gay militants who were committed to a utopian vision encapsulated

Parade participants ride past the site of the original Stonewall Inn in New York's Greenwich Village during the annual Gay and Lesbian Pride Parade, 1989. AP/Wide World Photos.

by the slogan "revolution in our lifetime" had to figuratively "kill the Father" by openly challenging the authority of the older generation.

For gay radicals, then, Stonewall functioned as an enabling fiction in their conflict with the homophile movement, and the metaphorical connotations of the bar's name and its compound parts—stone and wall—helped to make it a sign for an event of resistance. No poet or novelist could have intentionally devised a name more expressive of the characteristics of the "new" Gay Liberation Movement. The name connotes toughness, solidity, resistance, and steadfastness. A stone wall is also a line of demarcation, separating two spaces absolutely from one another—one side and the other or, metaphorically speaking, the before and after. Would Stonewall have been so easily mythologized if the bar had been named something else? Is it any accident that the word "Inn"—with its pretentious connotations of country comfort, hospitality, and old English warmth—almost never appears in mythologizing references to "Stonewall"? The first act of creating the icon, then, was to drop the "Inn" from the proper name out of which the mythical sign was fashioned.

Not at all coincidentally, the gay militants chose the name Gay Liberation Front for their organization, in homage to the Vietnamese guerrillas. The name also refers to a marked difference between gay radicals and their predecessors. Gay liberationists considered themselves a component of the decade's radical movement for social change, part of a "front" in the political sense of the word (a collection of groups). They saw gay oppression as one social issue among many, and they also opposed capitalism, racism, sexism, and the war in Vietnam. In the words of Allen Young, writing in 1971, "gay liberation is a total revolutionary movement" (24). Along similar lines, the sign "Stonewall" was in the beginning essentially tied to the sign "Riots." By semiotic correspondence, the sign "Stonewall Riots" ties the gay and lesbian movement to the 1965 Watts Riots in Los Angeles, the student uprisings at Kent State University in Ohio and Jackson State University in Mississippi (among others), and perhaps most crucially, to the riots at the Democratic Convention in Chicago the preceding summer. This correspondence of "riots" figures Stonewall as normative, part of a larger movement for peace and (sexual) liberation.

In the late 1960s, homophile organizations such as Mattachine had a "reputation as the 'NAACP of our movement,' a damning description during years when groups like the Black Panther party were capturing the fancy of young radicals" (D'Emilio 2). Things had been decidedly different in 1950, when Mattachine was founded by five men in Los Angeles, among them the activist Harry Hay. The men had been members of the Communist Party, which was reflected not only in their tactics, but also in their early radicalism. The direction of Mattachine changed drastically in 1953 when a convention in Los Angeles marked the society's takeover by a more assimilationist strand of gay thinking, and the end of involvement of many of the original founders. In fact, the new leaders threatened to turn over to the FBI the names of any members who were also members of the Communist Party, unless they re-signed. The "Stonewall generation," then, pioneered neither the radical stance of the gay movement nor its militant tactics. In fact, it could be argued that gay militants in the early 1970s picked up where the founders of Mat-tachine had left off in the early 1950s, continuing a tradition of radical gay politics established by the early homophile movement.

It is ironic that, as was the case with the homophile movement, radicalism did not remain the dominant tendency of the "post-Stonewall" movement for long. Almost from its inception, the Gay Liberation Front was the subject of sometimes severe criticism. Only six months after Stonewall, on December 21, 1969, nineteen people meeting in a Greenwich Village apartment created a platform for those who disagreed with the GLF's philosophy and tactics by constituting a new organization, the Gay Activists Alliance. Whereas the GLF considered the fate of gay people in the context of a broader "revolutionary" movement, the GAA was exclusively dedicated to securing basic rights for homosexuals by working within the system, rather than trying to transform it:

> The Gay Activists Alliance...and later more professional and organized efforts such as the National Gay Task Force (later renamed the National Gay and Lesbian Task Force and still in existence), soon took gay liberation down another path. The goals of 'gay rights'—assuming a place for us in existing society rather than pursuing a utopian vision—began to replace "gay revolution." (Jay and Young xxxix–xl)

Under the sign "Stonewall," gay and lesbian activists joined a larger movement for social change—"The Movement," as it liked to call itself—and so found a legitimacy that they had not had before. This transformation of Stonewall led to the hegemony of rights-oriented gay activists, for whom liberation means simply extending the legacy of American freedoms to homosexuals in a pluralistic society. Ultimately, the myth of Stonewall came to mean, after some historiographical work, that gay men and lesbians had joined the mainstream, even if this was admittedly the mainstream to the left. Originally conceived as a catalyst for a radical political change, Stonewall eventually became the central trope of a mainstream gay culture that grounded its conceptions of gay identity within the "specific experiences of urban, middle-class white men" (Bravmann 10). This shift in political strategy was also reflected by the iconography of Stonewall: in the decade following the riots, Stonewall was represented as a rebellion of *white men*.

The erasure was twofold. First, there was the effacement of gender and race in accounts of the riots, which do not mention that Puerto Ricans, drag queens, and lesbians were among the patrons at the Stonewall Inn during the first night of the riots. On a symbolic level, celebrating Stonewall as the "birth" of the (white) gay (men's) movement eclipses the history of those who came to gay liberation via the black Civil Rights struggle, who, as it were, proclaimed that "Black Is Beautiful" before they realized that "Gay Is Good." Furthermore, the exclusive focus on Stonewall erases female specificity by discounting the experience of lesbians who trace their own origins back to the Women's Movement or lesbian feminism rather than to Stonewall.

In addition, gay rights activists were—and are—characterized by a highly pronounced respect for the middle-class sensibilities of mainstream America. Lesbians, people of color, and the so-called "fringe elements" of the gay community, such as drag queens and leathermen, were no longer considered ideal poster children for a movement intent on assimilating into mainstream culture by convincing the white, heterosexual, male powers that be that "we are just like you"—except for that one minor difference which eventually came to be known as sexual orientation. Paradoxically, while today's gay movement traces its origins to the radicalism of the "Stonewall generation," what seems to have endured is a peculiar sense of respectability, which clearly is more reminiscent of the later homophile movement.

Only in the mid-1980s did gay historians begin to challenge the traditional representation of the events at the Stonewall Inn as an all-male, all-white revolt. According to more recent accounts, gay men and lesbians fought back in 1969, and many of them were of color, and many were drag queens. While the participation of several Puerto Rican drag queens in the riots has been incorporated, albeit reluctantly, into the lore of Stonewall, the lesbian presence at Stonewall remains contested. According to one view, the arrest of a cross-dressed lesbian (and her violent resistance) was *the* incident precipitating the riots, while other accounts firmly deny that a lesbian was even present in the bar (qtd. in Duberman 190, 196–97). The changing iconography of Stonewall thus reflects the gay movement's historical difficulty in acknowledging the ways that race complicates sexual identity and the difference that gender makes.

In the continuing struggle over the meanings attributed to Stonewall one can distinguish two different approaches. To this day, a number of writers and historians persist in their attempts to ground "the symbolic Stonewall in empirical reality" (Duberman) and to "present the clearest possible picture of what happened and why" (Carter). This trend raises the question of whether the appeal to "empirical reality" and the promise to finally tell the "full story" still have any persuasive relationship to contemporary theories of history that have called into question the notions that the historian controls the facts and that history conveys an objective truth. In addition, the notion that it would be possible to establish some reliable historical narrative seems particularly questionable in the case of accounts such as Duberman's and Carter's, which, to varying degrees, are based on oral history interviews with people twenty-five years or more after the events they are being asked to recall.

An alternative to this idea of a "total history" of Stonewall can be found in Nigel Finch's film *Stonewall* (1995), which in its opening credits is characterized as a "fictionalisation based on the book by Martin Duberman." Finch's dramatization of the Stonewall Riots and the weeks leading up to this event is narrated by one of the film's fictive characters, a Puerto Rican drag queen called La Miranda (Guillermo Diaz). The difference between Duberman's and Finch's respective approaches to the question of historical representation becomes apparent with La Miranda's first words. In a direct address to the camera, she tells the audience:

> See, there's as many Stonewall stories as there's gay queens in New York, and that's a shit load of stories, baby. Everywhere you go in Manhattan or America or the entire damn world, you gonna hear some new legend. Well, this is my legend, honey. Okay? My Stonewall legend.

History, La Miranda reminds us, tells "stories" and creates "legends," thus calling our attention to the constructed nature of all representations of the past, however ostensibly "real" they might be.

It might be helpful to follow La Miranda's example of cheerfully abandoning the quest for a total history that would provide us with an objective, reliable, and definitive historical narrative of what happened at Stonewall. Because any historical representation is necessarily partial, we need to question the notion that Stonewall has some kind of settled, definitive meaning. La Miranda's history writes race, gender, and class into her account of the riots in order to enable a future politics that includes people of color, women, and those "fringe elements" of the community symbolized by the figure of the drag queen. As I have argued elsewhere, a greater number of queer fictions of the past will allow us to challenge the notion of a unitary gay community with a single shared history, to acknowledge the diversity that exists among queer historical subjects, and to proliferate the number of approaches to the project of gay liberation.

WORKS CITED AND RECOMMENDED

Bravmann, Scott. *Queer Fictions of the Past: History, Culture, and Difference.* Cambridge: Cambridge UP, 1997.

Carter, David. *Stonewall: The Riots that Sparked the Gay Revolution.* New York: St. Martin's, 2004.

D'Emilio, John. *Sexual Politics, Sexual Communities: The Making of a Homosexual Minority in the United States, 1940–1970.* Chicago: U of Chicago P, 1983.

Duberman, Martin. *Stonewall.* New York: Dutton, 1993.

Jay, Karla, and Allen Young, eds. *Out of the Closets: Voices of Gay Liberation.* 1972. 20th anniversary ed. New York: New York UP, 1992.

Kaiser, Charles. *The Gay Metropolis: 1940–1996.* Boston: Houghton Mifflin, 1997.

Piontek, Thomas. "Forget Stonewall: Making Gay History Perfectly Queer." *Queering Gay and Lesbian Studies.* Champaign: U of Illinois P, 2005.

Stonewall. Dir. Nigel Finch. 1995. BMG Home Video, 1998.

Young, Allen. "Out of the Closets, Into the Streets." *Out of the Closets* 6–31.

Suburbia

Philip C. Dolce

Suburbia often is seen in alternate images, as an American dream or dilemma. The remarkable growth of the "middle landscape" in the last half of the twentieth century established the United States as a suburban nation. Today more Americans reside in suburban communities than in rural areas or cities. The post–World War II suburbs still heavily influence our views of suburbia. Massive numbers of families bought single-family houses and established a lifestyle based, in large part, on the well-being of children. The suburbs seemed to be the new promised land that signified the middle-class success of its residents.

Yet, suburbs were neither new nor simply middle-class. There always have been many different types of suburban communities, including working-class suburbs, black suburbs, ethnic suburbs, industrial suburbs, and in-city suburbs, among others. None of these suburban communities were seen as representing the image of the American middle landscape. In fact, until recently, most of these suburban communities were underrepresented in literature and in popular culture. In addition, the iconography of suburbia rarely deals with suburbs as specific places, but rather with suburbia as a state of mind. The iconic image of the American suburb evolved into one of a white, middle-class community of nuclear families.

The development of suburbia and its dominant image was unforeseen just over 100 years ago. With both anticipation and trepidation, the city was viewed as the major force in American life in the late nineteenth century and early twentieth century. The city would give upstart America the powerful and sophisticated image needed to rival European nations. In a sixty-year span between 1870 and 1930, American cities bloomed with great museums, concert halls, skyscrapers, corporate headquarters, and other developments that marked these urban centers as world-class venues. The 1920 census established that more Americans lived in cities than in rural areas. The urban destiny of the United States seemed assured. There also, however, was a darker side to the image of urban America, including slums, crime, vice, and overcrowding.

At the same time, rural areas and small towns came to stand for a simpler, premodern America. Historically, countless numbers of Americans left rural areas and small towns for better opportunities in cities and later suburbs. Yet, a 1990s Library of Congress exhibition stated, "America remains in beliefs, in values, in spirit and soul, a small town nation." The need for urban amenities and the nostalgia for the small town would become part of the iconography of the American suburb. The duality of image for the middle-class suburb was that it was to represent urban modernity while preserving the mythical, home-grown virtues of the small town.

In the late nineteenth century, the image of suburbia began to take shape. For privileged members of society who moved to the suburbs, the middle landscape represented a way of escaping the worst aspects of modern, urban life. It also allowed well-to-do families to be in close contact with nature without having to give up the modern comforts of the city. Urban amenities would be cloaked in a rustic atmosphere. Roads would wind, and unique

Walkerville, a suburb of Butte, Montana, 1905. Courtesy of the Library of Congress.

single-family houses on large pastoral lots would be the norm. Nature also would be converted to residents' desires. Each house was set in a sort of personal botanical garden where only certain trees, flowers, and bushes were permitted to grow.

Suburban residence also connected strongly with an older view of how domestic life should be lived in the United States. The cult of domesticity stressed the house as a nurturing shelter in which a wife would establish a physical and moral environment for her family in a natural setting beneficial to all. A single-family house in suburbia, therefore, was more than a physical location. It was designed to be a home which would strengthen family bonds, improve the character of each family member, act as a symbol of family prosperity, and reconnect those chosen Americans with an agrarian past, without losing the benefits of urban amenities.

These early elitist suburban communities, such as Llewelyn Park, New Jersey, were not viewed with alarm for America's urban promise. It was believed that only the affluent few would live there, and that the city would dominate in terms of image, economy, and population. However, the availability of mass transit, the negative aspects of urban life, and the allure of the middle landscape, turned cities inside out as middle-class Americans from the professional-managerial class began to move to the suburbs in greater numbers. These newcomers, by and large, altered the elitist suburban dream of a unique house in a pastoral setting with a pattern-book house on a smaller lot. However, the idea of living in a homogeneous community of single-family houses on private lots, in which nuclear families would follow a prescribed pattern of behavior on a voluntary basis, demonstrated both an extension and a continuity in the allure of the suburbs. For the middle-class, home ownership not only fulfilled the needs of the cult of domesticity, but also offered a significant sign of upward mobility.

In the early decades of the twentieth century, some reformers saw the suburbs as a pristine landscape in which planned communities, based primarily on the British Garden City principles of Ebenezer Howard, would be built. An example would be Radburn, New Jersey, the "town for the motor age." This idea was popular enough that a display of planned, suburban, residential communities called Pleasantvilles was a major focus of the 1939 World's Fair in New York City. The belief in planned, suburban communities continues to this day. In short, suburbia as an icon has seemed to represent a new and better way of life, even if the images of what that meant were widely different.

This positive image of suburbia was partially offset by a more critical view of the middle landscape. In 1927, novelist Edith Wharton chided authors who situated their stories about modern American life in suburbia. Critics believed that the standardization, consumerism, and materialism of twentieth-century America seemed to be routine parts of life in suburbia. Cosmopolitan commentators pictured the suburban single-family house as a standardized dwelling filled with standardized furniture in a community of uninteresting, middle-class neighbors.

These criticisms did not deter a new generation which came into its own after World War II. Federal government programs, the automobile, the availability of inexpensive land, and other factors allowed more blue-collar workers and middle-class professionals to move to the suburbs. They sought much the same ambience that earlier generations did in suburbia. Families with an income of $3,000 a year now could afford to buy a home. In the 1950s, 13 million new houses were built, and 11 million of these were built in the suburbs. In places like Levittown, New York, a whole new community was created consisting of 82,000 people living in over 17,000 new houses. The iconic picture of suburbia was focused not only on the traditional images of house, domesticity, upward mobility, and natural environment but also on other factors as well.

For instance, suburbia seemed to be the true melting pot for America. White working-class and middle-class families were leaving their ethnic neighborhoods in cities and living together in the middle landscape. It seemed that class and ethnic differences would be less important than individual preferences in suburbia. The long-term, American goal of *E Pluribus Unum* seemed possible in the suburbs.

Some motion pictures of the 1940s and 1950s depicted these symbolic values. In *Father of the Bride* (1950), for instance, suburbia is viewed as a middle-class haven where children grow up to be model citizens like their parents. The complex problems of modern life are missing in these early films. The biggest problem in a youngster's life seems to be whether a son can borrow dad's car and the details of a daughter's wedding. Long-running television series such as *Father Knows Best*, *The Adventures of Ozzie and Harriet*, and *Leave It to Beaver* reinforced the constant tranquility and un-complicated image of life in the middle landscape. This popular culture image of the nuclear family nestled in a colonial, ranch, or cape cod house filled with modern conveniences spoke to how suburbia came to embody the American past, present, and future while taming the dilemmas of modern life.

As the suburban population increased so did the hostility of critics. Concern over conformity, mass culture, and standardization had grown and seemed linked to life in the middle landscape. The works of Sloan Wilson (*The Man in the Gray Flannel Suit*), David Riesman (*The Lonely Crowd*), John Keats (*The Crack in the Picture Window*), and others addressed the standardization of houses and the conformity of people in the suburbs. To some commentators, the expansion of the American middle-class and the mass movement to suburbia represented a degradation of the more established professional-managerial class. The house in suburbia was no longer a guarantee of status and social privilege. To these critics, the suburban house was not a home or an individual refuge any more than the corporate offices white-collar professionals worked in.

More importantly, the suburbs seemed to have sidetracked America from its urban destiny that had looked so clear at the beginning of the century. The suburbs were seen as exploiting the resources of cities and giving little in return. This concern grew with the urban crisis that impacted American cities in the 1960s and 1970s, which was tied to "white flight" and the growth of suburbs.

Motion pictures began to question the cult of domesticity and prescribed pattern of behavior that were supposed to be hallmarks of suburban life. While the title of *Rebel Without a Cause* (1955) offered some reassurance, the film unnerved America. This motion picture strongly implied that there was something wrong with the American family, and living in suburbia was no cure. In the following decade, films such as *The Graduate* (1967) and *Goodbye Columbus* (1969) portrayed affluent youngsters disillusioned with their parents' self-absorption and focus on material possessions. In the 1980s young suburbanites simply mocked their parents' pretentious lifestyles or flaunted the "rules" of middle-class, suburban society in films such as *Risky Business* (1983) and *Ferris Bueller's Day Off* (1986). By the 1990s children of the middle-class landscape portrayed good reason to fear or despise their parents in motion pictures such as *American Beauty* (1999) and *Happiness* (1999). The majority of suburban films in the last forty years have featured white, middle-class families trying in vain to find the comfort zone that suburbia seemed to represent in an early age.

In part, this critical turn occurred due to the fact that American values were changing. Diversity came to be valued more than homogeneity, especially in matters of race and, later, culture. The salad bowl rather than the melting pot became the dominant cultural metaphor. The cult of domesticity also came under attack as suburban life was viewed as contributing to the powerlessness of middle-class women and confining them to the responsibilities of house and home. The expansion of new suburban communities has come into question, as seen in attempts to limit sprawl and foster sustainable development through smart growth. Today there are attempts to find metropolitan solutions to the mutual problems impacting cities and suburbs.

Demographics also are changing the suburbs. The reality is that by the start of the twenty-first century more people continue to live and work in the middle landscape than in cities or rural areas. However, the nature of this population is changing. Recent black migration to the suburbs has, at times, exceeded white migration. Over 40 percent of Hispanics now live in suburbia, and Asians are the most suburbanized group in the nation. We now recognize that the suburban population includes an expanding number of single-parent families, gay and lesbian couples, and single people. The United States is a suburban nation not only in terms of population but also in economics. Suburbs have a significant share of businesses and jobs in the United States.

Yet the image of suburbia, especially in novels, film, theater, and the popular mind still features a narrow, stereotypical, domestic view of the middle landscape. In a way, this shallow vision is understandable. The suburbs always have been seen as an icon—a representation of life—rather than the reality of

Aerial view of the suburbs of Orange County, California, 2002. Courtesy of Corbis.

lives lived. Unfortunately, the iconic image of the middle landscape often appears in an extreme, either as an American dream or troubling dilemma. This false dichotomy has clouded our vision and impaired our ability to understand the complex and evolving nature of the suburban society which has brought a degree of satisfaction to residents' lives, and is still a much sought-after place to live and work.

WORKS RECOMMENDED

Dolce, Philip C., ed. *Suburbia: The American Dream and Dilemma*. New York: Anchor Books, 1976.

Dolce, Philip C., and Rubil Morales-Vasquez. "Teaching The Importance of Place in the World of Virtual Reality." *Thought and Action* 19 (Summer 2003): 37–48.

Frey, William F. "Melting Pot Suburbs: A Census 2000 Study of Suburban Diversity." Washington, DC: The Brookings Institution, June 2001.

Jackson, Kenneth T. *Crabgrass Frontier: The Suburbanization of the United States*. New York: Oxford UP, 1985.

Jurca, Catherine. *White Diaspora: The Suburb and the Twentieth-Century Novel.* Princeton, NJ: Princeton UP, 2001.

Palen, J. John. *The Suburbs.* New York: McGraw-Hill, 1995.

Seis, Mary Corbin. "The City Transformed: Nature Technology and the Suburban Ideal, 1877–1917." *Journal of Urban History* 14 (Nov. 1987): 1–11.

Wharton, Edith. "The Great American Novel." *Yale Review* 16 (July 1927): 646–56.

Wiese, Andrew. *Places of Their Own: African American Suburbanization in the Twentieth Century.* Chicago: U of Chicago P, 2004.

Superman

P. Andrew Miller

Look! Up in the sky. It's a bird. It's a plane. It's Superman!
—opening of the *Adventures of Superman* television show

Perhaps the most famous introduction in American popular culture is for the last son of Krypton, the Man of Steel, Superman. While we may not be able to spot the blue and red streak flashing through the sky, the average American is very likely to encounter Superman on any given day, without ever walking into a comic book shop. It's not unusual to spot the big red S on the yellow shield as you walk through the mall or down the street. Scores of songs reference Superman as well. Every decade since his creation has its own television or movie representation of the American superhero, often propelling such actors as George Reeves, Christopher Reeve, Dean Cain, and Tom Welling into stardom. But what this character did for these actors is nothing compared to what he did for the superhero genre in comic books, television, and movies.

Superman's comic book origin is well known to most Americans. The planet Krypton was dying. Superman's father, Jor-El, a Kryptonian scientist, foretold the destruction of the planet but no one would believe him. The death of Krypton came too soon, when Jor-El had completed only a prototype rocket. Strapping his infant son Kal-El into the rocket ship, he sent him off to earth, and a crash-landing in a Kansas field. Found by Jonathan and Martha Kent, the baby was adopted by the couple and reared in Smallville, Kansas.

Less well known but equally important is the real-life origin of the character created by Jerry Siegel and Joe Shuster, two Jewish boys from Cleveland, Ohio. Siegel was the writer while Shuster provided the first visual representation of Superman. Like most creations, Superman went through several versions, including starting off as a villain. But the partners eventually created the heroic Superman as a series of comic strips. However, they could not sell their creation. Then in 1938, when DC Comics was looking for something to put in the new comic book format, Siegel and Shuster sold

Superman and he appeared in *Action Comics* number 1: He was an immediate success. Of course, there is more to the story than that, as Dennis Dooley and others detail in a variety of histories and essays devoted to Superman.

But the significance of that debut cannot be underestimated. It started a whole new genre in American culture, and many costumed heroes hit the newsstands over the next several years. Batman appeared the year after; then Captain Marvel, the most direct imitator of Superman and biggest newsstand rival; and then Wonder Woman. An entire league of heroes emerged, and the stories of caped adventurers reached their peak during the World War II era. Yet it is a genre that continues today, with new superheroes introduced every year. In *Super Heroes: A Modern Mythology*, scholar Richard Reynolds looks to *Action Comics* number 1 as defining the genre much as Aristotle looked to *Oedipus Rex* to define tragedy. Almost every theme and characteristic used in the genre since 1938 can be found in this comic book.

Much as Reynolds views the significance of Superman's first comic book appearance, John Kenneth Muir in *The Encyclopedia of Superheroes on Film and Television* credits the 1950s *Superman* television series starring George Reeves as one of the most influential examples of the superhero genre for the big and small screens. Muir argues that the long-lived series, running from 1952 to 1958, "set the tone for no less than five decades of superhero programming on the tube. Because it lasted so many episodes…, it eventually featured every story and superhero formula known to Hollywood, ideas that would one day become cliché" (9). In fact, story lines such as Superman's getting amnesia were redone in both a *Superboy* series and *Lois and Clark: The New Adventures of Superman*, starring Dean Cain as the Man of Steel.

Superman, in a variety of incarnations, has influenced the genre in a variety of media. His popular success is owing to a convergence of differing characteristics. Certain elements of the character had appeared before. The Phantom wore tights. Zorro had an alter ego. But many comic book historians point out that what made Superman innovative was placing the extraterrestrial superhero in Metropolis, a contemporary, if invented, American city. The children of the time wanted more and they got it; the next year Superman had his own comic book. There was no stopping the hero, not even with Kryptonite.

This spectacular hero with amazing abilities certainly spoke to the youth and readers in his Depression-era debut. And in the following years, Superman fit with Roosevelt's New Deal ideology as well as the fight against America's enemies. Siegel and Shuster penned a two-page story where Superman flies to capture Hitler and Stalin, and brings them to the League of Nations for judgment. Max Fleischer, in his stunning animated cartoons, has Superman battling "Japoteurs" as well as Nazis in some of his episodes. Superman readily suited his early audience. However, even after World War II and the congressional hearings of the 1950s that labeled comic books dangerous to youth, Superman persevered, staying in continuous production along with Batman and Wonder Woman, while most of the rest of the costumed adventurers vanished from newsstands.

His longevity brings one of the complications that attends any consideration of what Superman represents, and how his character and mythos appeal to Americans. Through the years, the character has evolved and been reinterpreted for different decades and different media. Nevertheless, some things remain the same. Superman is always the orphan from Krypton. He is always found by the Kents and raised in Smallville. He always heads off to Metropolis. He always has a girlfriend, whether it is Lana Lang during his teenage years or Lois Lane, from whom he is separated because of his abilities. And in most versions, he faces off against his arch-nemesis, Lex Luthor. These are the important and essential elements of the mythos. Different interpretations of the myth look at different aspects of the constant elements.

Jonathan and Martha Kent, for instance, are an important part of the Superman story. The orphaned Kal-El (and the orphan is often the hero in American culture) is adopted by this generous, loving, all-American couple who are Kansas farmers. Naming the extraterrestrial orphan Clark, the two instill in him the values of Truth, Justice, and the American Way. He is reared with the work ethic of the Midwestern farmer as well as the cultural values of small-town America. He learns to use his powers responsibly to help people. DC Comics has explored the importance of the Kents by doing Elseworld stories, stories set outside the main continuity of the comic books, to imagine what would happen if Kal-El had been found by someone else. For instance, *Superman: Red Son* has Kal-El's rocket landing in Russia. The importance of the Kents is also brought out in the television series *Smallville*. In the series, Clark and Lex Luthor start off as friends, but Clark's nurturing relationship with his adoptive father Jonathan becomes contrasted with the dysfunctional relationship between Lex and Lionel Luthor.

Gary Engle, in his essay "What Makes Superman So Darned American," looks at Superman's status both as an orphan and as an extraterrestrial to argue that Superman is the ultimate American immigrant. Because America is a nation of immigrants, the American public readily took to the alien child who comes to this country and adopts it and its values as his own. He remakes himself into an American, not just a Kryptonian-American. For Engle, his is the quintessential American experience, the need, perhaps even moral imperative, to remake oneself:

> Thus the American identity is ordered around the psychological experience of forsaking or losing the past for the opportunity of reinventing oneself in the future. This makes the orphan a potent symbol of the American character. Orphans aren't merely free to reinvent themselves. They are obliged to do so. (83)

Engle also sees Clark's abandonment of Smallville for Metropolis as following the patterns of many immigrants in the twentieth century, leaving the small towns and farms for the promises of the big city. The Clark Kent identity is essential for the myth of Superman to work, because Clark Kent is actually the identity that Superman assumes, and not the other way around: "This uniquely American hero has two identities, one based on where he comes from in life's journey, one on where he's going. One is real, one an illusion, and both are necessary for the myth of balance in the assimilation process to be complete" (85).

Superman in front of stars and stripes, forming a peace sign with his hand, 1970. Courtesy of the Library of Congress.

Of course, most Americans don't look so deeply into the reasons they like Superman. For many it is fairly simple. Superman is a good guy, the ultimate boy scout. He has all these incredible powers that place him far above the rest of humanity, but he still loves his parents. He can fly to the other side of the world, but ordinary Jimmy Olsen is his pal. He can shatter meteors with his fists, but he still has trouble asking Lois for a date. For many of Superman's male readers and fans, he is the ultimate wish fulfillment: if only the girl of my dreams really knew what I could do. For others, he offers an escape, not just in his adventures, but in his origins. He may have been raised on a farm with boring parents, but secretly he is much more; he just has to discover it for himself (a common theme echoed in the popular Harry Potter series). And what cool super powers he has! Super strength, flight, x-ray vision, bulletproofness. Who wouldn't want such powers?

Superman's appearance is also significant, especially because many people know of Superman only through his appearances on the small and large screens. He is often played by an actor with classic boy-next-door good looks. Women particularly are targeted in the choice of actors. Christopher Reeve, the Superman of the 1970s and 1980s, Dean Cain, the Superman of the 1990s, and Tom Welling, the Clark Kent of the 2000s, have all been attractive actors and have made it to pin-up status. Their handsomeness is appropriate because Siegel and Shuster based Superman's appearance on Hollywood romantic heroes such as Douglas Fairbanks, Senior. The various incarnations of the Man of Steel have played up Superman/Clark's sex appeal in a variety of ways, including an episode of *Smallville* where Clark is thrown into a furnace and emerges naked, because all his clothes burn off. Of course, the actresses playing Lois Lane have also reached varying degrees of pin-up status, especially Terri Hatcher, the Lois Lane to Cain's Clark Kent. Kristin Kreuk, Lana Lang on

Smallville, has also appeared in magazines and television commercials after her starring role on the show.

Every good superhero must also have a good supervillain, or villains, and Superman is no exception. Lex Luthor is the archnemesis for the Man of Steel. The bald Luthor is almost as recognizable as his rival. Luthor has gone through a few more changes than Superman, however, with more numerous reinterpretations depending on the decade of the updates. Originally the mad scientist with nifty evil machines, he eventually became the evil CEO during the 1980s revamp of the title and in subsequent TV portrayals. For a while, in the DC Comics universe, he was even the President of the United States. In such ways, Luthor has evolved more than the very static Superman. His "villainy" gets updated with the times, unlike Superman's moral identity. Of course, his basic animosity toward Superman remains the same: Luthor knows Superman is not human and refuses to let the alien run free and retain power and respect.

Only a few superheroes have come anywhere near to being as recognizable as Superman. Batman, debuting the year after Superman, has seen nearly as many incarnations as the Man of Steel. John Kenneth Muir lists the 1960s camp *Batman* series as the most influential superhero television show, even above the 1950s *Superman*. The movie franchise that started in the late 1980s and through the 1990s brought the Batman back to the forefront of the American public's attention, in a darker, scary kind of way. Batman represents different things, though, than Superman. For one, he is completely human, with no super powers. Training himself to the peak of human capabilities and having a wide array of cool "toys," Batman follows the tradition of Zorro and other masked, human crimefighters. He is also an orphan. However, while Superman's birth family died with Krypton, it is a remote loss that the baby Kal-El did not witness or experience in a personal connection. Batman's personal origin lies in the murder of his parents while he watched. He is born of pain and trauma and anguish; and, while readers might want to drive the Batmobile or have the nifty Batbelt, most would not want to spend the rest of their lives in emotional distress like the Batman characters.

Spider-Man, Superman's much younger cousin (coming some twenty-five years later) also comes close to matching Superman in iconic stature. The spider emblem, like Superman's shield and the Batsignal, is easily recognizable and reproduced on a variety of clothing, thanks to merchandising campaigns. Also the star of a live-action television series and many different cartoon series, Spider-Man really jumped in popularity with the successful movies starring Tobey Maguire. With excellent special effects, a recognizable star, and a beautiful damsel in distress, the movies played well around the world. Because Superman's contemporaneous incarnation was stuck on the small screen and costume-less in *Smallville*, Spider-Man took center stage in public awareness. Obviously, Spider-Man has many similarities to the Man of Steel, such as wearing glasses. Peter Parker, a science geek, is bitten by a radioactive—or genetically modified, depending on the version—spider, and then gains great powers. However, he remains vulnerably human. Also an orphan, he feels responsible for the death of his father-figure, Uncle Ben (thus having something in common with Batman), because he refused to stop a thief who later killed his uncle. He has a family responsibility for his aunt and bills to pay, which he finances by photographing himself for the *Daily Bugle* newspaper. Yet, as comic-book veteran Danny Fingeroth points out in *Superman on the Couch*, Spider-Man also has fun being Spider-Man, and playing his alter-ego: "But the thing that makes Parker so modern—and so human—is not merely the combinations of emotions that spur him on, and hence his multiple innovations, but that he . . . is like all of us, capable of encompassing contradictions" (75).

Spider-Man and Batman echo other American heroes in their stature as "rugged individuals," standing on the border of society, much like the hard-boiled detective. Batman is a vigilante, Spider-Man painted as a menace by J. Jonah Jameson and the *Daily Bugle*. The X-Men, stars of comic books and blockbuster films, also exist in this border area. The X-Men are mutants, each born with their amazing abilities that, like Superman's, set them apart from the common masses. However, the X-Men are not welcomed as heroes but instead feared as dangerous threats to normal humans. Therefore, these individuals come together to find their own community, at Professor Xavier's School for Gifted Children. Orphans such as Scott Summers (Cyclops), Ororo (Storm), Logan (Wolverine), and Kurt Wagner (Nightcrawler), join together to protect humans from evil mutants and to protect each other from humans. They create their own family. This theme seems to be popular in superhero teams, especially those with teenage or young adult members. In an America where the family is not a constant, individuals are free to create their own families. The X-Men all live together in the mansion just like Buffy the Vampire Slayer and all her friends wind up living together as a family in her home in Sunnydale. If Superman is the ultimate American immigrant, the X-Men could be the metaphor of the melting pot, because the roster at times includes a Canadian, a German, a Russian, an Irishman, an African American, a Jew, and an American Indian.

What Superman started back in 1938 lives on into the twenty-first century. Despite several setbacks along the years, Superman and superheroes are still part of American culture and probably will be until we find a way to create such powers in ourselves. The reason is fairly simple. These costumed characters speak to Americans in a variety of ways and for a variety of reasons, from the ultimate immigrant Superman to the family metaphor of the mutant X-Men. So long as they do, they will be part of our culture.

WORKS CITED AND RECOMMENDED

Engle, Gary. "What Makes Superman So Darned American?" *Superman at Fifty: The Persistence of a Legend.* Ed. Dennis Dooley and Gary Engle. Cleveland, OH: Octavia Press, 1987. 79–87.

Fingeroth, Danny. *Superman on the Couch*. New York: Continuum, 2004.

Muir, John Kenneth. *The Encyclopedia of Superheroes on Film and Television*. Jefferson, NC: McFarland, 2003.

Reynolds, Richard. *Super Heroes: A Modern Mythology*. Jackson: UP of Mississippi, 1992.

Tara

Diane Calhoun-French

Before I was ever allowed to read *Gone With the Wind* (which in my 1960s Catholic girls' high school was kept off the shelves at the library and reserved for check-out by those deemed "mature" enough to read it), I knew about Tara, the legendary plantation home of Scarlett O'Hara, immortalized in David O. Selznick's 1939 film treatment of Margaret Mitchell's epic novel of the Old South. I actually "saw" it much before my long-awaited opportunity to meet Rhett and Scarlett on the screen finally materialized during one of the film's many re-releases. For on Griffith Avenue in Owensboro, Kentucky, there is a home whose façade is a copy of Selznick's Tara and, while it was slightly out of the way to take this route on the three-hour trips to and from Grandma's house, I always begged Dad to "drive us past Tara." The never-dulled excitement of these fleeting glimpses of "grandeur" is among my most vivid memories of frequent childhood journeys from Louisville to Owensboro. These memories furnish personal testimony to the iconic power of Tara in American popular culture. It represented for me then only some ineffable wonderfulness without specificity. Now I hope to explore its power and significance with more illumination—but no less appreciation.

The conception of Tara that dominates the popular imagination is far from what Margaret Mitchell envisioned when, in 1927, she began the untitled manuscript that she worked on for the better part of a decade. The house Gerald O'Hara, Scarlett's father, builds on a North Georgia plantation he won in a card game is made of whitewashed brick, "a clumsy, sprawling building...built according to no architectural plan whatever, with extra rooms added where and when it seemed convenient" (45, 53). Mitchell, who had a journalist's healthy fear of libel charges, always insisted that Tara was not modeled on any actual home, present or past—a fact she verified through extensive research and travel through Clayton County, its fictional setting. Despite her protestations, however, visitors to Georgia, particularly Atlanta, routinely request directions to it. If there was no "real" Tara, Mitchell was nevertheless adamant that the O'Hara dwelling and farm accurately reflected plantations of the Civil War era. Moreover, her version of Tara is consistent with—and emblematic of—her desire to look honestly at the South with all its warts (including hypocrisy and crudeness) and to interrogate the competing claims of the old Southern order and the new.

When Hollywood producer David O. Selznick bought the film rights to *Gone With the Wind*, however, his conception of what readers imagined and viewers wanted to see of plantation life was very different, grander in both scope and style. The Tara he created was its own imaginary place, almost wholly different from its antecedent in the novel. In her letters Margaret Mitchell recounts her struggles, along with those of film advisors Susan Myrick and Wilbur G. Kurtz, to restrain Selznick's ambition, both with respect to Tara and Twelve Oaks, the plantation home of Ashley Wilkes, another of the novel's main characters. They were almost wholly unsuccessful with the cinematic Twelve Oaks, which boasts two magnificent broad staircases in its interior and massive round white columns on its façade. Mitchell pleaded for a column-less Tara and considered it a small victory that, if Selznick would not agree to that, he did at least concede to a porch with modest square pillars. It is noteworthy that in the popular imagination, the "mansions" in the film version of *Gone With the Wind* (Tara, Twelve Oaks, and Rhett and Scarlett's house in Atlanta) have become conflated; the more modest Tara is routinely pictured and described as one of the large, round-columned extravagances to which Mitchell objected, so much so that architectural writer and columnist Jackie Craven, in defining the antebellum style, refers to Tara as "the palatial plantation home featured in *Gone With the Wind*."

More curious still are the descriptions, renderings, and floor plans of Tara that appear in Rosalind Ashe's *More Literary Houses*. Despite supposedly drawing inspiration from the novel (as opposed to the film) for its illustrations and narrative, Ashe not only describes a "typical gracious Southern home" in her paraphrase of the original text, but offers as well an altogether lavish imagined painting of Tara that features four massive columns and an elaborate two-story portico.

It is not surprising that Selznick's changes in the physical Tara reflect the film's thematic shift away from Mitchell's more balanced perspective on the Southern past. From the opening credits (preceded by a shot of Selznick's studio headquarters—itself a Hollywood-styled mansion much more akin to what he envisioned for Tara than what he eventually settled for), Selznick's vision of Scarlett's plantation home as a romanticized embodiment of an idealized world "gone with the wind" is everywhere evident: in the montage of idyllic agrarian scenes that accompany the credits, in the nostalgic invitation of the opening text (not found in Mitchell's book) to enter this bygone era, and, most clearly, in the dramatic, hyper-technicolor images of Scarlett silhouetted on the hills of Tara that mark the film's beginning, middle, and end. Clearly for Selznick, Tara epitomized an era of chivalry, comfort, beauty, and honor—the hallmarks of idealized antebellum Southern living which, if they could not be wholly regained, could nevertheless be celebrated and valorized. It is clearly Selznick's vision of Tara, altogether more gracious than the raw and rather crude setting described by Mitchell,

Vivien Leigh (as Scarlett O'Hara) runs from her stately mansion, Tara, in *Gone With the Wind*. Courtesy of Photofest.

that resonated with the popular psyche and remains rooted in the contemporary imagination.

Another part of Tara's iconic power undoubtedly comes from its name: its origins in the Latin *terra*, meaning earth, and its evocation of Ireland's Tara, the ancient seat of kings and sacred site for Celts, Druids, and Christians. (We can only speculate how American cultural history might have been altered had Mitchell persisted in calling the O'Hara home "Fontenoy Hall," the name she used until halfway through completion of the manuscript.) It has been argued that Tara itself is the most important "character" in *Gone With the Wind*. Indeed, Gerald O'Hara's assertion that land is "the only thing in this world that lasts . . . the only thing worth working for, worth fighting for— worth dying for" supports this reading (35). Max Steiner, composer of the Oscar-winning film score, believed that Tara was more important than any of the individuals in the story; this "is why the 'Tara' theme begins and ends the picture and permeates the entire score" (quoted in Ussher 165). In a perceptive essay titled "Gea in Georgia: A Mythic Dimension in *Gone With the Wind*," Helen Deiss Irvin explores the role of nature in the novel and particularly Scarlett as a "child of Earth" (57). Irvin convincingly argues that Tara not only represents, as Gerald O'Hara suggests, the permanence of land in an otherwise transient world but is also associated with mother earth, symbolically represented by Scarlett's two "mothers," Ellen O'Hara and Mammy, both of whom she associates with home.

The mythical Tara, then, embodies a constellation of values—grace, plenty, beauty, permanence, the safety of home and mother—that continue to exert a powerful influence in a world in which time and circumstance conspire to make such commodities scarcer and scarcer. Seeking to "lose" oneself in an epic novel or film whose fictional cosmos embodies them is one way to regain them; the enduring popularity of both the novel and film versions of *Gone With the Wind* attests to this compelling urge. Another way is to recreate or recapture the world out of which such values emanate. The continuing fascination with modern-day recreations of Tara and with items that bespeak its elegance and era has abundant evidence.

Contemporary Taras can be found not only in the South, but from Pennsylvania to Utah. Many feature Selznick-like architecture and décor; others do not. All, however, promise the elegance and gentility of Southern comfort, the world of Tara recreated—sometimes thorough direct reference to the fictional plantation and sometimes only indirectly. The Red Brick Inn of Panguitch, Utah, for instance, boasts rooms "Scarlet [*sic*] O'Hara would have cherished"; visitors at Rooms at the Inn in Hart, Michigan, or The Ballastone in Savannah can escape the everyday world in Scarlett's Room or Rhett's Retreat. The Chretien Point Plantation Bed and Breakfast in Sunset, Louisiana, proudly notes that it copied Tara's architecture for its own interior staircase. And Calhoun, Tennessee's Pinhook Plantation House declares that when visitors approach its ponds and rolling hills, they will see a vista much like what Gerald O'Hara enjoyed. Tara—A Country Inn is found not in Georgia but in Clark, Pennsylvania; despite its Yankee environs, proprietors Jim and Donna Winner promise "the grace, grandeur, and romance of the Antebellum South" to prospective guests. Most interesting of all in this connection is Tarleton Oaks near Barnesville, Georgia, billed as "the fictional plantation home of Brent and Stuart Tarleton," the young suitors bantering with Scarlett O'Hara on the porch at Tara as the narrative opens. This antebellum mansion is owned by Fred Crane, who portrayed Brent Tarleton in the film. The central hallway of the home has been transformed into the *Gone With the Wind* Hall of Stars Museum, featuring Crane's collection of rare memorabilia; and guests can be sure of a warm greeting from Rhett Butler, the Cranes' Missouri Fox Trotter horse.

Escapes from the hectic present to the elegance of Tara can be "manufactured" for those not lucky enough to retreat to antebellum mansions or modern-day plantations. Dean Bell Special Events of San Antonio will host themed *Gone With the Wind* parties. Spirits and wines popular in the Civil War era are served amid "large faux magnolia trees" and hothouse greenery flanking impressive rounded white columns. Tara's square-columned architecture is more accurately captured by Catered for You of Dallas/Fort Worth, which promotes similar events. Vintage Gardens of Modesto, California, promises luxury for weddings, banquets, and other events, and, while it does not specifically offer Tara-themed events, its Web site features a sample of the online wedding announcement provided for engaged customers. The happy couple? Rhett Butler and Scarlett O'Hara.

The places and settings described above provide both natural and architectural spaces reminiscent of Tara and the idealized Southern plantation. In addition, they frequently feature objects or replicas of objects that are part of the material culture of the antebellum South to enhance the experiences promised: period furnishings, art, dinnerware, and household decorations. Interestingly, with one conspicuous exception, neither Mitchell's nor Selznick's Tara is associated with particular objects or furnishings. Perhaps there's almost no borrowing because the principal action of the novel and film take place elsewhere, and scenes at Tara are relatively few, despite the overwhelming shadow cast on the narrative by Scarlett's ancestral home; or because the most prominent scenes at Tara feature the privations of the war and early reconstruction years. The exception of which I am speaking, of course, is Tara's green velvet draperies, one of the few items remaining after its Yankee occupation. Clearly, these have come to be emblematic of the lost comfort, elegance, and plenty the narrative elegizes. Even those who have not seen *Gone With the Wind* have heard the story of how Scarlett, desperate to impress Rhett Butler in order to get money to pay the taxes on Tara, fashions an elaborate dress, cape, hat, and purse from Miss Ellen's green velvet portieres. This ensemble, reputed to have weighed thirty-five pounds, is among the most reproduced of Scarlett's elaborate garments; it is certainly the most widely recognized. Today it is possible to secure both a modified "costume version" of the dress as well as an exact museum quality reproduction, complete with real gold-clad chicken feet. In an interesting reversal of the original metamorphosis, Terry Kowatch of Touch of Fabric created an award-winning fantasy window entitled "Tara—Gone With the Wind," using Scarlett's dress as a model for an elaborate green velvet window treatment.

In such instances, consumers are purchasing goods and services which—at least partially—achieve their desired outcome of enjoying the elegance or beauty associated with the plantation South: fine dining, gracious hospitality, comfortable furnishings, and elegant attire enjoyed in beautiful natural settings and architecturally interesting structures. One variation on this notion is, of course, the popularity of Tara-related merchandise. Indeed, *Gone With the Wind*–related items of all sorts are a veritable industry. Many of these are billed as "fine" collectibles: hand-painted miniature buildings, delicate china plates, porcelain boxes, hand-blown glass. To the extent that in materials or workmanship these objects represent modern-day manifestations of antique-quality objects from the past, we can view their acquisition as yet another variation on the desire to recapture past elegance. More significant, though, in a discussion of Tara's iconic power, is the desire simply to possess a recreation of its image or a product imprinted with its name: plastic Christmas tree ornaments, machine-made afghans, cross-stitch patterns, puzzles, and souvenirs such as combs, jewelry, and ballpoint pens.

Indeed, if one way to gauge the staying power of an icon is to determine the extent to which, over time, it remains capable of commercial and economic exploitation, Tara has demonstrated its endurance. Businesses, services, and products such as those described above show no signs of waning in popularity. In fact, the use of the World Wide Web permits even greater exploitation than before. Cursory internet searches will uncover the briefest, most tangential references to the object of desire: consider what happened when I "Googled" *Tara* and *plantation*. One link led to a law firm whose headquarters building is reminiscent of Tara. Another introduced me to Sims Stone, a company that manufactures patio materials; their "Tara" pavers create a "timeless weathered feel reminiscent of southern plantation charm." The Oak Grove Plantation Bed & Breakfast in South Boston, Virginia, did not explicitly associate itself with either Tara or Southern plantation life. It did, however, appear in my Google search because its Web site made reference to "Tara, our resident Dalmatian."

Perhaps the best evidence of the ubiquity of Tara in American culture is the extent to which its story, as well as its image, continues to be created anew. Three sequels have carried forward the story of Scarlett and Rhett, left so painfully unresolved at the end of *Gone With the Wind*. Two of these—Kate Pinotti's *The Winds of Tara* and Jocelyn Mims' and Melanie Pearson's *My Beloved Tara*—were unauthorized and are largely unknown and virtually unavailable today. Alexandra Ripley's *Scarlett*, which appeared in 1991, was a major bestseller and probably the most-anticipated sequel in literary history, although it was panned by critics and generally disappointed readers. Significantly, the source of reader dissatisfaction with both *My Beloved Tara* and *Scarlett* seems to be that *Gone With the Wind*'s major character—Tara— is nearly missing. While Scarlett retreats to her plantation home initially, the major action in both novels is set elsewhere—in Ripley's case, in Ireland. One wonders if both writers retreated from a narrative grounded in Tara because the task of recreating so powerful a mythic setting seemed too daunting.

Attempts to parody Tara, on the other hand, have proven quite successful, perhaps because parody acknowledges its object's iconic power without attempting to recreate it. In her provocative and controversial 2001 novel *The Wind Done Gone*, Alice Randall interrogates the master-slave relationship at the heart of *Gone With the Wind*. Ironically, however, Mitchell would almost certainly have approved of Randall's characterization of the plantation as the "Cotton Farm," something much closer to Mitchell's own vision of Tara than the one that dominates the popular imagination. New Line Cinema's *Gone With the Wind* Web site provides readers with the opportunity to post their own versions of classic scenes from Selznick's film, imagining directors and actors of their own choosing and modifying scenarios and dialogue as they wish: "There is no replacing *Gone With the Wind*, but participating in our homage to the greatest American romance ever told may just bring you a little closer to Tara." Responders to this program "As Directed By" envision how Peter Wier, Woody Allen, James Cameron, Quentin Tarantino, and others might have interpreted the movie's greatest scenes; whatever the changes, however, by implication, Tara remains sacrosanct and safe from meddling. Perhaps the most memorable parody was the "Went With the Wind" sketch on *The Carol Burnett Show*. The skit features Starlet O'Hara sweeping down the staircase at Terra to meet Rat Butler wearing a dress made of green velvet drapes and tassels—complete with curtain rod! At seventeen minutes, the laugh that greeted her entrance is often cited as the longest in television history.

As this brief discussion illustrates, the mythical Tara exerts its power into the twenty-first century. It remains a part of our collective imaginations. Its image still works its way, both directly and indirectly, into our material, literary, and popular culture. Helen Taylor, British scholar and author of *Scarlett's Women:* Gone With the Wind *and its Female Fans*, perhaps sums it up best:

> However much I know of Hollywood's historical distortion...[I] absorb an interpretation of America's real and legendary past, more vivid to me than any verbal re-creations I have read in my researches into American history and literature.... [T]he South's agricultural past will be for ever Tara. (15)

WORKS CITED AND RECOMMENDED

Ashe, Rosalind. *More Literary Houses.* New York: Facts on File Publications, 1983.

Craven, Jackie. "House Styles." *About.com* 30 June 2005 <http://architecture.about .com/library/bl-antebellum.htm>.

Dean Bell Special Events San Antonio. Advertisement. 24 June 2005 <http://www .deanbell.com/gwtw2.html>.

Gone With the Wind. "As Directed By." New Line Cinema. 26 June 2005 <http:// www.newline.com/sites/gonewind/directed/>.

Irvin, Helen Deiss. "Gea in Georgia: A Mythic Dimension in *Gone With the Wind.*" *Recasting*: Gone With the Wind *in American Culture.* Ed. Darden Asbury Pyron. Gainesville: UP of Florida, 1983. 57–68.

Mitchell, Margaret. *Gone With the Wind.* 1936. New York: Pocket Cardinal, 1964.

Oak Grove Plantation Bed & Breakfast. Advertisement. 24 June 2005 <http:// www.bbonline.com/va/oakgrove>.

Red Brick Inn of Panguitch. Advertisement. 24 June 2005 <http://www.redbrick innutah.com/html/so_comfort.html>.

Sims Stone—Plantation Series Pavers. Advertisement. 24 June 2005 <http://www .simstone.com/body_plantation.html>.

Tara—A Country Inn. Advertisement. 23 June 2005 <http://www.tara-inn.com/ accommodations.htm>.

Tarleton Oaks. Advertisement. 24 June 2005 <http://roadsidegeorgia.com/site/ Tarleton_oaks.html>.

Taylor, Helen. *Scarlett's Women:* Gone With the Wind *and Its Female Fans.* New Brunswick, NJ: Rutgers UP, 1989.

Ussher, Bruno David. "Max Steiner Establishes Another Film Music Record." Gone With the Wind *as Book and Film.* Ed. Richard Harwell. New York: Paragon, 1987. 160–69.

Tattoo

Karen Aubrey

We see them on nearly every singer on MTV, on movie stars, on television stars, on supermodels, on sports celebrities, on soccer moms, on many of the "heroes" of popular culture, and on those who shape the cultural habits of Americans. Tattoos are everywhere. In the twentieth century Americans have gone from disdain of the tattoo to such widespread cultural acceptance that it seems more people under 40 are tattooed than not. Even the association of tattoos with biker culture has been forever tamed due to the television series *American Chopper*, where Paul, Sr., sports the traditional biker/tattoo look, yet allows us to see the underlying middle-class "family" man at heart. He's no outcast, just another middle-class American trying to make money while raising a family.

Why has the tattoo gone from being a symbol of the primitive and un-civilized to a poetic statement of the middle-class self and of one's spiritual connection to the world and beyond? What has made the tattoo a part of today's fashion? What changes in tattoo designs and in societal attitudes contributed to the creation of this American icon?

In *The Tattoo History Source Book,* Steve Gilbert tells us that an amazing number of ancient Greek and Roman writers, including Plato, Seneca, and Aristophanes, discuss tattooing, and almost always associate it with bar-barians. Those societies used tattooing as a means of identifying prisoners, slaves, and deserters from the army. The Romans used the term "stigma" for tattoo, and that original meaning for "stigma" still exists in modern dic-tionaries (15). This early attitude of associating disgrace with tattooing car-ried into European encounters with the tattoo practices of other cultures, and has existed until very recently in America.

Most accounts of the history of tattoos and tattooing begin it in Polynesia over 2,000 years ago, though evidence of tattooing has been found in all regions of the world. Gilbert mentions that tattoos were even on the Iceman, a 5,000-year-old mummy found in a glacier between Austria and Italy (11). But the American design of tattoos has been especially influenced by the Polynesian islands of Tahiti, Samoa, and Hawaii. Samoa is thought to have developed the most artistically sophisticated tattoo designs. In fact, Samoan tattoo artists today are still regarded as being the best in the world.

The Polynesian style of tattoo design for males, extremely painful to receive and taking years to complete, would cover the entire body from between the waist to just above the knee. This included the genitalia. Traditional female designs cover a smaller area. Polynesians associated tattooing with spiritual and social issues. Early tattoos in Polynesia usually signified rank, including passage into manhood or into a leadership role, and were a primary means of beautifying the body. To refuse to be tattooed would ensure that one would become a social outcast with doubtful success in courtship. Incomplete tattoos were just as much a sign of shame. Some Polynesian cultures tattooed the full body, but most cultures have negative connotations with tattooing the face and head.

When eighteenth-century British sailors, like Captain James Cook, came into contact with these Polynesian cultures, they regarded the tattoos as primitive yet exotic curiosities. Very quickly, these sailors began to get small tattoos themselves from the native islanders and brought those designs back home to Europe. Also, native tattooed Polynesians were taken to Europe to be displayed as oddities. Thereupon, as anthropologist Margo DeMello notes in her book *Bodies of Inscription*, the initial Western reaction to tattoos was to begin "constructing a narrative about tattooed people as savages" who were shown as exotic displays (47).

Anthropologists find that, almost simultaneously, native islander designs began to exhibit elements of European influence. So Europeans were exposed to Polynesian design images, yet the Polynesians began to use Western images that were shown to them by the British. This cultural exchange has continued to today to influence modern tattoo designs.

Negative social attitudes toward tattoos appeared quickly in European minds, primarily as a result of missionaries' declaring that tattoos were unchristian and should be prohibited. This attitude may have been an attempt of missionaries to subvert the religious, spiritual, and cultural significance tattoos had in Polynesian society in order to further the influence of Christian practices. But missionary prohibition of tattoos was a total failure among the native islanders. Among Europeans, the prohibition did little to stop sailors from getting tattooed; however, it had a profound effect on the direction in which Western social attitudes toward tattooing would develop.

By the end of the eighteenth century, the display of tattooed people had become a "freak show" industry where the tattooed put themselves on display for a fee. The first tattooed sideshow exhibits consistently developed their explanations of how they received their tattoos by typically claiming to have been captured and held against their will as they were tattooed over a period of months by savages. Then, DeMello writes, "In 1840, P.T. Barnum... [brought] the freak show to prominence. It was here that...tattooed people were exhibited alongside people with disabilities, natural wonders like wild animals, native people, and 'gaffes,' or manufactured fakes" (54).

Over time, more white Europeans began to show their tattoos, especially sailors; and the tattoo began to represent different ideas to the white working-class male: travel, adventure, and freedom. The tattoo in America became particularly "Americanized" by soldiers in wartime. DeMello notes that perhaps the first professional tattooist in America, Martin Hildebrandt, who owned a tattoo shop in New York City by 1846, reported that he not only tattooed sailors, but also tattooed soldiers on both sides in the Civil War (49–50). After the Spanish American War and particularly after World War II, tattooing became a way of showing one's patriotism and became very closely associated with those who served in the military.

Probably due to advances in tattoo techniques which made it easier, faster, and cheaper to create tattoos, tattoos became available to the lower classes. As with many things in society, when the lower classes can participate, the upper classes avoid the practice. So tattooing became associated with the lower classes early in American history. Because many who serve in the military tend to be from the working class, the connection of tattooing with the working class was further reinforced.

A sailor being tattooed, World War II. Courtesy of Corbis.

The designs of tattoos during this time were images that would appeal to military men, names of beloved individuals such as "Mom" or a girl-friend, images of hula dancers or pin-up styles of scantily dressed women, military insignia, one's own initials or name, or designs which would signal bravery, patriotism, and traditional American ideals. Classic American tattoos also tend to include images from popular culture, such as cartoon characters. It seems that these American tattoos express an association with love of family, country, and American culture.

Most who study tattooing agree that, beginning around the 1960s, the attitude toward tattoos began the shift toward general acceptance in America. Ironically, as a result of widespread concern about blood-transmitted disease, better cleanliness practices were developed in the tattoo industry, and tattoo machines were designed which facilitated ease of cleanliness. In fact, today, walking into a high-end tattoo shop is more like walking into a medical office. Such increased focus on receiving a "healthy" tattoo is more palatable to the mainstream. Although, during the 1960s, tattoos were often associated with bikers, gangs, hippies, and others who were societal outcasts, the general atmosphere of freedom of self-expression, including the freedom to express oneself in ways that had formerly been taboo, included acceptance of the tattoo. Public entertainment figures began to publicly display tattoos, like Janis Joplin, Joan Baez, Peter Fonda, Flip Wilson, and Cher (DeMello 75).

The women's movement, too, especially influenced American tattoo designs. With freer control over their own bodies, American women getting tattoos encouraged more "feminine," subtle, smaller tattoo images. These more "tasteful" designs often had undertones of the philosophy of the freedom and peace movement of the times. So images of peace signs, peace slogans, and images from the psychedelic movement became popular. Tattoos became an expression of ideology rather than of exoticism or of patriotism. Those tattooed were seen as expressing their individuality and their own spirituality, rather than simply being marginalized from society.

Mainstream media plays a large role in the current acceptance of tattoos. In 1982 the first tattoo magazine aimed at the middle class was founded, *TattooTime*. This magazine was considered middle class because it did not feature biker images or sailor-style Americana tattooing designs. It also had a large educational component to its content (DeMello 80). Today, many tattoo publications also emphasize the tattoo's cultural history and cultural significance, making the tattoo a form of cultural acknowledgment. Tattoo magazines are prolific and don't have to be found at your local cramped, seedy tattoo parlor. They can be bought in the grocery story checkout line. These types of magazines have allowed people to write letters, ask questions, view tattoo designs, and read about tattoo artists and techniques.

Tattooing has also become a marketable and saleable commodity, again placing it squarely into mainstream values of middle-class American life. Partly through contests or the display of tattooists' works and through massive advertising of anything tattoo-related, tattooing has become, according to the online article "Attitudes about Tattooing," the sixth-fastest-growing retail business in the United States; middle-class suburban women make up the fastest growing clientele.

With all of the heightened talk about tattoos in the last twenty years, tattoos are getting attention from journalists and scholars as well as the tattoo community. University professors now research tattooing and the cultural attitudes toward it. Many tattooists advertise themselves as "better" because they have Fine Arts degrees. Museums are offering exhibits dedicated to tattoo design and the art of tattooing. As described in "Attitudes about Tattooing," the tattoo parlor has become more of an

A modern tattooed couple. Courtesy of Corbis.

art studio setting with "the ambiance of an upscale beauty salon," requiring appointments. These studios draw the "same kind of clientele as a custom jewelry store, fashion boutique, or high-end antique shop." Some tattoo magazines have furthered the tattooist-as-artist view by refusing to print "anonymous" tattoo images, and insisting on naming the artist of each pictured design.

Instead of a tattoo's being explained as something one did while drunk one Saturday night, tattoo magazines allot space for the tattooed to express why they got tattooed and what meaning their tattoo design has for them. These expressions of personal meaning lead to the overall impression that getting a tattoo is a long thought-out process, for a permanent change to the body, which has significant meaning rather than a drunken impulse behind it. Such forums have allowed the shameful aspect of getting a tattoo to disappear. They, too, present the tattoo as a conscious, moral or sentimental statement which has an uplifting purpose for the bearer. Tattoos can almost be seen as a mark of spiritual triumph. If the tattoo was chosen for its aesthetic beauty, the values inherent in fine art are expressed.

More frequent tattooing may also be a result of mainstream Americans' wide acceptance of a range of permanent body modifications. The popularity of "extreme makeover" television shows attests to this approval, as well as a look at the number of plastic surgery procedures that are advertised in mainstream newspapers and magazines, and discussed on afternoon talk shows. Elective body modification and cosmetic dentistry have surged in popularity and availability. Breast implants are now so common that they are given as high school graduation gifts to daughters. So the general attitude toward body modification is one of wide acceptance; tattoos are just another form of this practice.

Tattoo conventions, tattoo Web sites and chat groups, as well as tattoo publications, have all given the tattooed a sense of group identity, and the middle class generally finds group identity comforting. Rather than being an expression of individuality *outside* of the mainstream, as tattoos once were, tattoos now express an individuality *within* the context of remaining a part of the middle-class embraceable group. There is even a Christian Tattoo Association with its own site on the internet where issues such as the law against tattoos in Leviticus 19:28 ("You shall not make any cuttings in your flesh for the dead, nor tattoo any marks on you: I am the Lord.") are discussed on "The Bible & Tattoos" page. So the tattooed are both different, individualized by their particular image design and by their particular reasons for choosing to be tattooed, yet they are also part of the accepted group of middle-class Bible adherents. Because their designs are more philosophical and personal rather than expressions of rebellion or of the exotic, their tattoos do not offend mainstream sensibilities. So a mix of individualism and group dynamics is involved with modern American tattooing.

This seemingly contradictory mix of individuality and group dynamics seems particularly "American" to me. Instead of blending as in the common "melting pot" metaphor, Americans celebrate differences in culture and ethnicities, while retaining a group identity that is somehow "American." Where once the tattoo "community" was only the group that frequented a particular tattoo shop, now that community expands as far as the Internet will reach. So tattoos simultaneously signify one as an individual and as a member of a group.

One example of the Americanization of a tattoo design that has carried the spirituality aspect palatable to the middle class involves the "tribal" designs. Tribal designs, from Polynesia, tend to use heavy black lines without a lot of intricate detail. At its origin, it has social and cultural significance. Once the tribal designs became popular and widespread, tattooists began modernizing them and creating new designs which only look non-Western. One such example, discussed by DeMello, is the "Hawaiian Band," a tribal-looking motif that is designed to wrap around the upper arm. White tattooist Mike Malone designed this style in the 1970s. "Not only do native Hawaiians wear these tattoos…but Malone has seen his 'Hawaiian' tattoo appear in the *National Geographic* as a representation of traditional Hawaiian tattooing" (91). So the acceptance and prevalence of tattoos act to influence the very roots of tattooing traditions.

Other evidence that society has embraced tattoos is the abundance of "tattoo-like" products. There are temporary tattoos for sale at almost any large discount store or applied in many tattoo shops. These temporary tattoos are often elaborate, barely distinguishable from the real thing, and are routinely used by children under eighteen; so the acceptance of tattoos begins at an early age. Temporary painted tattoos are offered at fairs. Bathing suits with cutouts provide natural suntanned tattoos on the body. Stickers cut into various shapes, such as a heart, can be bought to cover a spot on the skin to prevent it from tanning, resulting in a "tattoo" of sorts.

As to the trendiness of being tattooed, one tattooist DeMello interviewed described the attitude toward tattoos as becoming part of a fashion statement: "because of all the attention it's getting, you know MTV, the media, it's like anything else where the kids see something on TV, whether it's a tattoo or a pair of shoes or something, they treat it as the same thing" (191).

I realized just how entrenched the tattoo is in our culture when I saw a parody of the tattoo on a recent Miller Lite beer commercial during prime-time television. Two men are fishing in a boat while a football referee stands thigh-deep in the water next to them. The referee blows his whistle and announces a "penalty" on one of the men in the boat for having a tribal arm design tattoo. The referee accuses him of using the tattoo as a clichéd attempt to fit in.

If we can now get the humor of a particular tattoo design being a cliché, we're certainly used to seeing lots of tattoos, whether we've thought about it or not. According to the online "The Vanishing Tattoo," *Esquire* magazine estimated in 2002 that 1 in 8 Americans has a tattoo. I'm surprised that number wasn't higher. As a college professor, I look at my students on hot Georgia days, when they're wearing as little clothing as modesty permits, and nearly every one of them has at least one visible tattoo. We're in an era where Americans have enthusiastically accepted the tattoo, but only after we changed its cultural meaning and raised it to iconic American stature.

WORKS CITED AND RECOMMENDED

"Attitudes about Tattooing." *The Art of Tattoo*. April 2003. 8 Sept. 2004 <http://www.msu.edu/~krcmari1/individual/att_cur.html>.

"The Bible & Tattoos." *Christian Tattoo Association*. 2004. 17 Nov. 2004 <http://www.xtat.org/tattoosbible.php>.

"Christian Tattoo Association Community." *Christian Tattoo Association*. 2004. 8 Sept. 2004 <http://com2.runboard.com/bchristiantattooassociation.fmainchat.t393>.

DeMello, Margo. *Bodies of Inscription: A Cultural History of the Modern Tattoo Community*. Durham: Duke UP, 2000.

Gilbert, Steve. *The Tattoo History Source Book*. New York: Juno Books, 2000.

Levins, Hoag. "The Changing Cultural Status of Tattoo Art." *Tattoo Artist*. 1998. 8 Sept. 2004 <http://www.tattooartist.com/history.html#top>.

"Tattoo Facts." *The Vanishing Tattoo*. 2003. 10 Sept. 2004 <http://www.vanishingtattoo.com/tattoo_facts.htm>.

Henry David Thoreau

Daniel S. Kerr

I wish to speak a word for Nature, for Absolute freedom and wildness, as contrasted with freedom and culture merely civil, to regard man as an inhabitant, or a part and parcel of Nature, rather than a member of society.

—Henry David Thoreau, opening sentence of his
posthumously published essay "Walking."

Few causes have so conscripted a writer as the modern environmental movement has conscripted Henry David Thoreau. The nineteenth-century icon best known for his association with Ralph Waldo Emerson and the American literary movement called Transcendentalism, and once observed to have been too "self absorbed to be politically diplomatic" (Lucas 267), has taken up a new mantra in popular culture more than a hundred years after his death. And, of course, Walden Pond is mecca, drawing nature-loving pilgrims from around the world. Noting the importance of the place and the writer who immortalized it in American life, Robert Sattelmeyer comments that "Walden is not only a literary shrine but also a cultural site that provides a focal point for a series of environmental concerns and beliefs that continue to be central to our collective social life a hundred and fifty years after Thoreau moved back to town" (235). The enshriner of Walden Pond becomes an "environmental hero" in Lawrence Buell's oft-quoted book *The Environmental Imagination* (315), a work that, according to Sattelmeyer, documents "the successive possessions and repossessions of Thoreau and Walden Pond by disciples, publishers, literary scholars, environmentalists, and the public" (236). Buell names the latter third of the book for Thoreau's "Environmental Sainthood." In an older classic of American dissection titled *Wilderness and the American Mind*, Roderick Frazier Nash credits the Concord eccentric for "the classic early call for wilderness preservation" (102). Today his essay "Civil Disobedience" is sacramental to activists of all kinds. Cast in the attitudes and partiality of his own day, Thoreau's words do transcend time to live at the spiritual core of the modern environmental movement, affixed in the public consciousness as much to the struggle for the preservation of wilderness as to the great movements of passive resistance.

Yet, the relationship between today's environmental movement and Thoreau does not come easy. The slightest scrutiny shows a marriage forced and orchestrated, built on selection and omission. Little more than a cursory inspection of *Walden* and especially his essay "Walking" yields a more complex environmental philosophy immediately contradictory to itself and sometimes at odds with that of today, or at least to current portrayals of environmental sensibilities. Opposing his iconic role, Thoreau's writing instructs that, in the end, nature is not delicate and that humans are not inimical to nature, because humans are nature. Thoreau is an uneasy saint of modern environmentalism; but the words he did speak for nature, agreeable or not to today's polarized polemics, offer people hope for a more accessible relation to the natural world. Part of the problem today is that the nature movement has failed to heed those words.

The idea of a nature that flourishes despite a certain level of human use agrees with William Cronon's contested essay "The Trouble with Wilderness; or, Getting Back to the Wrong Nature," now infamous in certain environmental circles. The trouble he refers to "embodies a dualistic vision in which the human is entirely outside the natural" (80). Many of the most beloved figures of modern environmentalism embraced this false dualism, important as they are to shaping our heightened environmental awareness today. Rachel Carson, John Muir, Aldo Leopold, Paul Ehrlich, and David Brower are recognized as the "main inspiration" for the Deep Ecology movement, which arose with 1960s activism. The philosophical underpinnings have been traced back to Thoreau himself (Sessions ix–x).

Thoreau's nature is not so clearly defined, though, which is good because, as Cronon and many others before him have warned, the pristine wilderness so many of us seek is likely nonexistent. The most valuable lesson Thoreau the environmental icon offers us today is a more realistic view of our relationship with nature and a way to preserve it.

Henry David Thoreau, 1879. Courtesy of the Library of Congress.

WILDNESS AND WILDERNESS

In a world where the interests of people and animals seem increasingly to conflict, some environmental groups, such as Earth-First!, have asked that we place the interests of what they see as the real nature ahead of human interests. To many environmentalists best represented by what has come to be called the Deep Ecology or the New Environmentalism, wilderness demands the complete absence of humans. Nature activists and rhetoricians today often enlist one particular passage of Thoreau's essay "Walking" to encapsulate this environmental saga. Often misquoted as "in Wilderness is the preservation of the world," the Thoreauvian phrase "in Wildness is the preservation of the world" ("Walking" 61) became the title of the well-known Sierra Club book. Susan Lucas writes of the selection's extensive environmental service: "Again and again we see this statement extracted from the essay and wildness used to promote wilderness preservation" (269). Like much of Thoreau's writing, these words hold significance for many thoughtful environmentalists today, and justifiably so; yet latent in this apparent salvo for wilderness preservation lies a concept contradictory to the movement's most basic tenet that, by definition, wilderness cannot coexist with humans. Thoreau said that, rather, one does not necessarily portend the end of the other. Humans and wilderness share a commonality he called the Wild. Thoreau found sustenance in such wildness and not necessarily in wilderness. Contrary to much of contemporary environmental rhetoric, the philosopher sought wildness both in wilderness and in civilization—and there lies the threat to environmentalists who seek foremost to preserve islands of wildness in designated wilderness refuges, mythological places defined by the absence of anything human.

To understand that Thoreau's "Wildness" is not synonymous with his wilderness is to understand that Thoreau thinks of nature not as fragile and susceptible to destruction by humankind, but, rather, as resilient and able to coexist with responsible humans—to understand Thoreau's "Wildness" is, in his words, "to regard man as an as an inhabitant, or part and parcel of Nature" ("Walking" 49).

Wildness alone attracts us to "Literature," explained Thoreau in "Walking," an essay one editor condensed and renamed "The Value of Wildness." Nature writing is not what Thoreau means, necessarily, but "the uncivilized free and wild thinking in 'Hamlet' and the 'Iliad,' in all Scriptures and Mythologies, not learned in the schools" (64). Wildness sustains—or preserves—the world: wildness drives the plow and fills the sail, trees seek it beneath ground, and "cities import it at any price." Wildness is sustenance for governments as well as for individuals: "The founders of every State which has risen to eminence have drawn their nourishment and vigor from a similar wild source." Even domestic animals retain "wild habits and vigor" ("Walking" 61, 66). Thoreau's wildness exists outside of wilderness, a point environmentalists are wary to concede, perhaps understandably in consideration of such opposing dialectics as "Wise Use," the motivations of which are at best dubious.

In Cronon's landmark essay the environmental historian reminds us that "*wild*ness" (as opposed to wilderness) can be found anywhere: in the see-

mingly tame fields and woodlots of Massachusetts, in the cracks of a Man-
hattan sidewalk, even in the cells of our own bodies" (89). Thoreau, according to critic Barbara Nelson, was trying to formulate "a more realistic
definition for a wild American heritage," not the "American continent as
empty, wild, and pristine, newly delivered from the creating hand of God to
his chosen people." The phrase "in Wildness is the preservation of the world"
never implied that wild nature is delicate. "He does not say wildness needs
our condescending protection, but that wildness will protect us," Nelson
continues: "Although Thoreau definitely values wilderness, wildness and
wilderness are not interchangeable signifiers in his mind" (257–58).

THE INEXORABLE AND TRANSFORMABLE WILD

At first this idea of a resilient nature seemed to me either self-interested or
antique, set against the contemporary environmental fatalism of the so-called
Deep Ecology, which more often maligns humankind as a disease of nature than acknowledges the species as part of nature. Later, however, I remembered an example of nature's resiliency from my own region's ecological
history. Where I grew up on the southern high plains, concerted efforts to
eradicate predators to enforce the agroecosystem of livestock were tragically
successful in the nineteenth century. Government provisions of poison and
settler-supplied firepower made short work of the well-adapted wolf, a key-
stone species that won its place at the top of the plains' ecological hierarchy
through thousands of years of evolution. But unsentimental nature adjusted.
The wolf's former prey nourished the smaller, more versatile coyote, which
quickly assumed the lobo's place at the head of the table, the ancient ecological superstructure. These are the same "wily" animals that hunt and
reproduce in New York City, along with the Red Tailed Hawk, which also
shares my home. The shameful extermination impoverished my relationship
with an older form of my home, yes; human interference sent the ecosystem
into a tumult. Unlike more progressive places where wolf populations have
rebounded, the predator's reintroduction in the Texas Panhandle won't come
anytime soon. But instead of collapsing into environmental cataclysm, nature
rebounded, other predators held the numbers of prey animals in check, and
people continued to coexist with the morphing ecology of the Llano Esta-
cado. Today if I walk across the high plains or through a canyon, there I can
still enjoy the wildness of nature. The wolf's disappearance left a shameful
mark on the region's environmental history, but the unquellable force of life
drove nature relentlessly forward, if in new form.

Thoreau shows his confidence in nature's regeneration when he writes in
Walden of finding the "potato of the aborigines," or ground nut, decimated
by cultivation:

In these days of fatted cattle and waving grainfields, this humble root which was
once *totem* of an Indian tribe, is quite forgotten...; but let wild Nature reign

here once more, and the tender and luxurious grains will probably disappear before a myriad of foes, and... the now almost exterminated ground-nut will perhaps revive and flourish..., prove itself indigenous, and resume its importance and dignity as the diet of the hunter tribe. (154)

THE LACK OF CREDIBILITY

Environmentalists deserve credit for calling attention to the consequences of our tendency to transform nature for our exclusive benefit. And Thoreau did cast the human as a potential environmental antagonist, as he cast the "surveyor," another vocation of the writer, as "The Prince of Darkness," in "Walking" (53). The modern environmental consciousness does much to compensate for the justification many people have taken from Judeo-Christian teachings to use nature without thought to the obligations involved. Both Romantics such as Thoreau and Deep Ecologists have sought to over-throw this anthropocentric worldview, despite the Christian vocabulary he slips in and out of in his writing, and despite the spirituality modern environ-mentalists often impose on their "wild" surroundings. Animism and Deism

Site of Thoreau's hut, Lake Walden, Concord, Massachusetts, 1908. Courtesy of the Library of Congress.

offered both groups, Thoreau's associated Transcendentalists included, what traditional Western religious teachings did not: a view of the earth as something other than man's personal garden, as something autonomous, as something wild. Romantics of contemporary ilk still worship nature because they see in it a tangible promise of immortality and, thus, transcendence.

Still, today, for all the gathering knowledge that local actions have global consequences, our general public attitude of self-righteous arrogance concerning the environment has been humbled little. A debate between anthropocentrists and ecocentrists may be understandable, but the verbal contest has polarized people, and has paralyzed any satisfactory movement toward sustainability, as the ongoing consequences of our mindless exploitation of nature attest so unfortunately. The sides have become entrenched. Despite our new environmental awareness, we have accomplished little in curbing the excessive behaviors that have brought emergency alerts.

The capacity of humankind to alter the global system of life in drastic and dangerous ways is now undeniable to all but the most stalwart ideologue, thanks more to our enhanced powers of observation than any kind of religion or spirituality, Christian or environmental. Those observations tell us something else: we belong to Thoreau's "Wild" earth as much as any creature before us. The arguments for pristine nature in environmentalism today fail because people reject any message telling them they do not belong in nature as other animals do.

With the stakes so high, a compromise is desperately needed. Confidence in nature, in some form of nature, to survive the deliberated affronts of humankind might seem at first naïve from today's perspective, framed by what has become traditional environmental thinking. However, considering the adaptability in nature, Thoreau's deliberation on the profound-yet-limited effect of humans appears from my perspective to be more honest—less rhetorical—than the Deep Ecology. We need to ask questions that will direct us to ways to minimize the impact we will inevitably make. What kind of nature will we leave for the next generation? How much human-induced change is acceptable? Correctly or not, a great many people sense rhetorical overstatement on both sides of the nature debate today. Consequently well-meaning environmentalists become labeled "treehuggers" and lose credibility, to the detriment of nature, which includes us. The ostensible distance between human-centered and nature-centered philosophies need not be as wide as the extremes insist.

As inhabitants of the world, people bear a responsibility to sustain a symbiosis with nature, at their own certain peril. Equally important for nature, those who live there must also be able to use the place in relation to their sustenance, both physical and spiritual, without the moral condemnation many in the environmental community today thrust upon humanity as an inherent destroyer of nature. Such a hard line is too easily dismissed by the majority of Americans. If people are encouraged to accept themselves as a working part of the environment, as many already have, to protect that natural whole will become more of a responsibility, whether it means occasionally we seek solitude and efficiency in the woods or that we just decide to pay more for the "all natural" label. If the interests of the earth and its human inhabitants are seen clearly, as one and the same, then the difference between the anthropocentrism that Deep Ecologists decry as the root of environmental degradation and the ecocentrism they demand as the solution would cease to exist. Credibility is the single most critical problem that confronts environmentalists today. If embraced forthrightly, the nuanced environmental philosophy of Thoreau could offer the modern environmental movement the authority it so desperately needs.

ACKNOWLEDGING THOREAU'S GREAT GREEN MYTH

That nature writers and advocates in the contemporary environmental movement have overlooked these philosophical conflicts to embrace Thoreau as compatriot and even a potential savior—a messiah for the natural world—has become a conspicuous rhetorical stance. They have drawn a line in the sand and simplified and distilled his environmental philosophy into a polarized battle of evil against good, land developers and politicians against the sacred mother earth. Thoreau, instead, embraced the complexities of his American culture and American environment from the standpoint of his time and place, incorporating humankind as "part and parcel of Nature"—not inherently destructive. Thoreau saw nature not as something to put aside and protect in veneration, but, rather, as something to celebrate in sustained, responsible use.

The unbending stance of man as the destroyer of nature is a rhetorical simplification that precludes a more honest assessment of the human place in nature, that of component and, therefore, dependent. Thoreau no doubt ranks among the first nature advocates in a line that stretches to the nature writing of today, but his relation to nature is more complex than the idea forwarded by many who revere the man as an environmental saint. Thoreau was an original, but he necessarily viewed the world through the lens of his own times. As Lawrence Buell points out, the myths that grow around authors are, though important, "popular simplifications" (314). To understand them as such can lead to nothing but a clearer picture of not only the author's world, but ours, as well.

Thoreau suffers the fate of any cultural icon. His appropriation is necessarily incomplete, hardly a full reflection of the man's ideals, aspirations, and partialities; but the reverence of nature that his iconic status encourages can serve as an important check on human exploitation of nature. Environmentalists today are too often and too easily marginalized as "wild-eyed liberals." Thoreau offers a kind of reconciling hope that potential social reformers must take, if we are to gain the credibility to effect the cultural reform that our environment—our home, my home—needs so badly. If the more radical strains of the modern environmental movement accommodate the human place in the natural world, the message Thoreau has come to represent will resonate with a wider audience, even if that message takes what it may from his legacy and leaves the rest. Thoreau's philosophy of a resilient nature can propel the all-important cause of environmentalism into the mainstream of American values. If acknowledged, it must.

WORKS CITED AND RECOMMENDED

Buell, Lawrence. *The Environmental Imagination: Thoreau, Nature Writing, and the Formation of American Culture*. Cambridge, MA: Belknap–Harvard UP, 1995.

Cronon, William. "The Trouble with Wilderness; or, Getting Back to the Wrong Nature." *Uncommon Ground: Rethinking the Human Place in Nature*. Ed. William Cronon. New York: Norton, 1996. 69–90.

Lucas, Susan M. "Counter Frictions: Writing and Activism in the Work of Abbey and Thoreau." *Thoreau's Sense of Place: Essays in American Environmental Writing*. Ed. Richard Schneider. Iowa City: U of Iowa P, 2000. 266–79.

Nash, Roderick Frazier. *Wilderness and the American Mind*. 4th ed. New Haven, CT: Yale UP, 2001.

Nelson, Barbara. "Rustling Thoreau's Cattle: Wilderness and Domesticity in 'Walking.'" *Thoreau's Sense of Place* 254–65.

Sattelmeyer, Robert. "Depopulation, Deforestation, and the Actual Walden Pond." *Thoreau's Sense of Place* 235–43.

Sessions, George, ed. Preface. *Deep Ecology for the 21st Century: Readings on the Philosophy and Practice of the New Environmentalism*. Boston: Shambhala, 1995. iv–xxviii.

Simmons, Nancy Craig. "Speaking for Nature: Thoreau and the 'Problem of Nature Writing.'" *Thoreau's Sense of Place* 223–34.

Thoreau, Henry David. *Walden; or Life in The Woods*. 1854. Ed. Philip Smith. New York: Dover, 1995.

———. "Walking." *Civil Disobedience and Other Essays*. Ed. Philip Smith. New York: Dover, 1993. 49–74.

Tractor

Robert T. Rhode

In suburban gardens; on rural lawns; in flame-shooting, dirt-cloud-gushing contests; and in presents to children, we further our devotion to the tractor. That nostalgic icon of American culture, the farm tractor, evolved slowly and contributed to various values that developed in the country's history.

The origins of the tractor are to be found in the great age of steam power. When, in 1805, Oliver Evans's amphibious steam dredge named Orukter (or Oruktor) Amphibolos waddled down the streets of Philadelphia and splashed into the Schuylkill River, there had already been several attempts to make a steam engine pull itself along a highway by its own might. Although various steam historians give Evans the credit for having designed and constructed the first successful traction engine, the evidence shows that traction engineering dates to the time of the drafting of the United States Constitution.

Jack Alexander's *The First American Farm Tractors: Developments to 1917* offers several examples of early experiments in traction engineering. In 1790, Nathan Read of Salem, Massachusetts, applied for a patent for a steam carriage. David Burgess Wise's *Steam on the Road* suggests that a prototype of Read's machine may have been driven through the streets of Warren, Massachusetts. Wise also mentions a Dr. Apollos Kinsey, a contemporary of Read, who drove a steam carriage in Hartford, Connecticut. Alexander's *Steam Power on California Roads and Farms (1858–1911)* substantiates that traction engineering was advancing in California in the late 1850s.

In 1858, the Newark Machine Works in Newark, Ohio, was building a traction engine described as "self-propelling." According to *The Ohio Farmer* for July 21, 1860, one of the machines made a spectacular forty-six-mile round trip up and down the hills of Cadiz, Ohio.

The September 29, 1860 issue of the *Scientific American* announced that, on September 14, John Walker of Mount Vernon, Ohio, had exhibited at the United States Agricultural Society Fair in Cincinnati a self-propelling locomotive that powered a crosscut saw.

From 1916 through 1917, the *American Thresherman* carried a series of articles by C. M. Giddings, a designing engineer for the Russell Company of

Massillon, Ohio; Giddings reported that a farmer near Mount Vernon, Ohio, designed a traction engine in 1868 and 1869. It was steered by a team of horses harnessed to a tongue.

In its *Twenty-sixth Annual Report*, published in 1872 but covering events in the year 1871, the Ohio State Board of Agriculture noted that Hulburt & Page of Painesville, Ohio, had built a self-propelling steamer for threshing small grain such as wheat, oats, or barley. Threshing was one of the most important activities of the rural calendar. First, machines called reapers mowed fields of mature grain. The mowing was the initial phase of harvesting. In various regions, the mowed grain was formed into bundles; machines called reaper-binders paired the functions of mowing and bundling the crop. The bundles were arranged in shocks, or small stacks, and allowed to rest, or cure. After a few weeks, the shocks were loaded on wagons and brought to a threshing machine, or thresher, which separated the grain from the stalks on which it had grown. Threshing helped to clean the grain, which was saved for food and for planting future crops. Variations on this process were found in different locales. The Hulburt & Page steam engine provided power to run a threshing machine by a belt extending from a wheel on the engine's crankshaft to a pulley on the thresher. Since the 1840s, stationary and portable steamers had been belted to threshers, but self-propelled steam engines were still a novelty in 1872.

In 1874, the Ohio State Board of Agriculture presented to Job E. Owens and the firm of Owens, Lane & Dyer Machine Company of Hamilton, Ohio, a gold medal for a traction engine that Owens had designed.

By the late 1870s, several American steam engine manufactories were producing traction engines. Chains or gears were employed to this end. With its ideal location west of the mountains on the border of the most fertile land of the day, and with its all-important proximity to railway centers, Ohio developed the largest number of traction engine factories, thirty-one in all. As Alexander has explained, early traction engines went under a variety of descriptors: steam carriages, road engines, road locomotives, and field locomotives among them. By the turn of the last century, the term of choice was *traction engine*.

The era of the agricultural traction engine's greatest popularity dates from the latter half of the 1870s through the 1920s, with farm steamer production continuing into the 1940s. In the late teens, the noun *tractor* began to appear in advertising. Although most historians associate the word *tractor* with the kerosene- and gasoline-powered machines that eventually eclipsed the agricultural steam engine, ads for late-model steam engines frequently called them *tractors*.

Almost from the beginning, the tractor became an icon. In the late 1800s and early 1900s, steam was king, and children admired farm steam engineers. Despite their simplicity of both design and function, agricultural steam engines were dauntingly complex machines, and a relatively small proportion of farmers could master their intricacies. As engines and associated equipment

Engraving of a turn-of-the-century tractor. Courtesy of the Library of Congress.

like threshers and sawmills were expensive, only a few agriculturists could afford steam rigs. For these reasons, engineers occupied a high status in rural communities. In turn, engineers were to lead exemplary lives. Early textbooks for operators of farm engines often addressed the lifestyle of the engineer and urged cleanliness and temperate living. Images of the steam tractor became associated with technological savoir-faire, authority, wealth, and power. More than a hundred prominent agricultural steam engine factories published annual catalogs depicting and describing their machines. For farm families, these catalogs were a source of literature, and writers employed to compose the catalogs invoked a host of tropes to proclaim the virtues of their wares. Steam engine companies further promoted their products through commemorative buttons, watch fobs, small mirrors with advertising on the back, matchboxes, and iron toys.

In a 1910 survey, the U.S. Department of Agriculture found there were over 100,000 working steam engines on American farms. An indeterminate number of steamers had been junked before 1910, and several thousand more were produced through the teens and twenties. In World War II, thousands of steam engines and kerosene- and gasoline-powered tractors were scrapped to contribute to the production of ammunition.

In spite of the scrap drives and perhaps in reaction against them, a movement to restore old iron and to preserve agricultural history gained momentum. This movement had begun in the late 1930s, and it aimed to celebrate the legacy of threshing and sawmilling with steam engines. The first "threshing reunion," sponsored by the Stark County Threshermen's Association, was held at the F. E. Slutz farm near Battlesburg, Ohio, in 1939. In that same year, Lyman Knapp of Blackwell, Oklahoma, and Paul R. Woodruff of Ponca City, Oklahoma, staged what was probably the first public exhibition of steam plowing as it had been performed in the "good ol' days." In 1941, Joseph T. "Steam Engine Joe" Rynda of Montgomery, Minnesota, held a threshing bee. In that same year and in subsequent years, Ben Markley near Wichita, Kansas, collected engines and hid them in a woods to keep them from junk dealers and scrap hounds. After the war, steamers hidden from the scrap drives were hauled from storage and put in preservation. On September 19, 1947, Nelson L. Howard, who had begun collecting and preserving steam engines in 1944, attended a meeting of a new thresher club named the Indiana Brotherhood of Threshermen, and he was elected president. In 1948, the group hosted its first show; in 1949, the name of the organization was changed to the Pioneer Engineers Club of Indiana. The club was based at Rushville, Indiana. LeRoy Blaker began hosting a steam gathering at his farm near Alvordton, Ohio, in 1945, and a formal association rapidly developed. In 1948, Guy Sams named the organization the National Threshers Association. It was incorporated in 1950. The NTA reunions later were held at Montpelier, Ohio, and still later at Wauseon, Ohio.

In 1948, Arthur S. Young presided over the first meeting of the Rough and Tumble Engineers Historical Association at his farm equipment dealership near Kinzers, Pennsylvania. Young had collected engines since the steam-power era itself. In that same year, President of the Illinois Brotherhood of Threshermen Dan S. Zehr of Pontiac, Illinois, originated the Central States Steam Threshers Association. Ray Ernst of Wayland, Iowa, began the reunion at Mount Pleasant, Iowa. It eventually became the largest event of its kind in the country. In the beginning of the restoration movement, the shows featured steam engines and the earliest kerosene tractors, which were as large as the largest steamers. Year by year, exhibitions included more and more of the relatively small gasoline tractors that became popular after the steam era had faded.

A woman in the midwest driving an Oliver tractor, ca. 1940. Courtesy of the Library of Congress.

Threshing reunions and similar events honoring the history of agricultural machines proliferated at a rate far more rapid than anyone had the right to expect. The 2004 *Farm Collector Show Directory* listed over 1,300 vintage iron shows throughout the United States. In addition to these exhibitions, numerous county and state fairs showcased agricultural implements. These gatherings spawned a myriad of items to be purchased by enthusiasts. Lamps in the form of tractors, lampshades depicting tractors, photo mirrors, pillowcases portraying tractors, souvenir plates, stationery, postcards, rubber stamps, jigsaw puzzles made from tractor photographs, belt buckles, belts stamped with tractor designs, watch fobs, calendars, embroidery, coffee mugs, neckties, key chains, buttons, handkerchiefs, saw blades painted with scenes of tractors, and mailboxes shaped like tractors appealed to the tractor aficionado.

Television personality, author, humorist, and erstwhile professor Roger Welsch of Nebraska has published a handful of wildly popular books on tractor restoration, including *Love, Sex and Tractors*. Welsch is only one of numerous authors who have contributed books on vintage iron. Entire catalogs are devoted to tractor books available from booksellers who specialize in titles ranging from classic automobiles to heavy equipment. Shelves in chain bookstores are laden with books on the art and science of preserving antique tractors. As Farm Bureau statistics for 2002 indicate that farmers are only 1.9 percent of the population, booksellers wishing to earn a profit have no incentive to appeal only to an audience of agriculturists. Clearly, inhabitants of rural areas are not the only people bitten by the tractor nostalgia bug.

Fair and show organizers have recognized that tractor pulls are a real pull, attracting thousands of spectators from farm and city alike. At such events, tractors, which have been rebuilt to be more powerful than their manufacturers ever intended they should be, struggle to draw massive weights along parade routes in front of grandstands packed with cheering devotees. Churning up clouds of dust, the tractors belch fire and lunge forward in the present-day equivalent of the medieval joust. Such machines are the proverbial far cry from the simple, sputtering, modest little tractors that pulled two-bottom plows across America's heartland in the late 1940s, yet the souped-up puller is emblematic of the unpretentious plower. While not every old-iron enthusiast is a fan of tractor pulls, fairs and exhibitions that host these events fill the parking lots.

Part of the motivation behind the first threshing reunions was nostalgia, or a compulsion to prevent a glorious past from disappearing into obscurity. During the steam century, grain harvesting and threshing in many regions constituted a grand communal endeavor. As not every farmer could afford a steam rig, farm families joined rings, also known as *runs*, to collaborate in threshing. The steam-powered threshing machine made the rounds of the ring of farms, and the families that formed the run met at each other's farms to assist with the process of mechanically separating the grain from the stalks on which the grain had grown. For years after the passing of the threshing epoch, people who had experienced steam threshing spoke nostalgically about steam engines and the golden age of American agriculture that such machines had helped to induce. This nostalgia arose partly from fascination with the machinery and partly from awareness that the steam technology had fostered an enjoyable camaraderie. At one time, most Americans had intimate knowledge of threshing. Just before the 1920 census, over half the people of the United States were farmers or were engaged in pursuits that assisted agriculture.

A host of factors led to the end of the threshing epoch, not the least among them the widespread adoption of the combined harvester, known as a *combine* (pronounced with the accent on the first syllable), which united in one machine and one operation the mowing of the crop and the separating of the grain from the straw. The rise of the combines occurred with the symbiotic availability of small, affordable gasoline tractors to pull them. (Later, combines became self-propelling.) When each farmer owned a tractor and a combine, communal threshing disappeared.

At the time of this writing, the people who remember steam threshing are few, yet the nostalgia they have felt has grown exponentially. In the masses of the newly nostalgic are farmers whose memories include small gasoline tractors but not steam threshing, and city dwellers who took summer jobs on farms. These two groups account for only a tiny percentage of those who buy tractor books, purchase tractor memorabilia, or attend tractor pulls. The nostalgia for a golden age of agriculture permeates a large segment of the population that perceives the rural past of the United States as enshrining significant values, including the work ethic, Christian religiosity, and a secure hearth and home. From the creation of threshing reunions, through the efforts to preserve steam engines during the scrap drives of World War II, through the old-iron restoration movement, through the hundreds of tractor shows and fairs, to the current tractor pulls and tractor books, the tractor has emerged as the icon of these values.

WORKS CITED AND RECOMMENDED

Alexander, Jack. *The First American Farm Tractors: Developments to 1917.* Tigard, OR: Binder, 2003.

———. *Steam Power on California Roads and Farms (1858–1911).* Tigard, OR: Binder, 1998.

Farm Collector Show Directory. Topeka, KS: Ogden, 2004.

Giddings, C. M. *Development of the Traction Engine in America.* Rpt. from *American Thresherman.* 1916–1917. Lancaster, PA: Stemgas, 1980.

Rhode, Robert T. "The Birth of the Steam Preservation Hobby in America." *Engineers and Engines Magazine* 44.3 (1998): 26–29.

———. "Famished for Reading: How a Harvest of Machinery Catalogues Fed Rural America." *Iron-Men Album Magazine* 52.5 (1998): 24–27.

———. "The First Ohio Traction Engine? Pushing Back the Date of Traction Engineering in Ohio." *Steam Traction* 57.4 (2003): 9–10.

———. *The Harvest Story: Recollections of Old-Time Threshermen.* West Lafayette, IN: Purdue UP, 2001.

———. "King Steam's Gallant Knights." *Iron-Men Album Magazine* 48.5 (1994): 23–26.

———. "Lehmer Update." *Steam Traction* 57.4 (2003): 3.

———. "The Mystery of the Lehmer Model: An Old Traction Engine Model Leads to a Modern Mystery." *Iron-Men Album Magazine* 57.2 (2002): 6–12.

———. "Ohio Engines." *Steam Traction* 58.3 (2004): 9–10.

———. "Ohio Origins." *Steam Traction* 58.5 (2004): 7–8.

———. "Update on Isaac Lehmer." *Steam Traction* 57.5 (2003): 4.

———. "When Steam Was King…and Cincinnati Was Queen." *Iron-Men Album Magazine* 50.3 (1996): 2–7.

———. "Who Built the First Traction Engine in America?" *Engineers and Engines Magazine* 44.2 (1998): 14–15.

Welsch, Roger. *Busted Tractors and Rusty Knuckles.* Osceola, WI: MBI, 1997.

———. *Everything I Know About Women I Learned from My Tractor.* St. Paul, MN: MBI, 2002.

———. *Love, Sex and Tractors*. Osceola, WI: MBI, 2000.

———. *Old Tractors and the Men Who Love Them*. Osceola, WI: MBI, 1995.

Wik, Reynold M. "Farm Steam Engineers: Pioneers in Rural America." *Iron-Men Album Magazine* 34.6 (1980): 5.

Wilson, Mitchell. *American Science and Invention: A Pictorial History*. New York: Bonanza, 1960.

Wise, David Burgess. *Steam on the Road*. New York: Hamlyn, 1973.

Young, Mehl. "The First Reunion?" *Steam Traction* 58.1 (2003): 8–11.

Tupperware

Judith Hatchett

"It has to burp," my Aunt Mallie solemnly explained to my sister, my two younger male cousins, and me, as we, equally solemn, watched her practice her Tupperware demonstration. Then we got a chance at the Wonder Bowl ourselves, until we too had mastered the magic burp that would keep food fresh, possibly forever so far as we knew. We were too young to really care about the freshness of food, surely an adult problem, but we could easily grasp that there was something inherently modern and exciting about Tupperware, its colors, its variety of containers, even its very plasticity. We lived in a world where something new and brilliant was always being created to replace the old and dull, and Tupperware appeared to be a logical part of this progression graciously planned for our generation.

My Aunt Mallie was a farm wife and a Tupperware dealer. I'm sure that the money she earned through the amazing plastic containers replaced the egg money saved by earlier generations of farm women. For my cousins, my sister, and me, Tupperware meant adventurous drives down country roads to isolated farmhouses where women eagerly awaited the delivery of their Tupperware, not to mention the visit. It also meant that Aunt Mallie had a great deal of Tupperware herself, and we thoroughly enjoyed the Popsicle makers and unbreakable orange and turquoise tumblers and looked forward to each new incarnation of Tupperware. We had no idea that we were very small parts of a revolution in American consumerism fueled by science, war, Yankee ingenuity, Southern extravagance, subversive women, suburbia, and of course that amazing burp.

The first point to establish in a discussion about Tupperware is that everything about it is amazing in a distinctly American way. That a plastic kitchen container is recognized worldwide as an American icon seals the special place of Tupperware in twentieth-century consciousness. Although the iconography we associate with Tupperware is part and parcel of the 1950s, even now Tupperware is sold in over 100 countries, and every 2.5 seconds a Tupperware party is beginning. A second point is that because Tupperware burst on the scene already iconic in its design and construction, the plastic phenomenon has been analyzed and researched by scholars, designers, and business people, its significance and impact measured and debated. A third point is that while all analysts agree on the basic story of Tupperware—its origin, function, artistry, economics, and major players—they certainly do not agree on how to interpret it. This entry offers the Tupperware story and examples of varied interpretations including my own, which have, not surprisingly, changed over time. The most thorough treatments of the Tupperware story are Alison J. Clarke's *Tupperware: The Promise of Plastic in 1950s America*, published by the Smithsonian Institution, and *Tupperware!*, a 2004 *American Experience* video which acknowledges its debt to the Clarke book. The following summary is based on those sources.

First comes the basic story. Earl Silas Tupper, a New England tree surgeon and amateur inventor, developed Tupperware from polyethylene, a plastic used as a seal in World War II industry and aviation. While others had recognized the unique qualities of polyethylene—it "bridged the gap between categories of rigid and non-rigid plastics, retaining toughness and flexibility at extremely low and comparatively high temperatures" (Clarke 38)—it was Tupper whose many experiments established that the plastic could be molded into an infinity of forms. It could also be produced in many colors. When in 1949 Tupper patented the Tupper seal, which he had modeled on the sealing of a paint can, his "revolutionary, generic kitchenware"—water-tight and air-tight—was born (Clarke 35). An office memo of 1949, in which Tupper describes his plastic, affords a glimpse into his quirky personality: "With the end of the war [polyethylene] was another young veteran that had accelerated from childhood to a fighting job. It had done its job well but like all young vets returning from the wars it had never had civilian adult experience" (Clarke 37). Tupper would gain fame and fortune providing that experience.

Ironically, the art world embraced the revolutionary kitchenware before American housewives did. In 1956 the Museum of Modern Art in New York showcased a variety of Tupperware containers for a national exhibit of "outstanding twentieth-century design," having determined that "Tupperware embodied the machine aesthetic of technologically determined, functional form" (Clarke 36). This accomplishment was less impressive to thrifty postwar housewives, however, who did not flock to department stores to purchase the new product. Financial success came to Tupper in the form of Brownie Wise, a divorced single mother who persuaded him to sell Tupperware exclusively through home parties, whose benefits she had learned through a tenure with Stanley Home Products. Tupper and Wise formed an "unlikely but perfect match" (*Tupperware!*), with Wise heading the marketing side of the business, which she soon moved to Kissimmee, Florida; Tupper handled the production side, continuing to design personally each new piece of Tupperware.

Wise knew women. She knew the frustrations and isolation of 1950s housewives who were expected to erase Rosie the Riveter from their mem-

Women gathered at a Tupperware home party, 1958. AP/Wide World Photos.

ories and confine themselves to the domestic sphere of the new suburbia, reigning over home and hearth and never challenging the breadwinning status of their husbands. She knew how much having their own spending money could mean and how to create a business empire that would enable women to get that money without shedding their lady-like, stay-at-home-status. Wise developed a structure wherein the Tupperware party was also and equally a social event. The dealer recruited women to give the parties, invite friends and relatives to their homes, feed them light refreshments, and offer them the opportunity to buy the water- and air-tight (also vermin-free) containers that would, after all, save money by preserving food. There were also games and demonstrations, breaking the ice and showing how to achieve that all-important burp. For her efforts the hostess received free Tupperware and the opportunity to become a dealer herself. Very successful dealers could become managers, earning larger commissions and overseeing and recruiting more dealers. Top managers had a chance to become distributors. Because Earl Tupper was always designing new products, and because the parties were considered pleasant social events, the supply of friends and relatives willing to attend and make purchases would not necessarily diminish over time.

In Kissimmee, Wise developed a pilgrimage site for her empire of the Tupperware sales force, where beginning in 1954 she held annual Jubilees—motivational reunions for the "Tupperware Family." In addition to lavish prizes, leading sellers won public recognition and acclaim. All received information and hints and advice for improving sales. The Jubilees also required some work: business education sessions with homework and a formal graduation ceremony. Jubilees also included enthusiastic rallies where participants sang songs and performed rituals Wise had created. Wise, always beautifully dressed, would sometimes spontaneously give items of her own clothing to high-achieving members of the Tupperware family.

Phenomenal success resulted. For several years Tupperware achieved an equipoise in which all its participants seemed happy with what the system provided. Brownie Wise became the public face of Tupperware—she was the first woman ever to appear on the cover of *Business Week*—and Tupper was content to remain in New England and design and produce more Tupperware. With success, though, came eventual strain. By 1957 Wise and her feminine kingdom had taken more orders than Tupper's factory could produce, and when Wise urged (or in some versions, demanded) increased production, Tupper was annoyed. Tupper, who had never even attended a Jubilee, began for the first time to question Wise's spending and judgment. Various interpretations of these events linger but the essential facts are these: Tupper fired Wise in 1958 and subsequently sold the company, which he owned outright, for $116 million. Brownie Wise received—but only after Tupper was pressured by others in the company—a severance package of $35,000. None of the properties in Florida, neither her house nor her clothes, were hers.

The Tupperware empire continued quite successfully without its two founders, becoming international in scope. Wise and Tupper seemed to remove themselves from the world. Tupper gave up his U.S. citizenship, divorced his wife, and moved to an island in Central America. Wise attempted a few ventures, none of which succeeded. The Tupperware patent expired in 1984, eliminating the product's uniqueness and opening the door for cheaper competitors. Earl Tupper died in 1983 and Brownie Wise in 1984.

That's the story. Branching from it are alternative versions and interpretations. As *Tupperware!* reveals, Wise's departure remained a mystery among the Tupperware family, with many assuming she had retired in the wealth and splendor exhibited at her Jubilees. Another version is that Tupper wanted to sell the company and knew that no one would buy it with so prominent a woman at its marketing head, so he picked the fight because "Bankers didn't talk to women" (*Tupperware!*). One version even declares that Tupper broke with Wise because she advocated a Tupperware dog dish. Certainly the ending seems to topple Wise from that savvy businesswoman pedestal. *Tupperware!*'s Laurie Kahn-Levitt explains in an interview that "Back then, things that are basic for women now weren't obvious. I don't think it occurred to her to ask for stock, for example.... So when Earl fired her, she didn't have anything."

Reading those words, I understood that "back then" leads to our various interpretations of the Tupperware narrative. Whether we can bring ourselves to an understanding of "back then" makes all the difference. From the vantage point of 2005, the exploitive dimension of the Tupperware setup seems obvious, the party games ridiculous, and the rituals of the Jubilees embarrassing if not humiliating. "Back then" women actually seemed to enjoy grabbing a shovel and digging for prizes buried in a Florida field or singing, with religious fervor, "I've Got That Tupper Feeling," to the tune of an old Sunday School song about having joy, joy, joy down in the heart. They didn't mind, or didn't seem to mind, the absurd party games or purchasing their own demonstration kits or inviting their friends and relatives to parties.

Watching the *Tupperware!* video, I seemed to split into two viewers: one who was genuinely moved by the reminiscences of the former Tupperware salespeople and another who was repelled by everything about the world they so fondly remembered. An anonymous Amazon.com reviewer, obviously much younger than I, also found the footage of the Jubilees to be a "sort of creepy and bizarre" reminder that "there was some pretty strange stuff going on in the 1950s." She and I would certainly never grab a shovel and dig for a prize; and we wouldn't want mink stoles even if we did dig them up. Yet careful attention to the interviewees' stories fleshes out the many poignant differences between then and now and explains why the opportunities offered through Tupperware did indeed improve lives. Most telling for me is that of a woman who learned at her first Tupperware party that the dealer had made ten dollars on the party. Nowhere, she explains, in the entire rural area where she lived, was there a job she could get, even working all day long, that paid ten dollars. Others describe how they identified what they perceived as luxury items—a television set, a new sofa—and counted the number of parties it would take to make enough to purchase them. Tupperware funded family vacations and college educations. Another woman recalls with pride that her earnings enabled her to support her elderly mother. Others remind us that many of these women had never completed high school, had never been honored in any way, had never seen their names in a publication; for them the Jubilee graduations and diplomas and Tupperware newsletters and personal notes from Brownie Wise were the most glorious affirmations of accomplishment they ever had or would receive, and they valued them highly and without cynicism.

The same gap emerges in attitudes toward Tupperware parties. I attended my last one in the very early 1980s, after I'd had my second child. As a "second wave" 1970s feminist I found the party silly, a pageantry in time warp, but at the same time I was suspicious that my life wasn't as different from those original suburban Tupperware partiers as I'd expected it to be. "Why can't you just relax and enjoy a night out?" asked my friend, who'd had her third child. Why not indeed? Many attendees at 1950s parties had no car during the day—it went off to work with the breadwinner—so a party in the neighborhood, like an earlier quilting bee or sewing circle, offered a welcome social outlet, communal childcare, and collective advice on husbands and children. Buying a bit of Tupperware was a small price to pay, and besides, Tupperware actually saved money. Perhaps my discomfort lay not so much with the party as with the reality that women like me, who unlike our 1950s forebears were both educated and employed, were still assumed by all (especially by ourselves) to be fully responsible for home and children. "Back then" was simply a lot closer than it should have been.

Attitudes toward the 1950s also shape reactions to Clarke's book. In "Life of the Party," Susan Porter Benson says that Clarke made her realize that "one of the many ways we second-wavers missed the boat was in failing to appreciate the subversive meanings lurking in the 1950s suburbia we were reacting against" (1). Certainly Brownie Wise got her women out of the house and making money in a culture that frowned on both actions. Second wave feminists may not like the way she did it, but they never walked in her shoes. Further, the women interviewed for *Tupperware!* firmly establish that they viewed themselves as rebels. In a contrasting current perspective, Susan Vincent in her review faults Clarke's book for presenting an unsuitably favorable view of Tupperware by emphasizing success stories and glossing over the exploitive features of the system. In another article, "Preserving Domesticity: Reading Tupperware in Women's Changing Domestic, Social and Economic Roles," Vincent argues more extensively that Tupperware's continued success is possible only because working women are driven to sell it to supplement inadequate salaries and because they are still responsible for the domestic sphere. "Back then" and "Right now" are the same for them.

Certainly both Clarke and the video emphasize Tupperware success stories rather than the many failures that there must have been. Both do convey, however, that those who became involved with Tupperware in the 1950s and early 1960s remained quite aware that it was enabling them to advance within a system stacked against their upward mobility. According to couples in the video, there was no point in objecting to the rule that when a woman advanced beyond manager to distributor—the most lucrative of all positions—she would then in effect work for her husband because it was he who was given the title and was expected to quit his job and relocate wherever more Tupperware was needed. That many couples did just that proves the genuine monetary advantage the system offered to those at the very top. But it is obvious that not all couples, even if able to attain this status, could accept it without conflict. Even Brownie Wise, credited by so many women with lifting their status and self-esteem, was an acknowledged Queen Bee whose helping hand never led another woman to the center of the hive. And although Clarke describes the Tupperware party as a "celebratory and consciously feminine activity" (107), April Austin counters that "the currency of social interaction has changed, making many women skeptical of a selling event masquerading as a party" (1).

The many tensions among the themes of the Tupperware story ultimately tell us that our degree of skepticism, or cynicism, or rebellion, is commensurate with our opportunities. Ingenious invention, kitchen container, modernist art, gender-bending sales revolution—Tupperware provided its extended family with money and social bonds gratefully welcomed during a crucial decade when rules and roles were changing on and beneath the surface. Those women (and some men) in the early Tupperware sales force would be astonished to know that highly educated people have analyzed Tupperware and written articles about it. What would not astonish them is that some of those higher educations are likely to have been funded by Tupperware sales.

Tupperware as icon, then, shifts in the eye of the beholder. For the most part Americans seem to regard it as a distillation of American ingenuity and 1950s kitsch. To me, Tupperware looms as a transitional item poised between the frugality of the Depression generation and the frivolity of the postwar boom, between the generation who would never throw away anything and the one whose foundation was planned obsolescence. My mother and my aunts saved jars, paper bags, rubber bands, and, yes, string; the idea of using an item and tossing it never occurred to them. The advertising campaign for cheap, disposable containers designed to replace Tupperware was based on the national awareness that Tupperware was a cherished item that could bear food to the picnic, potluck, or wake, but that must of course be treated correctly and promptly returned.

At the recent graduation party for Aunt Mallie's great-granddaughter, my cousin and I talked about the Tupperware days, and he produced one proudly saved item. It was a ham carrier. As we stared at the ham carrier, it really was like examining an artifact from the ancient past whose use we could barely fathom. Earl Tupper must have had a good time designing the handle that fit under the ham and could be used to lift it out. I could see Brownie Wise introducing the item as the latest boost to modern convenient living. And yet to us the container called up a world long gone, one of family picnics, church suppers held outdoors, cousins who actually knew each other, and kitchen items washed and dried after every meal and carefully put away. We remembered stacks of Tupperware ready to be returned after family deaths, and the box of Tupperware lids kept just for teething babies. Somehow, even though we admitted our use of those cheap containers whose ads mocked Tupperware's durability and a generation's values, we acknowledged that they can never really replace Tupperware. They lack its color and design, but even more importantly they lack its sense of fun.

Besides, they don't even burp.

WORKS CITED AND RECOMMENDED

Austin, April. "No More Lady of the House." *Christian Science Monitor* 17 May 2002. *Academic Search Premier.* EBSCOhost. Midway College Library, Midway, KY. 12 Oct. 2004 <http://web4.epnet.com/citation>.

Benson, Susan Porter. "Life of the Party." *Women's Review of Books* 17.6 (Mar. 2004). *Academic Search Premier.* EBSCOhost. Midway College Library, Midway, KY. 12 Oct. 2004 <http://web4epnet.com/citation>.

Clarke, Alison J. *Tupperware: The Promise of Plastic in 1950s America.* Washington, DC: Smithsonian Institution P, 1999.

"A Trailblazer, Rediscovered." *Inc.* 25.9 (Sept. 2003). *Academic Search Premier.* EBSCOhost. Midway College Library, Midway, KY. 12 Oct. 2004 <http://web4epnet.com/citation>.

Tupperware! Dir. Laurie Kahn-Levitt. PBS: *The American Experience,* 2004.

Vincent, Susan. "Preserving Domesticity: Reading Tupperware in Women's Changing Domestic, Social and Economic Roles." *Canadian Review of Sociology and Anthropology* 40.2 (May 2003). *Academic Search Premier.* EBSCOhost. Midway College Library, Midway, KY. 12 Oct. 2004 <http://web.4epnet.com/citation>.

———. "The Promise of Plastic in 1950s America." *Canadian Review of Sociology and Anthropology* 38.3 (Aug. 2001). *Academic Search Premier.* EBSCOhost. Midway College Library, Midway, KY. 12 Oct. 2004 <http://web4.epnet.com/citation>.

Underground Railroad

J. Blaine Hudson

When the Fugitive Slave Act was repealed on June 28, 1864, the work of the Underground Railroad, assisting fugitive slaves, was no longer a violation of American law. By the end of the next year, after the Thirteenth Amendment to the Constitution was ratified on December 18, 1865, there was no longer a legal institution of slavery in the United States from which the Underground Railroad might seek to deliver an enslaved African American. However, while the Underground Railroad belongs to the ever-receding American past, it remains a cultural icon, a powerful symbol of a multiracial human rights movement for racial justice on American soil. The congressional actions and National Park Service initiatives of the 1990s, the proliferation of Underground Railroad sites and freedom trails, a wealth of new research and publications, and the opening of the Underground Railroad Freedom Center in Cincinnati in August 2004 all attest to the enduring hold of this icon on the American imagination, and its power and vitality in our time.

The popular image of the Underground Railroad has flaws in its portrayal of history. In the facts related to this icon, though, we find one of those exceedingly rare cases in which the truth is actually more meaningful than the myth. We need only briefly to examine the history of both the icon and the Underground Railroad itself.

In his classic 1898 study, Wilbur Siebert defined the Underground Railroad as "a form of combined defiance of national laws, . . . the unconstitutional but logical refusal of several thousand people to acknowledge that they owed any regard to slavery" (Hart viii). The law in question was the Fugitive Slave Act (first of 1793 and then of 1850)—and the offenses criminalized thereby were several specific acts of rendering assistance to enslaved African Americans escaping from bondage in the antebellum South.

Understood properly, the history of the Underground Railroad brings together two overlapping historical narratives. The first, and more important, is the chronicle of enslaved African Americans who sought freedom through flight—who they were, why and how they escaped. Considering only the half-century before the Civil War, their numbers were anything but trivial, as summarized by the following table (Hudson 162):

Estimated Rate of Slave Escapes: 1810–1860

	East	West	Total
No. of Slave Escapes 1810–1829	24,000	16,000	40,000
Escapes per Year	1,200	800	2,000
No. of Slave Escapes 1830–1849	30,000	30,000	60,000
Escapes per Year	1,500	1,500	3,000
No. of Slave Escapes 1850–1860	15,000	20,000	35,000
Escapes per Year	1,500	2,000	3,500
Total (1810–1860)	69,000	66,000	135,000

Not only were the numbers of fugitive slaves significant, but the fugitive slaves themselves were often exceptional. For example, George Washington Williams, the true "father of African American history," concluded that slave escapes were "a safety valve to the institution of slavery. As soon as leaders arose among the slaves, who refused to endure the yoke, they would go North. Had they remained, there must have been enacted at the South the direful scenes of San Domingo" (58–59). Larry Gara observed that fugitive slaves were atypical individuals, noting that "it was the gifted and highly intelligent slave who enjoyed the semi-freedom of a hired laborer, and having greater sophistication and more freedom of movement, was better qualified than most bondsmen to conceive and put into action a plan of escape" (42–43). Similarly, Richard Wade stated that "the slaveholders' fear of fugitives was understandable. . . . [T]he traffic usually involved many of the best bondsmen—those with the highest skills, the most literate, the most energetic. Some were also the most obstreperous and ungovernable" (221). The "quality" of fugitive slaves was even cited by defenders of slavery as proof of the benefits of the institution. Responding to such claims, Frederick Douglass commented, "We give slavery too much credit, judging it by the fugitive slaves whom we see" (*The North Star*, 20 Oct. 1848).

Equally significant, although seldom noted, was the simple fact that most escaped alone and received little or no assistance on their desperate flight to freedom. Taken together, this fact and the massive numbers of fugitive slaves over time constitute the first flaw in the iconic representation of the Underground Railroad.

The second flaw is embedded in the popular interpretation of the historical narrative of the exploits of those who assisted runaways in violation of law and custom. Few "friends of the fugitive" could be found in slave territory, particularly in the deep Southern interior. There, fugitive slaves faced their greatest danger and succeeded or failed based largely on their own courage

The Underground Railroad by Charles T. Webber, 1893. Courtesy of the Library of Congress.

and/or good fortune. Once in the border-states, however, there was slightly less danger and a far greater likelihood of finding help, particularly in free black settlements and communities. The danger grew correspondingly less as freedom seekers moved farther North. As noted perceptively in the National Historic site nomination materials for Rokeby House in Vermont:

> The popular conception of the UGRR...is of brave, white abolitionists taking great risks to transport hotly pursued fugitives in deepest secrecy. As "agents" moved the "dusky strangers" along the "route" from "station" to "station," they were well concealed in secret hiding places.... Yet, the oral tradition of the UGRR...is more melodrama than history. The key to the popular conception is pursuit. All of the conventions of the popular understanding—the need to operate clandestinely, to communicate in secret, to travel at night, and to create hiding places—arise from the assumption of hot pursuit by a determined, ruthless, and often armed slave catcher. While many fugitives were in precisely such danger in the first days and miles of their escapes, it diminished as they put more and more distance between themselves and the slave south. (National Historic Landmarks Survey)

When assistance was rendered, "friends of the fugitive" could break the law in several ways. For example, they could "assist" or "entice slaves to escape" or, in a few instances, "conduct" fugitive slaves from slave to free territory, as did Harriet Tubman and John Parker. If they "harbored" fugitive slaves in their homes, barns, churches, or elsewhere on their property, these sites served as "stations" in Underground Railroad parlance at which fugitives could find sanctuary and from which they would often be "conducted" to the next "station," perhaps eventually to Canada. In some cases, an entire free African American community or a community in which blacks and whites worked collaboratively became a "junction" of sorts—in essence, a complex of individual stations. Still, before the passage of the Fugitive Slave Act of 1850, harboring fugitive slaves in such communities was not the work of an organization, but simply the result of persons of good conscience helping others in need, often African Americans simply helping one another.

Harriet Tubman, 1911. Courtesy of the Library of Congress.

Several hundred antebellum slave narratives—and postbellum accounts by William Still (1872), Levi Coffin (1876), Laura Haviland (1882), R. C. Smedley (1883), Wilbur Siebert (1898), William Cockrum (1915), and others—support the legend of an "elaborate, organized and far flung conspiracy" to assist fugitive slaves who could scarcely have escaped without such help. More recently, some scholars (Gara) dismissed the legend, while others (Blockson) revised it by assigning fugitive slaves and free people of color far more prominence. However, these were simply conflicting and competing interpretations of an historical record that remained largely unchanged for nearly a century.

The past decade has brought new empirical evidence (Franklin and Schweninger; Hudson; Switala, *Underground Railroad in Delaware, Maryland, and West Virginia*; *Underground Railroad in Pennsylvania*) against which to test the long-accepted interpretative framework—and, by extension, the cultural icon itself. This research affirms the centrality of fugitive slaves to their own "story" and the centrality of free people of color as sources of sanctuary and aid for freedom seekers, but adds that:

Deepening sectional divisions over slavery in the late 1840s and through the 1850s were the catalyst that wove isolated local efforts into such a larger network in the Kentucky borderland [and the North]. In other words, crossing this critical threshold transformed friends of the fugitive, collectively, into a more organized social movement. However, becoming better organized was not synonymous with becoming an organization and this movement spawned more formal organizations only in a few sites [nearby in the free border states]. (Hudson 158–59)

Still, simply establishing a new set of facts is not sufficient to repair the icon if these facts are viewed through an old interpretive lens. This distorting lens is the third and final flaw in the cultural icon, and is embodied in the controlling image of the Underground Railroad: one or more poor, befuddled and bedraggled fugitive slaves being assisted in some way by one or more noble and well-meaning whites, often Quakers such as Levi Coffin and Thomas Garrett. That there were such scenes is indisputable; however, the notion that they were representative is unsupportable. In other words, the predisposition to accept this image has less to do with the quality of historical evidence than with how and why the evidence is "constructed" along particular and predictable lines.

To understand this predisposition, and the exit from the dilemma it poses, it is necessary to confront how the construction of race in the United States changed fundamentally after the American Revolution and why this change made it virtually certain that, if the Underground Railroad became a cultural icon, it would be flawed. In the colonial period, many English men, women, and children were in bonded servitude, temporarily sharing the bondage of slaves; and racial differences seemed only "skin deep":

> Behind the most vicious assaults on the character of people of African descent during the first two hundred years of American slavery stood a firm belief that given an opportunity, black people would behave precisely like whites, which was what made African American slaves at once so valuable and so dangerous. (Berlin 364)

However, after the American Revolution, a new and radically different racial ideology of white supremacy was advanced to justify slavery, not on the grounds of "might makes right" or as a "necessary evil," but rather as a positive good. This ideology stood on assumption that persons of African descent were inferior in their abilities and character, and that these deficits were fixed and natural. Put simply, the raw reality of slave escapes flatly contradicted this assumption—making each fugitive slave "a living refutation of stereotypes of racial inferiority, African American dependence on and contentment with slavery, and the ubiquity of kindly and paternalistic masters":

> That the stereotypes seldom fit the facts created a rather thorny dilemma and its solution necessitated the fabrication of a complex illusion.... First, whenever possible, the number of slave escapes was minimized in an effort to deny the existence of the "problem." Second, when the evidence could not be denied, its meaning was interpreted within the limits of prevailing racial myths...and slave escapes were often blamed on "evil" whites who spirited away ignorant slaves. (Hudson 6)

As evidence of the lengths to which pro-slavery advocates were willing to go, a new category of mental illness—drapetomania, literally the "flight-from-home madness"—was even invented to account for this seemingly inexplicable behavior (Thomas and Sillen 2). Ironically, there were also those who opposed slavery in principle but could not view its living victims as their equals. From their perspective, African Americans were incapable of human agency and, hence, slave escapes were possible only if noble whites assisted witless and benighted blacks to freedom. Thus, the façade of the cultural icon masks the familiar illusion that there were only a handful of slave escapes, that fugitive slaves were either "crazy" or helpless—and that the "stars" of this drama were invariably white. Fortunately, the historical record supports a different and more balanced conclusion.

Perhaps, the Underground Railroad as a cultural icon might be represented most accurately by not one, but three controlling images—arranged, following the conventions of ancient Egyptian (Kemetic) art, by size to reflect their relative importance. The largest and most imposing image would be an African American escaping alone; next would be a free African American helping a fugitive slave—and the last, and smallest, would be the familiar image of legend. Each embodies the struggle for freedom, and their combined legacy is a powerful affirmation of the ideal of multiracial democracy—and a reminder that, apart from the Civil Rights Movement, the Underground Railroad was the only sustained multiracial movement for racial justice in American history. This legacy is also a lesson repeated often in American and global history that, in the haunting words of Frederick Douglass, "he who suffers the wrong must be the one to seek redress" and, in the case of white friends of the fugitive, that those who truly believe in freedom must find the courage to make common cause with others unlike themselves, even at the risk of their lives and of becoming outcasts among their own people.

In truth, this is a cultural icon that uplifts us all.

WORKS CITED AND RECOMMENDED

Berlin, Ira. *Many Thousands Gone: The First Two Centuries of Slavery in North America*. Cambridge, MA: Harvard UP, 1998.

Blockson, Charles. *Hippocrene Guide to the Underground Railroad*. New York: Hippocrene Books, 1994.

Cockrum, Col. William M. *History of the Underground Railroad, As It Was Conducted by the Anti-Slavery League*. 1915. New York: Negro Universities P, 1969.

Coffin, Levi. *Reminiscences of Levi Coffin*. New York: Augustus M. Kelley, 1876.

Drew, Benjamin. *The Refugee: Or the Narratives of Fugitive Slaves in Canada*. Boston: John P. Jewett and Company, 1856.

Franklin, John H., and Loren Schweninger. *Runaway Slaves: Rebels on the Plantation*. New York: Oxford UP, 1999.

Gara, Larry. *The Liberty Line: The Legend of the Underground Railroad*. Lexington: UP of Kentucky, 1961.

Hart, Albert Bushnell. Introduction. *The Underground Railroad from Slavery to Freedom*. By Wilbur H. Siebert. New York: Russell and Russell, 1967. vii–xiii.

Haviland, Laura S. *A Woman's Life Work*. Cincinnati: Walden and Stowe, 1882.

Hudson, J. Blaine. *Fugitive Slaves and the Underground Railroad in the Kentucky Borderland*. Jefferson, NC: McFarland & Company Publishers, 2002.

Jordan, Winthrop D. *White over Black: American Attitudes toward the Negro, 1550–1812*. New York: Norton, 1968.

National Historic Landmarks Survey. *Underground Railroad Resources in the United States*. Washington, DC: U.S. Department of the Interior, 1998.

Quarles, Benjamin. *Black Abolitionists*. New York: Oxford UP, 1969.

Ross, Alexander M. *Recollections and Experiences of an Abolitionist; From 1855 to 1865*. Toronto: Rowsell & Hutchison, 1875.

Siebert, Wilbur Henry. *The Underground Railroad from Slavery to Freedom*. 1898. New York: Arno P, 1968.

Smedley, R. C. *History of the Underground Railroad*. 1883. New York: Arno P, 1969.

Still, William. *The Underground Railroad*. 1872. Chicago: Johnson Publishing Company, 1970.

Switala, William J. *Underground Railroad in Delaware, Maryland, and West Virginia*. Mechanicsburg, PA: Stackpole Books, 2004.

———. *Underground Railroad in Pennsylvania*. Mechanicsburg, PA: Stackpole Books, 2001.

Thomas, Alexander, and Samuel Sillen. *Racism and Psychiatry*. New York: Citadel P, 1972.

Wade, Richard C. *Slavery in the Cities: The South, 1820–1860*. New York: Oxford UP, 1969.

Williams, George Washington. *History of the Negro Race in America*. 1883. New York: Bergmann, 1968.

Viagra

Bennett Kravitz

Before discussing the iconic status of the blue diamond, better known as Viagra, we should situate this phenomenon in the context of the revolutionary and perhaps outlandish behavior of Americans in regard to all prescription drugs. In 2003, retail drug sales worldwide were $317 billion, with American consumers spending just over half that amount. The pill-taking life is a trend that has its origins in the 1950s, but only recently has it reached alarming proportions. To mention just one example, we should acknowledge that never before have antidepressants been prescribed for preschoolers in such large amounts. It is as if one shouldn't wait too long before embracing a lifestyle dependent on drugs. Thus, I think it is fair to say that "Homo Pharmaceuticus" has arrived in America, as prescription drugs and the pursuit of happiness have become synonymous. As a result, what we once considered normal or a mundane part of the aging process is no longer tolerated. Baldness, incontinence, erectile difficulty, and even the very concept of aging are out. These unacceptable "deficiencies" have become cultural concerns that the medical profession is expected to address, of which the most urgent seems to be erectile dysfunction.

The journey to chemical perfection of the sexual experience received its biggest boost with the development of Viagra, whose name derives from an odd combination of the roots of the words *tiger* and *Niagara*, creating a vision of a powerful and erect stream of water. Viagra started out as a product for sexual enhancement in sexually dysfunctional elderly males, yet has transformed American society in ways that could not be imagined when the product first came to market. The drug companies refused, or we did, to accept the limiting marginalized role of the product, so that it has become as liminal as Emersonian philosophy. Who could have predicted the portrait in a current Viagra ad of a seemingly horned and horny middle-aged man with the message, "Get back to mischief"? Who would have imagined that Mike Ditka would be pushing Levitra, Viagra's dark other, to middle-aged men as a product of masculinity right on par with an outstanding football hit? Who would have thought, as did the creators of the Cialis campaign, that the best way to advertise a product of sexual enhancement initially targeting the elderly, would be to show a giggling thirty-something couple in a Jacuzzi, apparently imagining the sexual benefits of pharmacology?

The "blue diamond," Viagra, affects culture and society in so many ways, subtly and overtly, that it is reasonable to claim that the products of sexual enhancement, especially Viagra, have revolutionized American society, and established the blue diamond's status as an American icon. How? Let us count the ways.

To start our investigation, we should note that over half of American men over 40 either need or think they need a product of sexual enhancement to safeguard their sex lives. According to a Massachusetts survey, 52 percent of 1,290 males from ages 40 to 70 suffered from erectile dysfunction. The drug companies have come to rely on these and similar statistics to expand their market even though there is no attempt to sort out minimal sexual snafus from chronic dysfunction. Apparently, anything less than perfection is unacceptable in matters of sexual performance. As a result, any instance of problematic function over a six-month period qualified as erectile dysfunction and thus was counted as part of the 52 percent. Moreover, in a noteworthy shift from past medical thinking, the psychological component seems to have disappeared in the diagnosis of erectile dysfunction. Do problems of the psyche have no effect on sexual performance? Are they not worth exploring? If someone is able to have an erection while sleeping but is incapable of having one during a real time sexual encounter, should Viagra be the solution instead of psychotherapy? Apparently, in a society of the quick fix, the pharmaceutical takes precedence over the psychological approach, only partially because the latter is much more expensive. According to the new norm, one should take the pill and "get busy," without worrying about the underlying cause of imperfect sexual performance.

Because of the above phenomena, one might argue that erectile dysfunction has become a cultural disease or, at the very least, a malady, which, despite its physical and psychological causes, has become a social norm via cultural manipulation. In other words, once the surveys begin to show high numbers of males suffering from erectile dysfunction, the disease becomes pervasive and "real." In order fully to understand erectile dysfunction, we should approach it holistically and allow for a cultural as well as physical or chemical explication. Indeed, I would argue that the advertising for the "cure" to the problem to some extent creates the malady as well. In a bizarre reversal of fortune, the disease has become desirable for the simple reason that the "cure" is so attractive. Males of all ages find it easier to belong to a group suffering from a sort of universal erectile dysfunction without nuance or distinction, because the solution to their collective problem is so simple. Pop a sexy blue pill and the difficulties, real and imagined, go away. The disease may not even actually exist for many males who think they suffer from erectile dysfunction, but accepting such an "in" illness that has such a pleasurable solution is easier than undergoing psychological evaluation, introspection, proper diet, exercise, or any other regime that involves hard work. Why endure the discomfort of traditional self-help when better living through chemistry is available in an attractive shade of blue?

In an apparent endorsement of this attitude, approximately 6 million American men and 23 million men worldwide have taken Viagra for erectile dysfunction in the seven years since Pfizer released the "blue diamond" on the market in 1998. These numbers do not include the millions of people who have purchased counterfeit pills currently available around the world at discount prices. Furthermore, the new competitors of Viagra, Levitra and Cialis, have already captured an additional million clients of their own. These numbers pale, however, in light of the grand scheme of the pharmaceutical companies that produce these products: to entice 30 million of the 60 million males in America over 40 to use their product. This figure doesn't broach, of course, the numerous other middle-aged males worldwide or the young people in America and abroad who aren't necessarily suffering from impotence, but are looking for that dating edge. After all, not everyone has the wealth the rich and famous use, according to advertisements, to attract women, so taking a drug that is proven to prevent erectile dysfunction might be the next best thing. It seems that the ultimate goal of the drug companies that produce these products of sexual enhancement is to have all males indulge on a regular basis, situating the use of Viagra on the same level as that of popping an Omega-3 fatty acid dietary supplement. Why not start your day with Cialis, the long-lasting version of Viagra, and be prepared for any sexual encounter that might come your way?

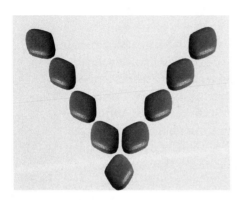

Pills of Viagra. Courtesy of Shutterstock.

But let us return to our investigation of sexual function, sex, and sexuality by reevaluating the original group of elderly sexually dysfunctional males who were offered Viagra to preserve and rekindle the sexual union of matrimony. Their problems were "legitimate," often the result of disorders that interfere with circulation, such as hypertension, heart disease, and diabetes. In retrospect, Robert Dole, Pfizer's first spokesman for the blue diamond, seems to have been the perfect Puritan spokesman for a product that was initially marketed as consistent with mainstream Republican family values. In line with seventeenth-century Puritan thinking on the topic, the earliest ads appeared to be saying that sex is okay, so long as it takes place only with one's heterosexual spouse. They also implied that a legitimate disease causing erectile dysfunction shouldn't necessarily put an end to an officially sanctioned couple's sexual activity.

Viewed in the above light, the Viagra phenomenon became a type of chemical self-realization, just as what was once said of Prozac. That is, the drugs of sexual enhancement do nothing more than to allow males to reassert their true selves. With that goal in mind, many users imagine that there is nothing artificial about a product that restores their "natural" abilities. After all, they might argue, is a product of sexual enhancement any more intrusive or unnatural than taking a pill to prevent manic episodes or to lower high blood sugar?

But the answer to that question, I would argue, is yes. We should at least acknowledge that there are problematic aspects of relying on Viagra and similar products for erectile function and that these products are over-prescribed and even abused. For example, once our original target group, these elderly males, discovered that the "blue diamond" delivered the goods, so to speak, many of them abandoned their Puritan mores. That is to say, they decided to "spread the wealth," and seek out partners more appropriate to elderly male fantasies. Thus age differential has become less of a factor in determining the limits or possibilities of a sexual relationship once an elderly male has the confidence and ability to enjoy solid penetration with a younger female. Moreover, regardless of the age of the partner, with sexual confidence comes more temptation and thus opportunity to have sex outside the officially sanctioned relationships initially promoted by the drug companies.

Another psychological/cultural complication of using Viagra is that the drug might also have a paradoxical effect, so that if one does not take it, the very concept of achieving an erection is beyond the pale. If men fear the sexual consequences of their not taking Viagra, that apprehension might easily become a self-fulfilling prophecy. Indeed, some physicians have already begun to refer to Viagra as psychologically addictive for a number of users.

A further difficulty inherent in the use of products of sexual enhancement is that we tend to view the disease (or dis-ease) of erectile dysfunction strictly through the perspective of patriarchy. How can we be certain, for example, that just because men find it easier to function sexually, women are necessarily overjoyed? Indeed, Viagra could also promote paranoia among the wives of sexually energized males: "Now that he can do it, who is he doing it with?" might be one such paranoid introspection. Women might also undergo undue sexual pressure from husbands or lovers. After all, if hubby or lover boy has taken the pill at $10 a pop, one should not be wasteful, even if one or the other has had a change of heart or is no longer in the mood.

In general, it does not seem that the desires of women influenced the development of the products aimed at preventing erectile dysfunction. Can we be sure that women are pleased that their elderly male husbands are now willing and able to have sex with them? Who says they are interested in having sex with their husbands, or having sex at all? We seem to have made the assumption that Viagra is every bit as pleasing for women as it is for men. In a seeming preponderance of this mode of thought, the next big Viagra project is to produce an effective version for women. But unlike its male counterpart, Viagra for women will have to function as a mood enhancer, if it is to have any value at all. At present, though, the drug companies' research indicates that there will be enough of a market for this product, or that they will able to create the market as they go along, just as they did with the male version of the blue diamond.

As I have already implied, the more the group of Viagra users moves to a kind of universal mode of behavior, the more cultural implications there are. As we have seen, although elderly married males were the original target group for Viagra, that reality has changed with a vengeance. For example, upon superficial reflection, one would suspect that the most unlikely group to embrace the use of Viagra would be males in their twenties and thirties. Yet there is no ignoring the ways that sexual practice among thirty-something and even twenty-something males has been influenced by Viagra and other performance enhancement drugs.

A typical night out for a representative of either group might begin as follows: to head out the door with a wallet, two or three condoms, and a blue diamond or two. No, the second pill is not for the overly ambitious, but in yet another twist of fate, Viagra has taken on the value of currency and is used as a tip at bars and other hip locations. More important, Viagra has become a kind of party drug, to be taken together with Ecstasy or crystal methamphetamine as if to combine erectile possibility with the enhanced desire other drugs offer. In fact, the potent combination of Viagra and Ecstasy is known as Sextasy. Nevertheless, an erection is an erection is an erection, and if one does not suffer from erectile dysfunction the drug on its own will not have much of an effect.

In this light, then, Viagra has become a misguided insurance policy for the sexually bold and restless. In accordance with its multiple possibilities, the pill might give one the confidence to consume alcohol with abandon, believing that Viagra will offset the effects of drinking. Moreover, in line with American optimism, there is always the hope that sexual prowess will increase even if there is no dysfunction to speak of. After all, the reasoning goes, if one has an opportunity to make a good thing better, why not go for it? Perhaps the overriding secret hope is that the pill will not only enhance sexual performance, but actually create desire where there is none. As one young forlorn male asked me in confidence, "Is there any chance that my using Viagra or Cialis will help me see my wife as sexy and attractive?" As amusing or pitiful as that might sound, to identify one's marital aspirations with the taking of the blue diamond is clearly a product of cultural rather than erectile dysfunction.

In this state of affairs, even teenagers feel they must somehow engage a Viagra rules world. One sex therapist reports that 16-year-old boys have come to ask for a prescription for Viagra in order to have sex for the first time or enlarge their penises. Thus, it is fair to say that products of sexual enhancement have developed their own versions of urban legends and rewritten basic cultural assumptions about their limits and possibilities.

Another problematic aspect of the Viagra phenomenon is the way products of sexual enhancement are advertised. Mike Ditka, the ultimate macho male, with a distinguished career as an NFL tight end who is also a Super Bowl–winning coach, insists that anyone not willing to try Levitra for improved sexual performance is simply too much of a sissy to do so. Millions viewing his commercials, no doubt, must be wondering what is wrong with their sexual prowess if they find no need for enhancement. The drug's brilliant advertising campaign has somehow created an equal alliance between virility and sexual dysfunction, with the latter leading to the former if one is "man" enough to use Levitra.

The sports macho advertising theme works well for Levitra even without Ditka, as it does in the ad with the middle-aged quarterback who cannot successfully thread the needle—throw his old football through a tire swing—until he is willing to try Levitra. The viewer can only imagine that as an added bonus, our rugged quarterback not only regains his sexual prowess but improves his football-throwing accuracy as well. His young, sexy female partner stands beside him adoringly as he throws the ball through the tire time after time. There is even a little suspense and uncertainty generated by the television commercial, as it is not quite clear what the couple's priorities will be: will they first embark upon a touch football game or a sexual encounter, with an outside chance of their combining the two activities in the bedroom? So whoever uses the product is apparently fortunate enough to recover two skills for the price of one. Rather than using sex to sell goods, sports are being used to sell satisfying sex. And if you can't march unimpeded down the field to score how good are you anyway?

But the ultimate Viagra cultural paradox questions and perhaps redefines the very nature of the sex act itself. I would argue that Viagra, because it encourages the phallocentric view of sex, seems to have limited rather than enhanced sexual possibility. As a result, the only sexual act that has meaning, at least according to the advertising campaigns, is reduced to penile-vaginal penetration. Must one have a perfect erection all the time for couples to enjoy sex? As this view becomes more entrenched, the holistic view of legitimate sexual activity diminishes accordingly. In such a scenario, all other sexual activities—touching, kissing, stroking, and so on—lose their value and meaning.

So what does all this tell us about our sexual and cultural future? While unable to answer this question specifically, I would argue that the most interesting issue for future exploration is not just how Viagra and other drugs have changed our lives and become cultural icons, but whether they have redefined what it means to be human. Past assumptions about the human condition must take into consideration a new chemical reality that prolongs the quality and length of life. An elementary question worth considering in light of the way we now live is whether or not human beings will become happier and more satisfied because of their altered chemical state. As just a small cog in the cultural machine, I suspect that it will take more than a pill to overcome the fundamental existential conundrums that have always troubled human life.

WORKS RECEOMMENDED

Altherr, Thomas L., ed. *Procreation or Pleasure: Sexual Attitudes in American History*. Malabar, FL: R. E. Krieger Publishing Company, 1983.

Koch, Patricia Barthalow, and David L. Weiss, eds. *Sexuality in America*. New York: Continuum Publishing, 1998.

Morgentaler, Abraham. *The Viagra Myth*. San Francisco: Jossey-Bass, 2003.

Sobel, Alan, ed. *The Philosophy of Sex*. Lanham, MD: Rowman and Littlefield, 2002.

Tracy, Sarah W., and Caroline Jean Acker, eds. *Altering American Consciousness*. Amherst: U of Massachusetts P, 2004.

Video Game

Ken S. McAllister and
Judd Ethan Ruggill

The video game is iconic in every sense of the word. It has been featured in news magazines, mocked on television programs, studied by academics, scrutinized by U.S. senators, worshiped by children and adults alike, and has spawned thousands of spin-off products, from shot glasses to feature-length films. In fact at one point during the early 1990s, Nintendo's mascot—Mario—"was more recognized by American children than Mickey Mouse" (Sheff 9).

Like all icons, the video game is simultaneously simple and complex, its iconicity at once masking and revealing a rich network of sociocultural, economic, and political meanings. In order to understand the iconic power of the video game, therefore, it is necessary to apprehend and historicize this network. In this essay, we will do precisely that: we will unpack the five major semiotic domains that constitute the meaning-making network of the video game. We will situate games technologically, aesthetically, psychologically, socially, and politically.

HOW VIDEO GAMES MEAN TECHNOLOGICALLY

Though video games are often thought of as distinct from the technology on which they run (e.g., game consoles, personal computers, cell phones), game hardware is a crucial contributor to the meanings games produce. Some of the first video games, for example, were designed for and played on oscilloscopes, devices that visually indicate fluctuations in electrical voltage and current. Though not especially expensive or difficult to obtain, oscilloscopes are by no means popular devices. Even today they tend to be used only by scientists, engineers, home electronics enthusiasts, and other "nerds," that is, by people so technically proficient that they can turn the complex behaviors of electrons into passable imitations of ping pong. In 1958, when *Tennis for Two* (arguably the first video game) was developed, oscilloscopes were even more arcane than they are today.

Early video games were also developed on industrial computers such as the venerable PDP-1 (e.g., *Spacewar* [1962]). Again, these devices too were then out of the mainstream, requiring a level of expertise to operate and program beyond even some computer scientists. As a result, the video game languished as little more than an inside joke among society's most elite technicians until the early 1970s, when affordable computer chips prompted consumer electronics companies and toy manufacturers to begin marketing home gaming consoles and handheld devices (Magnavox Odyssey [1972], Atari Pong [1975], and Mattel Football [1977]).

Though the video game has since been popularized, its icon still resonates with a highly technical "nerd" image. Console manufacturers brag about bus speeds, online service providers advertise ping rates, players compare polygon counts when shopping for hardware and software—all despite the fact that advances in consumer electronics design have made video-game play (and in some cases, design) simple enough for young children (e.g., *Walt Disney's The Jungle Book: Rhythm and Groove* [2000], *Dora the Explorer: The Search for Pirate Pig's Treasure* [2002]).

The icon of the video game resonates with other technological markers as well: modularly-designed arcade cabinetry that allows new games to be efficiently installed over old ones, input and output devices designed to simulate the hardware of genuinely dangerous occupations such as soldiering or race-car driving, and the equating of technical characteristics (i.e., floating point operations per second, storage device access speeds, gesture recognition algorithms) with game-play quality are just a few that endure in various guises today. The technologies that enable video games, therefore, not only shape the look and feel of games themselves, but define who gamers are, and how and where games are played.

HOW GAMES MEAN AESTHETICALLY

Aside from the actual technologies of the video game are the aesthetic decisions and boundaries that technology enables. How games look, sound, and "feel" are integral both to their commercial and iconic success. This is not to say that more realistic or elaborate aesthetics necessarily translate into sales, but rather that game aesthetics contribute directly to the play experience, a phenomenon that is often talked about in terms of "immersiveness" and "engagement." Old games such as *Space Invaders* (1978) and *Pac-Man* (1980), for instance, while not very complex by current audio-visual standards, were (and still are) powerfully engaging primarily because their gameplay aesthetics are extraordinarily high. The gameplay aesthetic is one of the components of the video game that makes it unique from all other media. It also makes it possible to reasonably compare an old game such as *Asteroids* (1979) to a new title like *Ace Commander 5* (2004). In its seamless combination of what the senses perceive and the ways that the player's body and mind respond to those perceptions in order to alter the game world, the gameplay aesthetic generates a fundamentally ineffable experience that can also be deeply memorable. Put another way, the gameplay aesthetic helps create iconic experiences.

Aesthetics contribute to making meaning and game iconicity in other ways. For example, the video game has always borrowed icons to tell its stories. From the crudely rendered spaceship in *Galaga* (1981), to the film noir symbolism of *Max Payne* (2001), filmic, televisual, and literary iconography is used by developers to combat technical limitations to meaning-making such as low processor speeds and lack of available memory. Embedding older, more established icons into game content allows developers to reference vast amounts of information without taxing the hardware that enables that information to be depicted audio-visually and kinesthetically. Naturally, as technology has improved, so too has the video game's ability to reference, reproduce, and repurpose iconography.

Interestingly, this ability to draw upon, adapt, and project virtually any icon is key to the video game's capacity to teach. Games use icons—or rather, the vast meaning sets icons signify—to teach multiple things in multiple ways, from simple hand-eye coordination to complex resource management skills. Granted, not everything games teach is necessarily appreciated. Sometimes parents, teachers, and lawmakers feel the need to regulate game content. Such regulation, of course, contributes to the iconicity of the video game too, at turns celebrating and vilifying the cultural work games do.

HOW GAMES MEAN PSYCHOLOGICALLY

Broadly speaking, aesthetics provide a baseline for how games mean. Like statistics, however, this baseline is useful only on a large scale. Applying a "video game aesthetic" to analyze individual player experiences inevitably results in mismatches, half-truths, and poor descriptions. The fact of the matter is that icons often mean different things to different people.

Consider the outcry against video games after the Littleton, Colorado, massacre. In 1999, Eric Harris and Dylan Klebold walked into Columbine High School and shot thirteen of their classmates to death. As people around the country struggled to process the tragedy, the icon of the video game— already seen as excessively violent thanks to such titles as *Contra* (1987), *Smash T.V.* (1990), and *Night Trap* (1992)—became a lynchpin linking media and real-life violence. Harris and Klebold had been passionate about *Doom* (1993), a popular first-person shooting game. The young men's passion simply confirmed what many parents already thought: video games are incubic, surreptitiously planting the seeds of evil into the minds of children.

Not surprisingly, the game industry has worked hard to combat this vision of its product. In the early 1990s, the major game publishers joined together to establish the Entertainment Software Ratings Board (ESRB), a game-content rating organization modeled after the Motion Picture Association of

America's Classification and Rating Administration (CARA). Much like CARA, the ESRB has done a great deal to assuage parental concern. As we noted above, however, icons are highly dynamic semiotic constructs, often meaning different things to different people. ESRB ratings thus can work against their intent, encouraging the misappropriation of restricted content. For instance, while parents may use ratings to ensure their children do not obtain "Mature" titles, many young gamers see the "Mature" rating as an attractor that promises particularly exciting gameplay. In this way, the icon of the video game is incredibly dynamic, especially at the level of how it affects psychological processes such as human responses to media content.

HOW GAMES MEAN SOCIALLY

While the video game was once an elite in-joke, it evolved into a cultural icon after being introduced into the public space of the bar, nightclub, and bowling alley in the 1970s and early 1980s. During this era, games were associated with such working-class pastimes as hanging out at the neighborhood bodega, occasioning the local pool hall, and "cruising," that is, staking out various public venues in search of a sex partner. Through the early 1990s, the video game was a focal point around which revolved a variety of bad habits: illicit sex, drugs, alcohol, smoking, gambling, gang activity, and so on. Like the penny arcade almost a century before, the video game arcade was seen by many as a den of iniquity.

A girl playing games on her Super Nintendo, 2002. Courtesy of Corbis.

Through the concerted efforts of home console developers such as Nintendo, however, this tarnish has been largely burnished away. From the mid-1980s to the mid-1990s, Nintendo ran an intense—some might even say "fascistic"—campaign to domesticate the video game. The company not only brought arcade-quality graphics into the home, but released toy-like consoles (the Nintendo Entertainment System [1985]), handheld devices (the Gameboy [1989]), and games (*Super Mario Bros.* [1985]). Nintendo worked hard to transform the icon of the video game into something child-friendly and wholly innocuous, qualities that to this day still mark the company's game devices and in-house games. In fact, so successful were these efforts by game companies to reverse the bad associations of video games that they are now largely—though erroneously—considered child's play, a consideration that in part explains the fierceness of the ongoing debate over violent game content.

HOW GAMES MEAN POLITICALLY

Like many icons, the video game has long been a political plaything. After the devastating crash of the game market in 1984, for example, the Federal Trade Commission (FTC) launched a probe into the trade practices behind what was widely perceived to be a highjacking of the industry by opportunistic developers. These developers, the probe proclaimed, had glutted the market with inferior product, in essence destroying a multimillion-dollar cash cow. Curiously enough, though the FTC probe was meant to protect the game industry, it prompted the creation of various video-game trade lobbies seeking to protect the developers from governmental inquiry and regulation.

In both 1993 and 2002, the federal government again turned its eye toward games. Instead of trade policies, however, these later investigations focused on game violence. The turn toward game violence is significant because overtly violent games such as *Soldier of Fortune* (2000) or *BloodRayne 2* (2004) are rarely top-sellers. And yet, Senators such as Joseph Lieberman (Connecticut) and Herb Kohl (Wisconsin) have spent years trying to control game violence, in the process so infusing the icon of the video game with the rhetoric of graphic violence and sexuality that even hard facts such as unit sales and net profits are ignored. Much of this rhetorical power is a consequence of politically motivated witch hunts, the kind ideal for tawdry media reportage and the careerism of socially conservative politicians and activists.

This is not to say that many video games are not needlessly violent, sexual, racist, and otherwise offensive. Rather, the issue here is that as the video game is subjected to politicized investigations, its iconicity changes accordingly. Instead of being discussed in terms of aesthetic merits or commercial strength, the video game comes to signify issues of constitutional rights (freedom of expression) and the ethics of free-market capitalism (equal access to the marketplace). Such political significations, while not usually at the forefront of most consumers' thoughts about video games, nonetheless shape how games mean generally. When senators, representatives, mayors, and even presidents weigh in on how games mean, public perception of games and gamers changes, and thus does the icon of the video game.

The video game is without question one of the definitive icons of contemporary society. It not only signifies the computer age in a most graphic way, but also links the development of digital technologies and methods of communication to one of the primary human instincts: play. Indeed, play is the "primaeval [sic] soil" in which "myth and ritual...law and order, commerce and profit, craft and art, poetry, wisdom and science...are rooted" (Huizinga 5). The icon of the video game thus embodies play in a simultaneously modern and ancient sense, a simultaneity seemingly at the heart of every icon.

WORKS CITED AND RECOMMENDED

Burnham, Van. *Supercade: A Visual History of the Videogame Age 1971–1984.* Cambridge, MA: MIT P, 2003.

Cohen, Scott. *Zap! The Rise and Fall of Atari.* Philadelphia: Xlibris Corporation, 1984.

DeMaria, Rusel, and Johnny L. Wilson. *High Score! The Illustrated History of Electronic Games.* New York: McGraw-Hill/Osborne Media, 2003.

Herman, Leonard. *Phoenix: The Rise & Fall of Videogames.* Union, NJ: Rolenta P, 1997.

Herz, J. C. *Joystick Nation: How Videogames Ate Our Quarters, Won Our Hearts, and Rewired Our Minds.* New York: Little, Brown and Company, 1997.

Huizinga, Johan. *Homo Ludens: A Study of the Play Element in Culture.* Boston: Beacon, 1955.

Kent, Steven L. *The Ultimate History of Video Games: From Pong to Pokemon—The Story Behind the Craze That Touched Our Lives and Changed the World.* New York: Three Rivers P, 2001.

Poole, Steven. *Trigger Happy: Videogames and the Entertainment Revolution.* New York: Arcade Publishing, 2000.

Sheff, David. *Game Over: How Nintendo Zapped an American Industry, Captured Your Dollars, and Enslaved Your Children.* New York: Random House, 1993.

Vietnam Veterans Memorial

Linda Marie Small

The Vietnam Veterans Memorial in Washington, D.C., is built of polished black granite that reflects the faces of visitors gazing upon its 140 panels of names. Etched upon the two lengths of wall that meet in an apex 10 feet, 8 inches tall are the 58,245 names of military personnel who died as a result of their service in the U.S. war in Vietnam from 1961 to 1975. Those named are deceased warriors, honored not for winning or losing a war unpopular at home, but honored because they served. Their sacrifice, rather than the rightness or wrongness of this conflict, provides the common ground of grief for the many who died. However, many more, 2.7 million Americans, served in the war zone, with 304,000 wounded in action, 75,000 permanently disabled, and more than 1,300 who remain missing in action. Most of their countrymen and women were affected in one way or another, in one degree or another, by this war that was televised in nightly news stories at home for over a decade. While "The Wall," as it is often called, commemorates those fallen in battle, it also stands for the travail of a whole generation of Americans.

The Memorial was built with $9 million in private donations. Congress allotted space for the Wall to stand—space at the nation's center. Jan Scruggs, who served from 1969 to 1970, started and shepherded the movement to honor America's Vietnam War dead. The Wall was designed by Maya Ying Lin, an architecture student at Yale who won the competition to design the memorial. The Wall is as bereft of the usual verbal and visual funerary language as it is free of any value judgments on the Vietnam conflict itself. The deliberate omission of such language is in keeping with the highly polished, reflective stone panels that form the wall, to define a place for reflection, for remembering, in the center of the U.S. capital. Dedicated in November of 1982, the Vietnam Memorial stands as if this shining monolith had erupted through a fissure in the grassy mall at the heart of the nation.

From the beginning the Wall emerged as a site of remarkably democratic ritual practices. Funerary greenery and material artifacts and letters were hand-carried to and deposited at the Wall. So important are the grave goods, that family members of the fallen enlist the help of neighbors, associates, and others embarking on travels to Washington to take the time to carry personalized grave goods to the Wall.

Rituals include searching the Book of Names, locating the panel bearing an individual's name, and making a rubbing of that very name engraved on the Wall's polished surface, as well as leaving grave goods. Visits to the Wall often include photographing these ritual processes. Sometimes strangers photograph tearful Veterans as each searches for the names of fallen comrades; that is to say, that a tearful person sporting military dress of any kind and searching at the Wall is given instant and public recognition as "returned Warrior Hero" such that even strangers want to take home a picture of a "national hero."

Although more organized by the turn of the century than at the time of dedication, there have always been veteran volunteers on site to serve as an honor guard and to help visitors find the names of the fallen. A cottage industry hastily grew up around the Wall to sell military insignia, flags, flowers, tracing paper and soft pencils, frames, statuettes, and other artifacts of commemoration so that no visitors need be left out of the rituals at the Wall because they had not come prepared to participate.

Since the Wall was dedicated, a replica of the Wall has traveled to cities throughout the nation and virtual Walls have appeared on the Internet. On one day in September 2004 an Internet search netted seven and one half million hits for Vietnam Veterans Memorial. There have risen Internet-based

Reflections of visitors are caught in the black marble of the Vietnam Veterans Memorial. Courtesy of Shutterstock.

organizations that offer volunteers to produce name-tracings from the Wall and then to send these, pictures, and other items to families back home. The Wall itself remains the most widely visited Memorial in Washington, with the number visiting the Wall estimated to be in the millions yearly. Surprisingly, quiet prevails at the site at all times of day.

After the first two years, National Park Service officials began nightly to collect the material artifacts, but not funerary greenery, left at the wall. This daily collection and curation (everything is preserved) confirms the participation of survivors of the conflict, and those who would remember the conflict, in the construction of its meaning. This curatorial practice doubtless has influenced what is left. Families leaving items at the Wall know that their gifts will enter into the nation's heritage. Thus, these grave goods link the living with their warrior dead while also preserving each hero's family line into the future of the Republic.

Reflection is encouraged and orchestrated by the memorial's design. And from the beginning the Wall has mediated a dialogue between Americans and the popular cultural experience of the Vietnam conflict by creating new connections between a people and its warrior heroes through image-making, rituals, and the deposition of grave goods. Unlike most war memorials, the focus here is not on the war itself or even an abstraction like "sacrifice"; rather, it is upon the individuals who perished. The long list of names, which seeks to be exhaustive, demands that attention be paid to particular persons. Moreover, also unlike most war memorials, the relationship of the visitor to the memorial is up close and personal. One can—no, one is invited to—touch it. Rituals of feeling the texture of the names, of tracing names, of leaving tokens allow visitors, both veterans and ordinary citizens, to make concrete connections with people. Indeed, grave goods left at the Wall have become an integral part of the experience of Vietnam Veterans Memorial. The memorial has initiated a popular reconstruction of national identity, of how a nation reenvisions itself after a season of social discordance.

The gifts left daily at the Wall are not grave goods interred with the deceased in burial rites such as archaeologists have uncovered in the material remains of other cultures from a distant past. These grave goods, rather, are hand-carried daily by the living to a place of remembering erected quite apart from grave sites. The artifacts are, however, just as totemic as those artifacts from the past deposited in actual graves. An incredibly wide variety of tokens are left at the Wall, including, for example, a hat worn in the field by a soldier, pictures of surviving children of the deceased, a motorcycle, a Christmas tree adorned with emblems of a hoped-for future—baby shoes, wedding rings, a football letter, a graduation cap, a birthday gift. And there are many many more, numbering more than 80,000 material artifacts and increasing daily. These grave goods assert a relationship between the living and the dead: a motorcycle representing past happier travels, pictures linking the deceased with descendant children, a hat as stand-in for a particular soldier. Grave goods left at the Wall are personal, often handmade, artifacts that extend in totemic fashion the ancestral lines of these deceased warriors, bridging gaps between the nation's past and her future, between individuals and families, and among generations, all unfolding in the popular reclamation of the sacred and the quotidian. So strong is the Wall's power that these objects began to appear even before its dedication.

Perhaps an initiating event is the tale of the soldier and the purple heart. The story first circulated in 1982; and having since been retold and retold, it has risen to the level of myth. On a day that the footings for the Wall were being poured, a soldier is reported to have passed by and tossed his brother's purple heart into the wet concrete. Thus commenced a popular cultural dialog conducted in part through the deposition of grave goods, and leading to a reconciliation of a nation once bitterly divided by the war and the unfolding of a common future.

Further evidence of popular culture's role in this process can be seen in some of the films appearing in the years after the war ended. These postwar films cast soldiers of the Vietnam War era as heroes within images of America's leatherstocking past. Vietnam Veterans are linked to this nation's pioneer history as typified by the rugged individualists that first hued out a nation in a new land. *The Deer Hunter*, for example, portrayed soldiers of the Vietnam conflict as rugged individualists, enduring much in the service of the same nation that had earlier produced the likes of Daniel Boone, Sam Houston, and other leatherstocking individualists from America's mythical pioneer history.

Statues at the Vietnam Veterans Memorial. Courtesy of Shutterstock.

As icon, the Vietnam Veterans Memorial functions as do many, possibly most, of the cultural signs associated with social upheaval and reconstruction—that is, it came to mark a move toward reconstruction of social identity and toward national reunification. Americans, for example, still negotiate Civil War memory and meaning in symbols, films, battle reenactments, cemeteries, memorials, living histories, commemorative ceremonies, and oratory, political and ceremonial. Memory thus manipulated reconstructs social identity, creating a popular notion of the past that advances the nobility of those commemorated, as well as advancing the standing of a nation and of its surviving citizens who remain to collectively remember. These devices elicit emotions quite apart from considerations of the rightness or wrongness of the war or conflict. The reworking of memories is a means of searching for and finding the sacred within the quotidian, the commonplace. At issue in the Civil War was the nation's unity, for which over 600,000 Americans died. For these Union and Confederate dead, hundreds of thousands survived to mourn and labor to construct a viable national identity out of a divided republic. Rituals of mourning and remembrance became a social duty. These activities proliferated after the war, with monuments increasingly erected in areas unassociated with graves, such as at town squares, government centers, American main streets, and city centers. Memorial sites became gathering places and served as set-apart spaces for rituals of remembering and for commemorative display including funerary greens. Memorials and rituals thus provided the living with geographical and cultural space to install all those who died in the conflict into the social category of the "honored dead." By agreeing on interpretations of the past, on what should be remembered, people employed shared categories, symbols, myths, and legends to legitimize a new social identity. These devices reestablish relatedness and exemplify the sacred so to underscore present social relations now governing those who together share a collective past.

In the new millennium we again see similar memorials put into place with regard to the Iraq conflict. Originally a collection of fifty pairs of combat boots was left along the footings of the Vietnam Veterans Memorial on one Memorial Day, an orchestrated display of remembrance. Repeating this thematic portrayal of sacralizing national service, is an array of pairs of footwear, one pair for each American who died to date in the Iraqi-American War. The footgear has been assembled into a traveling Iraq War Memorial as a collective remembrance of America's warrior dead from this more recent conflict that has spawned a new period of social discord at home. Such memorials imply a commonality of belief in image and personal relics as reflective of the souls of individuals. Thus, also noteworthy here is the effort of 200 artists in creating an iconographic memorial of the Americans who died in the Iraqi conflict—an exhibit consisting of individual portraits of the faces of each of America's war dead, a memorial display titled, appropriately enough, "Faces of the Fallen." A similar impulse drives the publication of the names and/or pictures of American service personnel killed in action in various newspapers, on *The*

News Hour on PBS, and in the comic strip *Doonesbury*. The names and images of the fallen in these instances stand in totemic relationship with these deceased warriors, their families, and their nation's collective history, just as the material objects and images left at the Wall also assert totemic connections of the named deceased with the American people.

As a nation we labor in search of the sacred. In a certain sense sacredness is a feeling directed toward what is great, what is transcendent, what is beyond the physical present and the commonplace. All memorials seek to mediate this engagement with the sacred, but it is mediated in a particularly American way and with signal effectiveness by memorials like the Vietnam Veterans Memorial, memorials which allow people to engage the sacred physically, to contribute to the creation of the sacred.

Most significantly, the Vietnam Veterans Memorial, as reflected in searching the book of names, in taking rubbings, and in leaving grave goods, ties individual visitors to particular deceased veterans of war. At its core, the exercise of memory that the Wall demands is far more focused upon the individual than the collective. Individual experience has far greater resonance than the sum of the conflict.

WORKS RECOMMENDED

Douglas, Mary. *Implicit Meanings: Essays in Anthropology*. London: Routledge and Kegan Paul, 1975.

———. *Purity and Danger: An Analysis of Concepts of Pollution and Taboo*. London: Routledge and Kegan Paul, 1976.

Hass, Kristin Ann. *Carried to the Wall: American Memory and the Vietnam Veterans Memorial*. Berkeley: U of California P, 1998.

Johnson, Robert A. *He: Understanding Masculine Psychology*. New York: Harper & Row, 1979.

———. *She: Understanding Feminine Psychology*. New York: Perennial Library, 1976.

———. *We: Understanding the Psychology of Romantic Love*. San Francisco: Harper & Row, 1983.

Levinson, Sanford. *Written in Stone: Public Monuments in Changing Societies*. Durham, NC: Duke UP, 1998.

Mayon, James L. *War Memorials as Political Landscape: The American Experience and Beyond*. New York: Praeger, 1988.

McCallum, Bradley. "Preserving Memory: A Study [Curriculum] of Monuments and Memorials." Yale–New Haven Teachers Institute. 29 Dec. 2005 <http: //www .Yale.Edu/ynhti/curriculum/units/1993/1/93.01.06.x.html>.

Miehelski, Sergiusz. *Public Monuments: Art in Political Bondage, 1870–1997*. New York: Reaktion Books, 1998.

Scruggs, Jan C., and Joel L. Swerdlow. *To Heal a Nation: The Vietnam Veterans Memorial*. New York: Harper & Row, 1985.

Young, James E. *The Texture of Memory: Holocaust Memorials and Meaning*. New Haven, CT: Yale UP, 1993.

Wal-Mart

Richard Daniels

I've made several shopping and observing visits to Wal-Mart discount stores and Supercenters in Washington state and Oregon, and I haven't once been "greeted" by anyone, although I haven't found the experience of being there particularly less friendly than what one finds in other "big box" stores, such as Sears/Kmart, Home Depot, Kroger/Fred Myers, Costco, or Target. Still, I'd heard so much about "greeters" and the cheerful helpfulness of Wal-Mart hourly wage employees, or "sales associates," as they're officially called, that I'm disappointed not to have met the legendary friendly greeter on first entrance into the domain of the world's largest corporation (by total sales income, $288 billion in 2005), even if I was there only to look around and maybe buy a t-shirt or fishing lure.

Once inside the stores (which, like other box stores, are essentially identical) I've made a point of browsing slowly through the departments and aisles, spying on both associates and customers as they sell and shop, occasionally stopping to check out a pair of shorts, a lamp, or a bag of candy, and noticed that in almost all cases the employees are trying hard to be friendly and helpful, but that they're also so very busy and constantly distracted by their many chores, such as the seemingly endless reshelving, that my main impression of them is like that of the white rabbit in the Wonderland story, frenetically hurried and looking about as if being watched at all times, constantly afraid of being late, or perhaps of being accused of stealing time. The result is that only when I actually come to the point of buying something, the point of consumption—a watchband, in one case—do I get a harried worker's undivided attention, and even then it's to answer a question about size and then to say, of another woman hastily unpacking stuff, "she'll help you put it on; that's not my job." With that she turns away, and the other worker—like the first a middle-aged woman—does help me out and take my money, but without saying a word that isn't strictly necessary.

I was beginning to feel like I must have some odd, unpleasant smell about me, but probably, I suspect, all the sales associates are simply showing the effects of corporate speed-up, the time-honored business method for wringing ever more work per unit of time, and thus ever more profits, out of employees (on the floor, mostly women). And this is clearly one of the ways Wal-Mart increases income year by year, even, it seems, hour by hour. As Lee Scott, President and CEO, writes in the 2005 Annual Report (readily available online):

> Global revenues for the fiscal year 2005 exceeded $285 billion, and net income surpassed $10 billion. We grew earnings faster than sales by doing the basics well—better in-stock, less markdowns and an improved merchandise mix. As a result, we generated higher profits for our shareholders without passing along higher prices to our customers.

Even with fewer markdowns? He does not mention the hourly workers, or associates, as part of the company's driving purpose, yet clearly their speeded up, disciplined, inexpensive productivity is essential to creating value for customers and, most important, stockholders. The average wage for Wal-Mart's 1.25 million U.S. employees is $9.90 per hour, two-thirds that of Costco workers; CEO Lee Scott makes approximately $10,000 per hour (Greenhouse 1). Wal-Mart puts employees first only in its contradictory, mystifying rhetoric.

Wal-Mart has clearly replaced General Motors and joined (if it hasn't yet replaced) Microsoft, Coca-Cola, and McDonald's as the most popular icons of corporate America, although this could of course change at any moment in the ups and downs of corporate capitalism—one need only remember the case of Enron, now little other than a business-page joke but just a short time ago thought to be the very model, or icon, of American corporate success as well as a terrific place to be employed, although no one ever quite knew exactly what Enron *did*. But Wal-Mart as a corporation is much more substantial and deeply woven into the fabric of American society and the ideology, the system of beliefs and feelings, that gives that society cohesion and emotional appeal. Thorstein Veblen observed a century ago that America is a business civilization, and Wal-Mart is now the chief icon of that civilization, like it or not.

My wife and I visited the new Lebanon, Oregon, Supercenter two weeks before its official opening on July 20, 2005, and walked around it (perimiterized the site). Quite big, tire center in back. Very shiny from the outside. Then we went to the old store only a block away, which will close when the new place opens, and everything inside of it seemed disorderly, rushed, the associates brusque and hurried, although I suppose understandably so. Every employee in a Wal-Mart store seems constantly busy restocking shelves (because of Wal-Mart's policy of perpetual inventory, made possible by instantaneous feeds from store to satellite to the monster computer in Arkansas, and back again), replacing customer discards, moving about from one area to another, stealing the odd moment of time to sigh or stretch.

Very American all of that—the shiny exterior, the bright, optimistic façade, but beneath the smiley face a sort of shabby, hurried, anxious interior, and all

Super-sized Wal-Marts such as this one in Ohio are springing up all over the country.
Courtesy of Shutterstock.

devoted (the company, if not the country) to wringing as much profit as possible from all concerned, customers as well as workers. In a business civilization, it's the owners and stockholders that count, finally; as for the rest, the devil take the hindmost.

The customers and associates are pretty much all of the same social class, lower-middle-class working folk (with some exceptions, of course), families who often are basically one paycheck or less away from slipping beneath the poverty line. The goods for sale reflect that condition, because they're mostly (although certainly not all) cheap stuff that will soon show their lack of quality. Still, that's what folks figure they can afford, and I can feel the same consumerist (and cheap) urges at work within me as I browse and shop, planning simply to observe but falling into the trap of trying to save money by spending it, buying unneeded items along with apparent necessities. More to the point, buying things—like a new table fan—that I didn't know I needed until I saw them stacked in neat rows among their fellows and remembered the hot sunshine outside. Indeed, I bought some items partly because I saw them, partly because I wanted the experience of buying things at Wal-Mart.

Of course, consuming experiences similar to this can be had pretty much anywhere in the United States, not to mention the rest of the "developed" world, and not just in a Wal-Mart store.

Since Sam Walton—who was a kind of ultra-parsimonious latter-day Henry Ford—started Wal-Mart in a disorderly store in Rogers, Arkansas, in 1962, the company has grown in deceptively deliberate stages until it is a huge international retailer (over 1,500 stores in other countries on four continents) and the world's largest corporation (again, in terms of income, $288 billion in 2005, from its over 5,000 stores). From its start, the company has reflected the small-town southeastern conservative populism and patriotism of its area and founder (sometimes called "cornpone populism"), colored by patriarchal Christian fundamentalism, and above all driven by the bottom line, the very American compulsion to find profits under every stone it stubs its toe on. These qualities have determined the company's astonishing growth into the present moment, while both company and qualities have been to an extent altered and disciplined by the competitive forces of the global economy they have become a significant part of.

Such qualities also account for the company's well-known sexist, anti-immigrant, and anti-union employment practices, as detailed for instance in Liza Featherstone's book *Selling Women Short*, a fine account of the record-size class-action lawsuit over a hundred female employees have brought against the company for exploiting the labor of more than 1 million women in often illegal ways—promises of promotions that are never kept, harassment on the job, lower wages than men doing the same work—while projecting the image of being the poor working woman's friend and benefactor. More than 60 percent of Wal-Mart's hourly workers but only a third of management are women (Featherstone 25). As a department manager said to a female worker, women "will never make as much money as men" because "God made Adam first, so women will always be second to men," the memory of which prompted the woman worker to say to an interviewer, "Isn't it incredible that [someone] could believe this crap?" (Featherstone 128). Not only do women workers at Wal-Mart in the United States face discrimination and harassment, but, in addition, most of the goods the company sells are made in China by poor, often underaged women working long weeks and hours in sweatshops, and disciplined by the Red Army (which has been known even to execute workers to enforce labor discipline [Greider 156]). And the company's price bargaining with employees and suppliers drives down wages and benefits in various U.S. businesses—such as Safeway, Albertson's, and other supermarkets in the Los Angeles area—and drives some even long-established companies out of business altogether, for example, Rubbermaid, in favor of always-cheaper overseas, mainly Chinese, competition ("Is Wal-Mart Good for America?").

Wal-Mart is also the major force instituting the new "push-pull" structural dynamic in the global economy. That is, Wal-Mart tells manufacturers what and how much to make, and what they will pay for the wares, and the manufacturers obey or run the risk of going out of business by being shunned by their biggest customer. (Things could, however, change in a hurry if China strengthens its currency versus the dollar, making imports costlier to the United States.) Wal-Mart thus plays the major role in making ours a retail-driven economy, not a production-driven one, which means among other things that wages and benefits decline and that the older manufacturing unions are largely obsolete, irrelevant to most contemporary workers' problems. It's not bad, of course, that unions should have to change with the times, but today—since the Reagan years—only about 11 percent of workers are union members (just 8 percent in the private sector), down from a high of one-third, which greatly decreases their ability to bargain for working folk. Unlike General Motors, which in the 1950s was the icon among American corporations, Wal-Mart, arguably today's iconic U.S. company, produces absolutely nothing (except surplus value), and is the surest sign that we live ever more in a low-wage, next-to-no benefit service economy that in reality focuses on the economic interests of stockholders, not those of working people. A business civilization, indeed.

A further problem with Wal-Mart, and a sign of its fundamental corporate hypocrisy, is that it's perhaps the biggest recipient of corporate welfare—immense public, taxpayer-funded subsidies in terms of public assistance (e.g., some employees on food stamps), Medicaid (which the company has encouraged its workers to apply for), local tax abatements, and free or cheap land and public services (again at taxpayer expense), job-training and worker-recruitment funding, and more (Dicker 200). These practices are hypocritical to say the least for a company that takes every opportunity to propagandize workers with the free-market, anti-union ideology of individual rights, right-to-work, and self-reliance. So Wal-Mart exploits its workers by paying always low wages and next-to-no benefits; its customers (mostly from the same class of women as the workers); and then all of these same people, who are of course taxpayers, yet again by feeding lustily at the public trough. As U.S. Rep. George Miller of California has written, "Because Wal-Mart fails to pay sufficient wages U.S. taxpayers are forced to pick up the tab. In this sense, Wal-Mart's profits are not made only on the backs of its employees—but on the [back] of every U.S. taxpayer" (Dicker 208).

As I've walked through various Wal-Marts, the impression has grown on me that they offer an illusion of plenty and choice. There are many departments, and certainly lots of stuff, but very few choices (sometimes none) of brand or quality *within* any department. One reason (aside from the "always low wages" workers complain of in private) the company can offer "always low prices—Always," is that they don't sell anything much that claims to be of substantial quality; that is, everything is cheap to begin with, from watch bands to Bermuda shorts to polo shirts, lamps, TV sets, CD players, bags of candy, the whole range of groceries, women's garments, and a thin selection of fishing lures and equipment (well, I'm a fisherman and know that market). Whole realms of possible choice involving quality simply are not there, a lack easily noted in a tour through the full service grocery section, say, of a Supercenter. Bread? Meat? Coffee? Choices strictly limited. Want fresh meat? Looks like mostly roughly butchered feed-lot specials. Particularly interested in healthful food, or organics? Next to nothing offered. In another department of the store, how about men's shorts or wash pants? You can indeed find enough very cheap ones, one or two brands, but little if any choice of quality; sometimes things that cost a little more wear and look better, last longer and thus make good economic sense. But the temptation and desire to buy cheap is palpable, and to me—a family man without a lot of cash—understandable.

What does this retail global behemoth mean? What is Wal-Mart's cultural resonance? Is it an evil business corporation, unlike all others in its exploitation of workers and customers for the sake of the bottom line and its stockholders, not to mention the multibillionaires of the Walton family? Critics gain nothing by trying to demonize the company. It has plenty of faults, contradictions, and moral failings, but surely not many more than the other mammoth corporations that make up American and global capitalism. Wal-Mart has a tremendous impact on business and trade decisions throughout the global economy, but this is because of its size, steady high growth, push-pull tactics, and evident success at making profits. Wal-Mart is the icon of American and even perhaps of global business today for these reasons primarily, and thus not radically different from other corporations in its practices—just better than most, more efficient at turning labor power, what its workers and others, including the Chinese, do, into surplus value and thus into the profits that go to major owners and stockholders. The worker becomes "a worker-in-general," in a "formation of *abstract labor*" (Laibman 301). Employee turnover at Wal-Mart averages over 45 percent a year; that is, every year over 550,000 of the company's 1.25 million or so employees quit (or are fired), and 550,000 or so new Sales Associates are hired—every year! (Dicker 30–31). Clearly, such workers are, as David Laibman characterizes them, "interchangeable and dispensable" (301), as indeed are vast numbers of working people around the world in this glutted labor market.

Wal-Mart in part represents the American consumer's addiction to the cheap, on the cheap. John Dicker (215) bluntly points out the depth and practical complexity of this problem when he contends that, as human beings,

> We require so much more than everyday low prices. One day perhaps we'll have the courage to realize that this entitlement to "cheap" is our new crack cocaine. In the meantime, those taking on Wal-Mart on so many disparate fronts must grapple with one of the most complex social-change questions of our time: How do you convince a poor person that a $28 DVD player sucks? (215)

Such a poor person might be a single mother trying to rear two kids on the $17,000 a year she makes working (almost) full-time at Wal-Mart, or an immigrant laborer trying to live with some self-respect while sending dollars back to Mexico or El Salvador and also saving to try to bring his wife and child to the better life he wants to build in El Norte. To compound the dilemma of the worker, consider that neither can afford health insuance.

Wal-Mart, as a sign of the power of corporations and of the global economy, represents a profound social and human disconnect, one of the great problems of our time, and one that involves every American whose income and whatever benefits, savings, and pensions ultimately derive from the corporate exploitation of the labor of the poor and other working-class people—here and in every continent and country of the world. Indeed, with the explosion of the service economy the vast majority of Americans *are* among the workers of the world, which pretty clearly suggests the struggle we're engaged in and the remedy we should be working toward, a struggle which includes but does not end with supporting the efforts of Wal-Mart's employees everywhere to organize to get better working conditions and a living wage.

WORKS CITED AND RECOMMENDED

"Annual Report, 2005." Wal-Mart Stores, Inc. 28 July 2005 <www.walmart.com>.

Dicker, John. *The United States of Wal-Mart*. New York: Penguin, 2005.

Ehrenreich, Barbara. *Nickel and Dimed: On (Not) Getting By in America*. New York: Henry Holt, 2001.

Featherstone, Liza. *Selling Women Short: The Landmark Battle for Workers' Rights at Wal-Mart*. New York: Basic Books, 2004.

Greenhouse, Steven. "How Costco Became the Anti–Wal-Mart." *New York Times* 17 July 2005, natl. ed.: C1+.

Greider, William. *One World Ready or Not: The Manic Logic of Global Capitalism*. New York: Simon & Schuster, 1997.

"Is Wal-Mart Good for America?" *PBS Frontline*. 16 Nov. 2004 <www.pbs.org/wgbh/pages/frontline/shows/walmart>.

Laibman, David. "Theory and Necessity: The Stadial Foundations of the Present." *Science & Society* 9.3 (2005): 285–315.

John Wayne

David Magill

Despite having been dead for over twenty-five years, John Wayne is still one of our most enduring icons. He ranks as one of the most popular and influential Americans; as late as 1995, he was still voted America's favorite actor and in 2004, he ranked in the top ten. Thanks to special effects wizardry, he has appeared in recent Coors Light and Coca-Cola commercials; in each case, he has appeared as one of his most famous figures (cowboy or soldier), conveying his masculine potency to the potables advertised. In 2004, the U.S. Postal Service honored Wayne with a stamp, while the army named an attack helicopter after him. Former actor and California governor Arnold Schwarzenegger headlined the 2004 Republican National Convention with a speech that garnered its loudest cheers when he reminisced about his boyhood days watching Wayne's films. Schwarzenegger's reference not only nostalgically revisited Wayne's political conservatism but also provided an important claim to American identity and masculinity by revealing a cinematic and political debt to "The Duke." No other actor has been more popular with moviegoers, and no other celebrity represents the American ideals of masculine courage and strength more forcefully than John Wayne.

Joan Didion captured it best when she wrote, "When John Wayne rode through my childhood, and perhaps through yours, he determined forever the shape of certain of our dreams" (30). John Wayne's iconic status arises from his embodiment of the ideal American male identity. He resolves the contradictions of both masculine and national identity for his viewers, creating his titanic star figure out of the ambivalences of modern life and exhibiting a mastery of those tensions: the quest for individuality balanced against the need for social conformity; the desire for women versus the desire of freedom from domestic life; the allure of brutal violence against the responsibility for social order. John Wayne was born Marion Michael Morrison, an unlikely name for the icon of the essence of American manhood. Yet Morrison chose his new moniker consciously to represent his masculine identity to film audiences, and he created his John Wayne persona with the same care, playing characters that accessed the mythic archetypes of the American hero in the service of the nation and shaped U.S. manhood after World War II.

A major tension of the post–World War II generation pitted the loss of individuality against the perceived need for moral and political unity in the Cold War struggle. John Wayne resolved that contradiction with characters that represent the rugged individualism of the U.S. frontier while also supporting larger ideals of justice, law, and duty to family and country. *Stagecoach*'s "The Ringo Kid" (1939), for example, is a loner and a gunslinger, yet he seeks revenge only against the criminals who murdered his brother and protects the stagecoach community on its journey. The Kid's introduction in the film supports this vision—the camera first swings in for a close-up that identifies him as apart and alone, then widens to a shot which includes him in the group. He is committed to his personal quest for retribution but also to communal ideals of justice and chivalry. *Stagecoach* also represents Wayne's masculine control over psyche and body. When asked why he seeks revenge for his brother's death, he answers quietly, "He was murdered," maintaining control of his faculties as well as the violence he will direct at the killers. Similarly, his powerful body often stands at ease, demonstrating to the audience his mastery of his own strength. But when action is required, the Kid does not hesitate; in one famous scene, he jumps from horse to horse to stop the runaway stagecoach. Thus, even in his earliest films we see Wayne developing the iconic persona that would bring him such adulation.

Although he headlined a number of films during the 1940s, *Red River* (1949) announced the beginning of Wayne's true stardom in its portrayal of another dominant masculine figure: Tom Dunson, an isolated cattle rancher who single-handedly built a productive cattle ranch on the frontier and now must drive his herd 1,000 miles to payday while training men, fighting the elements, and battling with his adopted son Matthew Garth (played by Montgomery Clift). Wayne's iconic persona is evident in this film in multiple ways: he plays the ultimate man who can out-work, out-shoot, and out-drink any man in the group. He lives by a simple code: a day's work for a day's pay, with no quitters allowed. He expects other men to follow his grueling lead, yet as the film's cinematography shows, no one is Wayne's equal. When Wayne surveys his herd and his workmen, the camera angle is always focused downward, emphasizing his higher status. And when the son Matthew challenges his authority verbally, Dunson responds with violence and threats that demonstrate his physical superiority. These two attributes come together as the film ends. Having tracked down his betrayer, Dunson marches through the herd, parting the cattle physically in his implacable quest for retribution. Gerald Mast notes of that scene, "[No one] can ever walk the way Wayne does, devouring space with his stride" (qtd. in Wills 147); visually it marks his unique masculinity. Wayne's manhood is hard and brutal, and his final battle with the son reflects it. But the restoration of family reflects Wayne's support for community.

Wayne depicts a similar resolution to this tension with the other central character he would play: the U.S. soldier, who further accented Wayne's "American" identity while also developing his masculine identity. In *Sands of Iwo Jima* (1949), for example, Wayne's Sergeant Stryker is both an independent leader who can shape his men through violent masculine competition and a willing participant in the military command structure. While Stryker breaks the rules to train his men (striking one with a rifle butt, for example), he also follows orders faithfully and leads his unit to victory, taking a sniper bullet for his country. He is a hero and a role model, converting even his staunchest rival to his views. Stryker has even lost his wife and child as a result of his military commitment, but he adheres to his duty nonetheless. Thus, Wayne creates another version of modern manhood that assuages the anxieties of contemporary men by enacting a model for emulation.

John Wayne as Hondo Lane in the 1953 movie *Hondo*. Courtesy of Photofest.

The Man Who Shot Liberty Valance (1962) portrays similar ideals of masculine identity and individualism within the community. Wayne plays Tom Doniphon, a gunfighter who renounces the love of his life to Ranse Stoddard (Jimmy Stewart) and protects that man's honor by secretly killing Liberty Valance and giving the credit to Stoddard. Wayne's portrayal makes clear his masculinity and its connection to individuality; in contrast to Stoddard's talk of law and civility, Doniphon represents the controlled violence that counters Valance's threat and reveals the need for individual men standing strong against evil. But Doniphon also recognizes the responsibilities of social order and supports them through his vindication of Stoddard. He allows Stoddard the spoils for killing Valance and the love of Doniphon's sweetheart because he recognizes that this sacrifice is necessary to support Stoddard's idealism and commitment to justice that will enrich the community. Even though he is the stronger man physically, Doniphon controls his own desires to support the communal good. Wayne's films thus create him as larger-than-life to demonstrate his overt manhood, yet these films always control that masculine vigor within a code of conduct. Wayne could play violent men because that violence was always directed through a conservative vision of justice and fairness, as in *Liberty*

Valance. He depicted the means by which men could do their duty and remain potent in their manhood.

The Searchers (1956) represents Wayne's most critically successful film, and while his character is far more troubled and negative than most of his other portrayals, Ethan Edwards fits within the trajectory of American manhood Wayne develops in his films. Edwards is a man on the line in multiple ways. He is connected to his brother's family by emotional bonds, yet, as the film's opening and closing shots reveal, he can never be part of that family officially. Edwards is always separate and alone, framed by the open door he does not enter and silhouetted against the frontier's mountain range and blue sky. Following a vicious Indian attack that kills Aaron and his wife, Edwards sets out to rescue Aaron's daughter Debbie from the treacherous Scar. Wayne's complex portrayal of Edwards critiques his racist ideals but also locates his transformation in Wayne's honorable manhood. While Edwards threatens to kill Debbie to remove the taint of her rape, and reacts violently towards Native Americans on several occasions, he controls his violence and his anger at the film's climax. His redemption lies in her rescue and return home, and Wayne's idealized manhood allows viewers to see Edwards's transformation as natural. The cost he bears, and the scars he hides, represent the sacrifices that American men must take willingly to secure the nation's future. *The Searchers*, then, is a vivid and powerful allegory of masculinity's duty to national interests. Wayne's American iconic persona stems from his portrayal of strong individuals who nevertheless obey communal ideals of duty, loyalty, and honor. By successfully melding the contradictory impulses of individual interest and group allegiance through strength and honor, he creates a masculinity which all can admire and emulate.

As John Wayne aged and faced the trials of cancer, he shifted his iconic persona from individual gunslinger to community patriarch. Later Wayne films portray him as a masculine figure that bestows knowledge and identity upon the younger generation. Thus, Wayne continued to represent masculine potency while also balancing the demands of community leadership and fraternal obligation. Wayne repeatedly portrays men who own property, love feisty women, and battle corrupt businessmen and ranchers in a fight for an egalitarian society where individual acumen is the primary measure of success. Of course, John Wayne's character is always the most successful figure. His later Westerns, such as *True Grit* (which won Wayne his only Oscar for lead actor) and its sequel *Rooster Cogburn*, follow this formula in that they create unique characters (Cogburn, for example, is a drunk with an eyepatch) who nonetheless fulfill their duties to communal order and justice by dispatching villains and protecting women.

His final movies, made as cancer wracked his body, cinematically represent Wayne's passing of the torch through a patriarchal motif. *The Cowboys* and *The Shootist* both involve an older cowboy teaching young men the ways of the West. In *The Cowboys*, Wayne hires schoolboys to accompany his cattle run when his regular hands run off in search of gold. The film's anticapitalist, nostalgic individualism cemented Wayne's persona as the father figure of American cinema. *The Shootist*, Wayne's final portrayal, is a referential portrayal of a cancer-stricken gunfighter who returns to his town to settle his life, bestow words of wisdom on a young man (played by Ron Howard, himself a figure of youthful innocence on television as Richie Cunningham and Opie Taylor), and then die with guns blazing. In both these films, however, Wayne's character teaches his young protégés the lessons of his life: live by a code of honor, fight for your principles, and act like a man.

Another attribute of several later films is Wayne's increasing conservatism. His patriotism and pro-America loyalties arise in several films to highlight his connection to an ideal "American" identity. *The Green Berets* marks both Wayne's turn as a director and his statement on Vietnam to a country divided. For Wayne, the war held no questions; and his portrayal of the steadfast Mike Kirby had its dramatic foil in the skeptical reporter who follows Kirby into battle and ultimately enlists. While critics panned the film for its heavy-handed portrayal of American patriotism, moviegoers flocked to see Wayne once again inhabiting the role of true American hero and man's man. So even though he would have been too old to fight and lead combat runs, Wayne's character not only leads his men into battle but presents a larger-than-life figure, thanks to filming angles that make him appear larger and more menacing than his men. Wayne's portrayal combines an overtly didactic patriotism with his typically strong masculinity to present a compelling figure of American manhood.

Wayne's other directorial project was *The Alamo*; in that story he found the American ideals that he supported as an actor and as a public figure throughout his life. Perhaps no speech summarizes Wayne's views better than the one he gave as Davy Crockett in this film:

> "Republic"—I like the sound of the word. . . . Some words give you a feeling. Republic is one of those words that makes me tight in the throat. Same tightness a man gets when his baby makes his first step, or his boy first shaves, makes his first sound like a man. (qtd. in Wills 213)

The speech links patriotism to manhood in a controlled sentiment voiced by a legendary American hero. The combination works so well because it taps into the mythos of American culture: the self-made strong and powerful man who succeeds individually yet lives by a code of ethics that puts country and duty ahead of self-interest.

Joan Didion writes,

> And in a world we understood early to be characterized by venality and doubt and paralyzing ambiguities, he suggested another world, one which may or may not have ever existed, but in any case existed no more: a place where a man could move free, make his own code, and live by it. (30–31)

Wayne represented a mythic fantasy of masculinity and individuality based in an ethic of freedom and choice; in other words, he represented the American ideal for men. Like Superman, he fought for truth, justice, and the American way, and like Superman, he is a mythic figure in American culture. He is a legend, and as his friend notes in *The Man Who Shot Liberty Valance*, "when the fact becomes legend, print the legend." Wayne became such an icon at a time when world war had shattered the globe, madmen dictators had killed millions, and nuclear annihilation seemed imminent; as such, he represents a simpler past nostalgically created to counter present anxieties, as well as a vision of a world where good and evil are easily discerned and right always wins out. But he also represents a humane heroism and a promise that someone is always there to protect the downtrodden and less fortunate from the dictates of evil. John Wayne is an American icon because he represents America's ideal vision of itself as a protector of individual freedom and choice.

WORKS CITED AND RECOMMENDED

Didion, Joan. "John Wayne: A Love Song." *Slouching Towards Bethlehem*. New York: Farrar, 1968. 29–41.

Ricci, Mark, Boris Zmijewsky, and Steve Zmijewsky. *The Films of John Wayne*. New York: Citadel, 1970.

Roberts, Randy, and James S. Olsen. *John Wayne: American*. New York: Free P, 1995.

Wills, Garry. *John Wayne's America: The Politics of Celebrity*. New York: Simon & Schuster, 1997.

Whistler's Mother

Elaine A. King

Throughout the twentieth century, James McNeill Whistler's painting *Arrangement in Grey and Black, No. 1: Portrait of the Painter's Mother* (1871) has functioned as an icon of motherhood, love, respect, and yet also indifference. This mother's stoic gaze is embedded in the part of our cultural fabric that does not seek powerful sensations or transcendence; she is not the kind of icon that invites being challenged or toppled; and, so she remains a well-known but idiosyncratic, and perhaps archaic, image of American culture. "Whistler's Mother," as the painting is commonly called, occupies a prominent position within American popular culture despite its chilly portrayal of maternity in a little lace bonnet and widow's weeds.

The quiet, enigmatic likeness of Anna Whistler along with Grant Wood's *American Gothic* and Leonardo's *Mona Lisa* are perhaps the three master-pieces most Americans are familiar with. A good part of its popularity, like theirs, stems from the number of derivations drawn by cartoonists, illustrators, and advertisers over the past 100-plus years. At the University of Pittsburgh in the Art History Slide Library, a drawer contains a widespread collection of popular culture's reinterpretations of art masterpieces, especially Whistler's Mother. In like manner at Stanford University the art historian Wanda Corn has amassed an impressive assortment of transformations of Wood's *American Gothic*. Her analysis can also be applied to the portrait of Whistler's mother: the simple compositional formula and the mute facial expressions of the couple made it possible for Americans to "use *American Gothic* as an all-purpose 'blackboard' on which to write their messages, voice their concerns, or hawk their wares. They have discovered, as the critics have before them, that the image is protean, capable of addressing an infinite number of issues" (134).

The emergence of the American icon from Whistler's brush has a greater peculiarity than does Wood's portrait from the midwestern heartland. Before the painting became popular as a protean icon of motherhood, it was revered as experimental Modern art by an expatriate American who had challenged the European art establishment and gained celebrity through controversy.

The son of a Lowell, Massachusetts, railway engineer, Whistler left the country for Paris at age twenty-one after failing at West Point, and thereafter lived in Europe, where he pretended to be a Southern aristocrat. The painting was created in England, purchased by the French government after much connivance by Whistler and his friends, and housed in a Paris museum. Whistler's idiosyncratic behavior, along with his radical ideas about art in the late nineteenth century when Modernism was beginning, contributed to his fame and to the love for this portrait. "One would like to think that Whistler the artist flies clear of Whistler the celebrity, the 'character,'" Robert Hughes points out. "Not so. On the one hand, his self-construction, his sense of the self as a work of art, remains as fiercely impressive as Oscar Wilde's. 'Float like a butterfly, sting like a bee'—he did that long before Muhammad Ali was born" (238). The portrait embodies Whistler's aesthetic philosophy that challenged "the traditional academic rule that the highest art must possess a high degree of finish and illusionistic detail at the same time as conveying moral narratives or ennobling ideas" (Bjelajac 274).

At first, Whistler's works were perceived to be unacceptable and shocking. At the Salon of 1863, Whistler's painting *Symphony in White, No. 1: The White Girl* and Edouard Manet's *Le Dejeuner sur L'Herbe* were rejected for essentially the same reasons—their technique and their "lewd" subject matter. In 1877 the renowned English critic John Ruskin blatantly charged that Whistler's *Nocturne in Black and Gold: The Falling Rocket* amounted to "the artist flinging a pot of paint in the public's face" (McCoubrey 182). Outraged, Whistler sued Ruskin for libel, but won only one farthing in damages. This trial almost ruined him financially. Whistler, however, was a master at using adversity, and made the most of the trial's controversy to further establish his reputation as an artist, and his notoriety as a critic of "devotion, pity, love, patriotism, and the like" in art, as he proclaimed in the London paper *The World* in 1878 (Bendix 33).

Whistler was aligned with the Aesthetic Movement; he and its artists argued that the primary quality of a work of art resided in its beauty, which translated into its formal elements of line, shape, and color. He admired the formal beauty and colors of Japanese prints, which influenced his specialized style of fusing figurative and abstract elements. Woodcut prints with sharply angled lines, bold cropping, and flat-pattern design appealed to him as ways to make supremely confident statements. In his resolutely simplified compositions— especially portraits—Whistler painted mostly solitary figures, and reduced them to a single form within a finite tonal scale. The monochromatic character of the portrait of his mother lucidly delineates what Whistler called his "tonal envelope." This composition remains one of the mysteries of American art, and yet, according to E. H. Gombrich, "perhaps one of the most popular paintings ever made" (400). In its carefully structured linear pattern, the mother subject is silhouetted and framed by the wall; she sits in profile fronting a light background. The horizontal lines of the skirting boards hold the elements in place. This painting is unlike maternal portraits painted by such other artists as

Whistler's Mother. Courtesy of the Library of Congress.

Dürer, Rembrandt, or Cassatt: Whistler was making an aesthetic design. In his collected writings *The Gentle Art of Making Enemies* he observed, "To me it is interesting as a picture of my mother; but what can or ought the public to care about the identity of the portrait?" It was, he insisted, an "arrangement" without concern for sentiments or imitation of its subject (128).

Whistler's acceptance as an internationally significant American artist began shortly after 1885 among Paris's creative and literary society. No previous American painter had been held in such high esteem. His reputation

flourished in the United States from the mid-1890s onward, when private collectors, notably Charles Lang Freer, and major museums began to acquire his work. His art appeared in six Carnegie Internationals between 1896–1907, where it can be said to have been a touchstone by which other contemporary painting was judged. (Strazdes et al. 480)

Following Whistler's death on July 17, 1903, many critics went through a period of mourning befitting the loss of a luminary American painter and controversial celebrity. Over a span of five years some eighty-eight articles appeared on the subject of Whistler, despite the many who questioned the significance of his position in the history of art (Knaufft 173). Within the realm of popular culture, a cigar was named after him because he had been a lifelong cigarette smoker, and a lithograph of the artist's image was made to grace the boxes of the Leopold Powell and Company of Tampa, Florida. Because he was a famed, sophisticated, and controversial American artist, his name and image naturally lent their allure to advertising and commodity marketing. A New York City department store produced a Whistler line of stationery, perhaps swayed by the success of his Metropolitan Museum show of 1910 and his contentious reputation. However, this burst of commemoration was short-lived. The last actual appearance of his work in the United States for nearly twenty years came in 1913 in Buffalo, New York.

The centenary celebration of Whistler's birth in 1933 prompted a reevaluation of his reputation and stature, with recurring showings of his work. A significant occasion that gave extra attention to his mother portrait among the American public was its inclusion in the traveling exhibition *What Is Modern Painting?* organized by Alfred Barr in 1933 for the Museum of Modern Art. *The Arrangement in Grey and Black* was loaned by the Louvre, and during the exhibition's half-year run an estimated 2 million viewers across the country were able to behold the famed mother portrait. Amid the remembrance and praise of his most famous painting, Whistler's reputation and reproductions of his work expanded, partially because of articles written on almost every aspect of his career. Stories of the vitriolic "Whistler versus Ruskin" libel suit and the artist's well-placed verbal barbs emanated in periodicals. Once again Whistler was a "hot" news item attracting attention among readers and viewers.

Well apart from his contentious life, Whistler's portrait of his mother gained importance as an image with iconic appeal among Americans during the Depression. It represented for a large segment of the public an object of art and one of mystery at the same time. The mother portrait's arrival and departure alone became the subject of news. When the painting was shown at the Modern in 1934, President Franklin Delano Roosevelt's mother posed in front of it for a photo which then appeared in newspapers. Moreover, the painting astonished the American public when they learned that the French Government insured the painting in 1933 for a value of $500,000 for the tour, and also that it had originally been purchased for only $800 in 1891. Such an increase in monetary value awed Americans and further broadened their interest in the distinguished portrait. Subsequently, among the general public Whistler's original title disappeared and it was simply dubbed "Whistler's Mother."

Moreover, a resurgence of realism in the United States produced a consummate milieu for a revival of Whistler's art, stimulated through President Roosevelt's response to unemployment with the Works Progress Administration. Many artists were employed to paint murals, paintings, and posters that celebrated American identity and civic life, for post offices, schools, trains, buses, air terminals, and housing projects. The works included illustrations of American nationalism, the work ethic, freedom, pre-industrial landscapes, and midwestern community life, by regionalist painters such as Thomas Hart Benton, John Steuart Curry, and Grant Wood.

As with Grant Wood's *American Gothic*, Whistler's Mother when seen as illustration evokes a homey Puritan tradition, in a pious mother likeness with caricature charm. It had appeal within the growing Protestant fundamentalism throughout the Midwest and South, suggesting the sovereignty of religion in rural America, as does John Steuart Curry's 1928 *Baptism in Kansas*. On the other hand, for the millions of recent immigrant, urban families it bore the dignified, modest image of old-world motherhood. For both, the Depression and war years brought emphasis to the importance of family. And as a picture, Whistler's Mother emanates a sensibility akin to Norman Rockwell's illustrations of American family life in the *Saturday Evening Post*.

The celebration of Mother's Day and the U.S. Postal Service also contributed to this painting's becoming an American icon. For the twentieth anniversary of Mother's Day as an official holiday, the Piedmont Chapter of the American War Mothers submitted a request on January 26, 1934, to President Roosevelt requesting that a stamp be issued. Mrs. William E. Ochiltree, National President of the AWM, claimed, "The granting of Mother's Day Stamp would not only express a loving remembrance of home and its queen, but it would give expression to the fact that Mother has always been a co-partner in our American life." News of the government's intent to publish a commemorative stamp prompted Earl F. Wood of Pomfret, Connecticut, to write Postmaster-General Thomas J. Farley inquiring if "a most suitable picture for the stamp [would] be the well known Whistler's Mother? Should we not do well to recognize this great American artist through circulating one of his greatest works and at the same time honor the mothers of America?" This recommendation took hold, and an estimated 250 million stamps were printed and made available to the American public on May 3, 1934. The stamp was promoted:

> As a means of stimulating interest in the forthcoming issue of the Mothers' commemorative postage stamp, the Postmaster, has had a supply of placards printed containing a reproduction of Whistler's portrait of his mother, that is the central design of the stamp, placed on display in post office lobbies, as well as in clubs and hotels. (Archives of United States Postal Museum)

Furthermore, the Post Office used mimeograph, radio, and other means to promote the sale of the Whistler stamp, as well as to advocate the importance of Mother's Day. The simple act of using a modified version of Whistler's portrait for the stamp's composition, and its massive distribution, turned an image that was never intended to be a cliché into a stereotype of motherhood in the United States. No longer was the image identified with high art, but instead a mass-produced item available to anyone for three cents.

The arts community was outraged by what they perceived as a mutilation of the original portrait. To make a more mass-appealing and sentimental image, the Postal design's revisions included cutting the mother's figure off at the knees, removing background designs, printing it in the color purple, and adding a pot of carnations. Numerous protests appeared in the *Art Digest* of May 1934, as well as national newspapers (Archives of the United States Postal Museum). Notwithstanding the critical outcry, the stamp contributed to the popularization of the painting. That stamp honoring the mothers of America, along with the original painting, now conveyed messages of devotion, pity, and patriotic value.

The Whistler stamp illustrates a curious coopting, for an idealization of motherhood. The original painting served as a point of departure for the stamp's image. The designer cropped the picture so as to gain access to the face and to close the distance. The added bouquet of carnations was to soften the austere space, as well as to invoke the Mother's Day custom in which mothers wore carnations; in the stamp they appear as if they were on a windowsill. Ironically, the very fact that Whistler's original composition was a tonal composition of blacks, grays, and white contributed to its mass distribution and reproduction. The work could readily be reproduced in magazines and newspapers in black and white and, despite the limitations of tabloid mechanical reproduction, the readers saw it pretty much as if they were actually seeing the museum painting. Because color technology was still in its infancy, its reproduction in black and white did not lessen its pictorial essence.

Subsequently the painting became an open subject for use in popular culture. Reproductions began appearing in elementary school textbooks, scout materials, and cartoons, as testimonies to being a good child. Cartoonists also steadily employed this image in humorous caricatures, and it continually underwent endless modification in books, cards, posters, and other items.

The painting's name went even further afield. During World War II a light bomber, the Douglas A-26 "Invader," was called "Whistler's Mother." It was used in attacks for bombing, strafing, and launching rockets. Silver models of "Whistler's Mother—A-26 Invader" can be purchased today on the Internet for $135.00. The visage took a different turn in 1945 when Disney Studios appropriated Whistler's Mother for comedy in a Donald Duck cartoon, *Don's Whistling Mother*. Since then Warner Brothers' Wile E. Coyote and numerous other cartoon characters have donned the guise for fun. Actual mothers and even President Reagan have been dressed and posed in it for social and political comment (Tedeschi 137, 133).

The uses of Whistler's Mother curiously presage adaptations in Pop Art, which emerged in the 1960s from such artists as Andy Warhol, Larry Rivers, and Roy Lichtenstein, who elevated banal everyday objects into icons in their art. Instantly these artists melded high art with popular culture by taking prevalent objects from advertising and real life—Coke bottles, Marilyn Monroe, Elvis, and newspaper comics. These icons are favored details in the endless symbiosis of modern culture that provides an illusion of social stability during relentless change. They represent a type of fusion of materiality and cultural meaning through the praxis of design and advertising.

After over 100 years, Whistler's Mother continues to be appropriated by popular culture, in derivations ranging from Looney Tunes kitchen canisters to versions on websites, to *New Yorker* cartoons such as Edward Sorel's menace-in-wait on the Mother's Day Cover of May 13, 1996. The plot of the 1997 film *Bean,* a slapstick comedy, revolves around the painting. Yet contemporary artists have also continued to respond to this work, as did Dean Brown with his 1983 color photograph *Barbie as Whistler's Mother.*

As with the *Mona Lisa,* the gaze of Whistler's mother is enigmatic—in the composition Anna Whistler appears cool and aloof, locked in a moment of deep reflection that the viewer cannot penetrate. She personifies in this composition a reserved old lady: her gaunt profile is austere, and accepting of her role as mother and widow. One might question whether this is a relevant image of motherhood in the twenty-first century; perhaps is it now merely a comfortable popular culture logo. Will it remain an icon as the youth culture persists in gathering momentum, and as mothers and grandmothers over the past decades have transcended the stereotyped role of "good mother" and taken on multiple identities? Will it maintain its power as a historical icon because we as a society continue being comfortable with nostalgic clichés of past values? Perhaps it will persist, because some icons come to make classic statements about a particular aspect of American culture, and they remain viable from one generation to the next.

WORKS CITED AND RECOMMENDED

Archives of the United States Postal Museum. Washington, DC.

Bendix, Deanna Marohn. *Diabolical Designs: Paintings, Interiors, and Exhibitions of James McNeill Whistler.* Washington, DC: Smithsonian Institute P, 1995.

Bjelajac, David. *American Art: A Cultural History.* New York: H. N. Abrams, 2001.

Corn, Wanda. *Grant Wood: The Regionalist Vision.* New Haven, CT: Yale UP/ Minneapolis Institute of Arts, 1983.

"Douglas A-26 'Invader.'" *Air Force Museum* 18 Feb. 2005 <http://www.wpafb .Af.mil/museum/research/attack/a4/a4-2.htm>.

Gombrich, E. H. *The Story of Art.* 6th ed. New York: Phaidon Publishers, 1954.

Hughes, Robert. *American Visions: The Epic History of Art in America.* New York: Knopf, 1997.

Knaufft, Ernest. "James Abbott McNeill Whistler." *American Monthly Review of Reviews* 38 (Aug. 1903): 173–76.

McCoubrey, John W., ed. *American Art, 1700–1960: Sources and Documents.* Englewood Cliffs, NJ: Prentice-Hall, 1965.

Morton, Frederick. "James McNeill Whistler, The Etcher." *Brush and Pencil* 12 (Aug. 1903): 305–19.

Prideaux, Tom et al. *The World of Whistler 1834–1903.* New York: Time-Life, 1970.

Strazdes, Diana et al. *American Paintings and Sculpture to 1945 in the Carnegie Museum of Art.* New York: Hudson Hills P/Carnegie Museum, 1992.

Tedeschi, Martha. "The Face that Launched a Thousand Images: Whistler's *Mother* and Popular Culture." *Whistler's Mother: An American Icon*. Ed. Margaret F. MacDonald. Burlington, VT: Lund Humphries, 2003. 121–41.

Walden, Sarah. "Rethinking Whistler's Mother: Restoration Reveals Secrets of an American Icon." *Architectural Digest* 48 (Sept. 1991): 42–46.

Walker, John. *James McNeill Whistler*. New York: H. N. Abrams; Washington, DC: National Museum of American Art, Smithsonian, 1987.

Whistler, James Abbot McNeill. *The Gentle Art of Making Enemies*. 1890. New York: Dover, 1967.

Oprah Winfrey

R. Mark Hall

All but the most reclusive Americans—indeed, citizens of the world—are familiar with television's most successful talk-show host, Oprah Winfrey. As an American icon, she is associated with some of the most dominant values and ideas in contemporary American popular culture. Among these, Winfrey represents a version of the American Dream narrative made famous in the rags-to-riches dime novels of nineteenth-century Unitarian minister and writer Horatio Alger. The American Dream, according to Alger's formulation, is available to anyone, no matter how disadvantaged or powerless, no matter how modest one's origins. If one perseveres, if one always does right and does one's best, then, through honesty, hard work, and determination, one can overcome any obstacles along the way and triumph over them to build one's own American Dream against the odds. Winfrey's personal legend, constructed and retold over the course of her long career, is a contemporary Horatio Alger progress narrative, or bootstraps myth, of upward transformation from humble beginnings against difficult odds, to extraordinary success through individual strength of mind and hard work.

The Queen of Talk TV was born in Kosciusko, Mississippi, the illegitimate child of Vernita Lee and Vernon Winfrey, in 1954. When her mother migrated to Milwaukee, Winfrey was left in the care of her grandparents. Though uneducated herself, Winfrey's grandmother, a strict disciplinarian, taught her granddaughter to read the Bible and to write by the time she was 3. As a young girl, Winfrey performed recitations at Sunday school. At 6, she left her grandparents' farm to live with her mother. Winfrey excelled in school, skipping ahead from kindergarten to first grade, and again from second to third grade. Shuttled back and forth between her mother in Milwaukee and her father in Nashville, at age 9, Winfrey was raped by a 19-year-old cousin; and until age 14 she was sexually abused by close male relatives and family friends. The abuse ended after Winfrey's mother attempted to place her daughter, who had become an uncontrollable delinquent, in a juvenile detention home. Turned away because the home was full, Winfrey was sent, instead, to live permanently with her father in Nashville. There she gave birth to a premature son, who died not long after birth. Afterwards, under her father's guidance, Winfrey became an honor student again. She graduated from East Nashville High School with a scholarship for her speaking ability to East Tennessee State. While a 16-year-old senior in high school, Winfrey began her broadcasting career by reading the news at WVOL radio for $100 a week. So began Oprah Winfrey's rise to celebrity.

Winfrey's life story reflects the idea, highly valued in American culture and made famous by Alger's novels, that material success results from dogged individual determination. This theme of transformation is fundamental to any understanding of Winfrey as an American icon. With a wide array of public images, Winfrey embodies the protean nature of the American icon. She is malleable and open to multiple interpretations. Winfrey's persistence and longtime success both result from and reflect her adaptability. In fact, change is a major theme on *The Oprah Winfrey Show*, which has itself undergone major transformations from time to time. For example, in 1996 Winfrey restructured her show, moving away from the tell-all, knock-down-drag-out daytime talk format of such competitors as Jerry Springer. She sought to reinvent *The Oprah Winfrey Show*, which she labeled "change your life TV," so that it would be more inspirational. In keeping with this theme came "Oprah's Angel Network," Winfrey's national effort to encourage viewers to make charitable contributions and do volunteer work.

After restructuring, doing well by doing good—another Horatio Alger trademark—became an enduring theme on the show, woven into the program's fabric of entertainment, self-improvement, and social reform. Winfrey's celebrity thus combines with the ideologies of self-improvement and cultural uplift to promote the American ideal of upward transformation. From the Greek word for "image," an *icon* has, as its core, a visual representation, and media images of Winfrey reflect the American ideology of rags-to-riches-and-recognition. For example, in 1997 Winfrey appeared on the cover of *LIFE* magazine. In a smart red suit, she smiles broadly, looking directly at readers, holding an antique leather-bound volume with pages edged in gold. The title announces, "The secret INNER LIFE of America's most powerful woman: OPRAH Between the Covers." Like so many other accounts of Winfrey's life, this one expands the legend of this American icon. The article's title presents the major themes of her Cinderella fairy tale: secrets, intimacy, power, and education.

Turning to the story inside, however, one is confronted with a very different figure from the confident, relaxed, happy, successful adult Winfrey on the cover. Filling the entire left-hand page is a stark black and white kindergarten class photo of Winfrey, grim-faced, staring blankly at the camera. Opposite, against a black background, is a quotation from her interview with *LIFE*. Winfrey's words offer a personal revelation, perhaps the single most distinguishing feature in the creation of this American icon, and the hallmark of *The Oprah Winfrey Show*: "No one ever told me I was loved. Ever, ever, ever. Reading and being able to be a *smart girl* was my only sense of value,

Oprah Winfrey presenting an award during the 76th Annual Academy Awards, February 29, 2004. Courtesy of Photofest.

and it was the only time I felt loved" (Johnson 45). The *LIFE* article illustrates that, in a sense, Oprah is herself a book. Put another way, her life is a carefully crafted story. Her progress narrative is told and retold in popular newspaper and magazine articles, television shows such as Winfrey's *Arts and Entertainment Biography,* and biographies such as Norman King's *Everybody Loves Oprah! Her Remarkable Life Story* and Nellie Bly's *Oprah! Up Close and Down Home.* As Winfrey has gradually revealed her life story on her show and in the popular media, fans have learned, over time, how education and hard work have led to her enormous fame and fortune.

As a poor African American girl growing up in the South during the Civil Rights era, among the obstacles Winfrey faced were her race and gender. Yet, at age 19, she became the youngest person and the first African American woman to anchor the news at Nashville's WTVF-TV. As the first black billionaire in the United States and the first African American woman to join the *Forbes* list of the world's richest people, Oprah represents the possibility of overcoming the double jeopardy of being black and female in a country whose history is plagued by discrimination against both. Winfrey is associated not only with the theme of triumph over adversity, but also with the prevailing concerns in the United States of racial and gender equality. Winfrey's life story is extraordinary, both for the proliferation of obstacles set against her and for her soaring achievement. For some, such a story provokes hope and optimism. At the same time, this American icon, like others, simultaneously incites the opposite reaction. Winfrey may also be seen as a potentially detrimental stereotype of African American women as invulnerable, indefatigable, persevering, and enduring against great odds without negative consequences. The American myth of the tough, strong black woman able to withstand any abuse and conquer any obstacle sets an impossible standard that may lead ordinary women to take on overwhelming responsibilities, to ignore the physical and emotional costs, never seeking or receiving assistance.

Winfrey also represents media imperialism and commercial domination, communicating widely, not only across the United States, but across the globe. She is mistress of all she surveys. Host of the highest-rated talk show in television history, with an estimated 30 million viewers each week in the United States, and broadcast internationally in more than 100 countries, Winfrey also established and now owns its production company, Harpo

["Oprah" spelled backwards] Studios. She is creator of *Dr. Phil,* the successful spin-off of *The Oprah Winfrey Show,* and co-founder of the cable television network Oxygen Media. Winfrey's dominion extends to film, as both actor and producer, with her best-known role as Sofia in Steven Spielberg's 1985 *The Color Purple,* for which she received an Academy Award nomination. As founder and editorial director of *O, The Oprah Magazine,* Winfrey is a major player in print media. According to her Web site, Winfrey's electronic presence is also vast, with Oprah.com averaging 3 million users each month. As the most important celebrity entrepreneur of our time, communicating extensively and marketing her fame in diverse media, Oprah stands for the American regard for the power and influence of the individual.

Herein lies a paradox in the iconography of Oprah Winfrey. On the one hand, her global influence via nearly every available medium is unparalleled. On the other, Winfrey simultaneously represents the ordinary, constructing the impression, highly valued in American culture, of "just folks." Winfrey is at once a larger-than-life celebrity and a regular gal. Anyone who has struggled to lose weight can relate to the Oprah who, in 1988, pulled a little red wagon filled with sixty-seven pounds of fat onto the stage of her talk show and proudly showed off her size-10 Calvin Klein jeans. From the early days of her talk show, Winfrey capitalized on her singular ability to coax ordinary folk to share their own traumas and tribulations—just as Winfrey herself does. Regular folk identify with the Winfrey who proclaimed, "Free speech not only lives, it rocks," after jurors rejected a multimillion-dollar defamation lawsuit by Texas cattlemen, prompted by Winfrey's caution during an episode of her show against the threat of mad cow disease. To critics, the accusation that Winfrey's remarks led to a cattle market plunge that caused $11 million in loses underscores the danger of placing too much power and influence with the individual, who may use that authority irresponsibly. For fans, Winfrey's story is emblematic of the American desire to see the little girl or guy triumph, David-over-Goliath fashion.

Likewise, in 2005, Winfrey reminded the world of the paradox of her celebrity-ordinariness. Thanks to rapid-fire, round-the-world Internet news and Web logs, the story of Oprah snubbed by upscale Paris boutique, Hermes, rose immediately to the status of myth, with multiple contradictory versions quickly circling the globe. The incident draws attention to the fact that Winfrey is not "just folks," attempting to dash into the Hermes shop on Faubourg Saint-Honore, a street lined with famous designer shops frequented by wealthy tourists and the well-to-do. At the same time, the story reminds us of the possibility that any African American may find herself similarly unwelcome in a tony boutique. The Hermes fracas brings to mind early episodes of *The Oprah Winfrey Show,* long before her online Oprah Boutique, with its exclusive Oprah's Book Club Pajamas for $64.00, in which Winfrey tackled the Klu Klux Klan or traveled to Forsyth County, Georgia to ask local citizens why, for more than seventy-five years, they refused to allow a black person to live in the county. Winfrey's studio confirmed a version of the story that suggests a racist motive for barring her entrance: Harpo Productions compared Winfrey's experience to the film *Crash*, which explores racial tolerance in Los Angeles, tracking the heated intersections of a multi-ethnic cast of characters ("Luxury Store..."). Whatever the facts of the Hermes rebuff, anyone who has experienced racial hostility may connect with Winfrey's plight, an ordinary, everyday encounter for many Americans.

By contrast, other versions of the Hermes incident cast Winfrey as an arrogant, wild-spending celebrity diva, rudely insisting on entrance even though Hermes had closed for the evening. While fans may view Oprah as a successful American capitalist, who, through hard work, has earned the privilege to spend without guilt, to critics, Winfrey's yearly "Oprah's Favorite Things" list of high-end products such as $312 hand-painted tea service, or a $465 Burberry quilted jacket, reflects and promotes the message that buying more and more brings happiness. A product endorsement by a celebrity tastemaker of Oprah's status creates demand where no genuine need exists. To critics, such conspicuous consumption leads to global conformity and social alienation. It also has a detrimental effect on the environment and the world's poor.

Essential to Oprah as icon are multiple and contradictory interpretations such as these. To fans, Oprah is a sacred cow. But the very status of icon invites both adoration and satire. Artist Bruce Cegur illustrates both points of view in his digital print of Oprah as religious icon. One image, "The Crucifixion," shows Winfrey as a glowing Aunt Jemima figure hanging on a cross of steer horns. Cegur allows negative but also positive interpretations of the image as a symbol of spiritual power, community leadership, an African American woman's strength and authority. Superimposed over this figure is a wider, glowing female form, which pokes fun at Winfrey's weight-loss struggles. At the same time, Cegur suggests that this image may also represent the struggle faced by black women for respect and recognition. Beneath this figure is one the artist titles "The Last Supper," a stylized version of Leonardo Da Vinci's famous painting, lampooning Oprah, seated center, in the place of Christ, surrounded by Book Club guests and other famous women television talk show hosts. The label above reads, simply, "SYRUP," reminding us that critics view Winfrey as a gifted actor, master of the con, trafficker in base sentimentality and empty psychobabble.

However we interpret Winfrey as icon, she has perhaps influenced American popular culture most by making the personal public, by sharing the private details of her life, and, at the same time, persuading her guests to do likewise. As she has risen in popularity, Winfrey has disclosed more and more details of her life, more and more secrets. These details stress her extraordinary success against daunting barriers, while they emphasize her human frailty. As a result, viewers of *The Oprah Winfrey Show* may feel that Oprah is both television's richest entertainer and also "just like me." A 1986 *Woman's Day* article quotes Winfrey as saying, " 'People out there think I'm their girlfriend; they treat me like that. It's really amazing'" (Tornabene 50). Likewise, popular biographies of Winfrey promulgate her reputation for intimacy. Bly quotes the *Washington Post*'s characterization of Winfrey's distinctive style among talk show hosts: "If Jane Pauley is the prom queen, Oprah Winfrey is the dorm counselor.... People want to hold Barbara Walters' hand. They want to crawl into Winfrey's lap" (52). Readers of Winfrey's biographies know, for example, the "inside" story behind the public story of Winfrey's weight loss battle. They know not only the Winfrey who dragged a load of fat across stage, but also the Winfrey who secretly binged on a package of hotdog buns bathed in syrup. This imagined intimacy is the hallmark of Winfrey's career. On her show, Winfrey enters the personal space of guests, touches them, sustains lingering eye contact, and appears to listen carefully when they speak. Such behaviors establish a sense of sympathy and sociability between Winfrey and her guests and viewers. Viewers invite Winfrey into their homes—their own private spaces—and in return she brings them the private lives, not only of her guests, but also of herself. In short, Winfrey uses intimacy strategically to attract and maintain audience interest and loyalty. Telling a secret about oneself, as Winfrey sometimes does, breeds affection and loyalty because such a revelation both reflects and engenders trust. Not only do viewers feel they can trust Winfrey because of the intimacy she constructs, but they may also feel flattered, in a sense, and therefore closer to her, because she trusts them with the details of her personal life.

In this way, *The Oprah Winfrey Show* challenges notions of what "counts" as evidence in public debates and gives voice to women whose sentiments, interests, and concerns might otherwise go ignored. Winfrey's message of individual empowerment resonates strongly with her mostly female audience. This message is one that led popular culture critic, Steven Stark, to compare Winfrey to Mr. Rogers. While acknowledging that "The mission is to sell us something, which is the goal of all commercial television: 'I buy; therefore, I am' is the theology of most TV," Stark calls Winfrey "another rather old fashioned TV performer when you think about it, who, while not formally trained in religion, has turned her show into a similar kind of uplifting ministry of empowerment, in her case, for women rather than children." While critics deride Winfrey's brand of therapeutic talk TV as treacle, the force of that sensibility is illustrated in the vehement responses to a 2000 article in the *Washington Post*. In the "Style" section, well known for its sardonic wit, staff writer Libby Copland offers a mocking critique of *The Oprah Winfrey Show* in "Our Lady of Perpetual Help: In the Church of Feel-Good Pop Psychology, Spiritual Rebirth Means Starting at O." Indeed, as an American icon, Winfrey has become an image with sacred significance. In this case, Winfrey is depicted as a satirical religious icon, with flowing white robes, a star-topped staff in hand, a twinkling halo about her head. Winfrey is the Goddess of New Age spiritualism, which takes individual empowerment as its central tenet. Surrounding "Our Lady" in monks' robes are four self-help "experts" who once frequented her show: Gary Zukav, Dr. Phil, Suze Ormon, and Iyanla Vanzant appeared regularly to offer strategies for changing one's life for the better.

One week after Copland's "Our Lady" critique of Winfrey, vehement letters defending Winfrey's aim to improve both the lives of individual viewers and the communities in which they live appeared in the Op-Ed section of the *Post*. One fiery response takes Copeland's "sarcastic Oprah-bashing" to task for ignoring Winfrey's good works—and her ability to inspire generosity among viewers: "Your June 26 Style article charges her television show with encouraging self-absorption and simplistic guru-ism but conveniently leaves out a major theme of the Oprah show: charitable giving and volunteerism" (Summers). As Copeland's piece and the responses to it demonstrate—and as the long-time popularity of *The Oprah Winfrey Show* illustrates—there is a significant place for the sensibility Winfrey advocates on her show. She speaks to the desire for hope, optimism, and the power of positive thinking to improve one's life, fundamental values in American culture. Winfrey's optimism, of course, is viewed by some as naïve and self-aggrandizing, but the history and power of its appeal are essential to understanding twenty-first-century American popular culture and Oprah Winfrey as a representative icon.

WORKS CITED AND RECOMMENDED

Bly, Nellie. *Oprah! Up Close and Down Home*. New York: Kensington, 1993.

Cegur, Bruce. "Saint Oprah." Online image. Cegur.com. 1 Aug. 2005 <http://www.cegur.com/html/frameOprah.html>.

Copeland, Libby. "Our Lady of Perpetual Help: In the Church of Feel-Good Pop Psychology, Spiritual Rebirth Means Starting at O." *Washington Post* 26 June 2000, sec. Style: 1.

Johnson, Marilyn. "Oprah Winfrey: A Life in Books." *LIFE* Sept. 1997: 45–60.

King, Norman. *Everybody Loves Oprah! Her Remarkable Life Story*. New York: William Morrow, 1987.

"Luxury Store Apologizes to Oprah." CNN.com. 22 June 2005. 1 Aug. 2005 <http://www.cnn.com/2005/SHOWBIZ/TV/06/22/oprah.apology/>.

"Oprah Winfrey." *Arts & Entertainment Biography*. A&E. Boston. 23 Mar. 2000.

Stark, Steven D. "Mister Rogers." *Weekend Edition—Sunday*. National Public Radio. WUOL, Louisville. 26 Nov. 2000.

Summers, Kathleen. "Giving and Passing It On." *Washington Post* 1 July 2000. Style Op-Ed: A23.

Tornabene, Lyn. "Here's Oprah." *Woman's Day* 1 Oct. 1986: 50.

Witch

Linda Badley

The "evil" witch flying on her broomstick, black cat in tow, is as important to the American observance of Halloween as the turkey is to Thanksgiving. In Disney's "Golden Book" versions of classic European folktales, in Disney's *Snow White* (1937), and in *The Wizard of Oz* (1939), she often upstaged the adolescent heroine—gloating over her cauldron, proffering poisoned apples, or cackling and swooping down on her victims. But by the 1960s, in the popular television sitcom *Bewitched* (1964–1972), the witch, Samantha, starred in her own suburban fairy tale, and by the 1990s her nemesis the "wicked witch" stereotype was politically incorrect or at best an anachronism. The Harry Potter phenomenon (1997–present) made witchcraft a metaphor for the sense of agency and power that comes with adolescence. So did television dramas such as WB's *Charmed* (1998–), whose sisterly heroines cast spells to wage war on evil, and ABC's sitcom *Sabrina the Teenage Witch* (1996–2003), in which the plucky heroine's talking feline familiar, played by a sardonic animatronics puppet, is named Salem. At the same time, paradoxically, the witch had become scarier than ever to one growing segment of the American population: the Christian fundamentalist right, for whom Harry Potter, Sabrina and, for that matter, Halloween alluded to or even consisted of a dangerous pagan, hence "Satanic," ritual.

The key term in this controversy, of course, is provided by Sabrina's Salem. Stereotypical images of the witch are often coupled with what Elizabeth Reis calls "one of America's most shameful and tragic moments: the large-scale accusation and execution of 'witches' during the 1692 Salem witch trials" (xi). Even if Perry Miller had asserted in 1953, in his influential study, that the witchcraft episode was a blip on the screen of colonial history (191) as subsequent scholarship and popular culture have revealed, Salem's witches would not have not gone away. Possibly the "single most intensively studied event in colonial North American history," according to Bernard Rosenthal, Salem haunts discussion of the Puritan origins of American identity, has shaped our image of persecution, and has "found a city to contain its symbol" (213). The trials took place in what is now Danvers, and many accused and accusers were from elsewhere, but the modern city of Salem, Massachusetts, claims the namesake: the witch on a broomstick is on police badges, traffic signs, tourist brochures, and the masthead of the *Salem News*. The debate represented by the episode, moreover, continues. On Essex Street one finds the Essex Institute, which houses a great range of documents pertaining to the witch trials; directly across is Crow Haven Corner, the store of Laurie Cabot, the "Official Witch of Salem" (as proclaimed in 1977 by then-Governor Michael Dukakis) and founder of the Witches' League for Public Awareness. Cabot sells an alternative story about a coven of real witches punished for practicing an innocuous religion (Rosenthal 205).

Outside of Salem, the world associates "witch city" with the superstition, ignorance, and persecution that enlightened modern people have largely superseded. No image demonstrates this association so dramatically as the confusion of Salem, where the condemned were hanged, with the contemporary neopagan/feminist myth of the "Burning Times," in which the European witch-hunts of the mid-fifteenth to the early eighteenth century are imagined as a Holocaust in which 9 million witches were burned at the stake (historians' numbers range from a few thousand to 200,000 or more [Guiley 39]).

"Salem" has become singularly mythic and highly politicized. Occurring just as the enlightenment was beginning to be felt, it was the last, the longest (from January 1692 through early May 1693), and the largest of the New England witch hunts, with 141 accused and over 50 accusers (Guiley 288–96). That most of the accused were women was not unusual, but the fact that most of their accusers were also females, most of them claiming to be "afflicted" or possessed and many of them children and servants, was. Once spent, the hysteria came to confirm an image of the original American character as "Puritan" in the most stereotypical and negative of senses, supporting the myth of founding fathers convinced of their "election"—unilateral and indomitable in a quest to seek out, name, and destroy "evil." In the 1996 film adaptation of Arthur Miller's *The Crucible*, Judge Danforth (Paul Scofield) frames the issue:

Title page of *The Wonders of the Invisible World: Being an Account of the Tryals of Several Witches, Lately Executed in New-England...* by Cotton Mather, 1693. Courtesy of the Library of Congress.

> You must understand, sir, a person is either with this Court or against it; there
> be no road between. . . . This is a new time, a precise time; we live no longer in
> the dusky afternoon when evil mixed itself with good and befuddled the world.
> Now, by God's grace, the good folk and the evil entirely separate!

Here Danforth stands for the Puritan dream of a New Eden without the moral ambiguity of the Old World past. "Puritan" in this sense also came to mean patriarchal: the old Eve and the first witch—the first person accused of consorting with the devil—clearly had no place in this new world.

As the hysteria subsided in the fall of 1693, the Salem trials were distinguished once again by being almost immediately recanted and confessed as a sin to be expiated. On January 14, 1697, an Official Day of Humiliation was called for public apology and fasting; in 1711, authorizing restitution to victims and families, Massachusetts Bay became one of the first governments to compensate victims of its mistakes (Guiley 296). The Salem witch thus came to represent white male guilt and reparation, merging with an American Gothic literature of gloomy self-examination and confession—one haunted by the conviction that America is doomed to repeat this particular folly. From Nathaniel Hawthorne's *The Scarlet Letter* (1851) and *The House of the Seven Gables* (1851) to Arthur Miller's *The Crucible* (1953), we find the accused "witch" configured as the fallen woman and martyr victimized by the Puritan minister or judge. In "The Custom House" prologue, Hawthorne confesses that he is haunted by the "persecuting" figures of his first ancestors including Salem Judge John Hathorne,

> who made himself so conspicuous in the martyrdom of the witches that their
> blood may fairly be said to have left a stain upon him. . . . As their representa-
> tive, I take shame upon my self for their sakes and pray that any curse . . . may
> be now and henceforth removed. (8–9)

In making *The Scarlet Letter*'s Hester Prynne one of the central tragic heroines of American literature and forcing the Reverend Dimmesdale to confess his adultery and hypocrisy, Hawthorne is thought to have attempted to right the balance. His "Young Goodman Brown" (1835) is even more instructive: once Brown ventures into the woods and discovers (or dreams) a witches' meeting in which his innocent wife Faith is inducted into the devil's tribe, he becomes incapable of seeing anyone other than witches.

This association of witchcraft with hypocrisy, paranoia, and guilt returned in the 1950s with *The Crucible* (1953), in which Arthur Miller discovered in the story of Salem the seeds of the McCarthyite panic over Communist subversion. In exploring American susceptibility to community hysteria, the play brought out issues of gender and sexuality that feminists would later seize on. In Miller's account, the accusations spark from an affair between teenager Abigail Williams, Salem's Reverend Parris's niece, whose age is raised from 11 to 17, and a John Proctor much younger than his actual

61 years. The conflict between the Puritan patriarchy and unleashed adolescent female sexuality charged this already politically volatile courtroom drama. When the wife of the Putnam family, Reverend Parris's strongest supporter, accuses the sage Rebecca Nurse of murdering her unborn children, the theme of the witch as maligned healer and midwife, soon to be taken up by neopagans and feminists, was given a stage.

The next decades produced two counter-cultural movements whose contemporary importance cannot be overestimated. The first was the neopagan religious movement Wicca, or modern witchcraft, founded by Gerald Gardner in the 1950s in the United Kingdom, in which worship of nature, as figured in the goddess and the horned god her consort, was central. The other was the second-wave feminist movement, in which the witch had become highly politicized. Beginning in 1968 with the WITCH movement (Women's International Terrorist Conspiracy from Hell) led by Robin Morgan, and as traced by Morgan and Diane Purkiss, feminists claimed solidarity with the persecuted witches of the "Burning Times." A radical-left political movement with a hip Marxist spin, WITCH employed the stereotype for its shock value and performative potential. It also drew feminist attention to the history of the witch. According to Barbara Ehrenreich and Dierdre English, the witch craze was influenced by the rising male medical profession's desire to eliminate midwives and assume control of women's bodies. In *Gyn/Ecology*

Agnes Moorehead dressed as a traditional witch. She played Endora on the television series *Bewitched*. Courtesy of the Library of Congress.

(1979), Mary Daly claimed that the dead witches of the "Burning Times" were victims of "gynocide" and a male design to cleanse the world of Hags analogous (if not equivalent) to the Holocaust's elimination of Jews. In *Beyond God the Father* (1985), Daly asserted that feminism and Christianity could never be reconciled, and the witch became the priestess of a prehistorical religion eradicated by Judeo-Christian patriarchy. (For relevant commentary, see Purkiss, *The Witch in History*, 7–28.)

The witch soon became central to empowering myths within feminist literature and criticism—for example, the female Gothic tradition celebrated by Ellen Moers, and Sandra Gilbert and Susan Gubar's *The Madwoman in the Attic* (1979) and represented in the poetry of Anne Sexton and Sylvia Plath. Plath's suicide poems "Lady Lazarus" and "Daddy" fuse the Burning Times myth with Holocaust imagery to read like self-empowering curses. (See Showalter, *Sister's Choice*, 127–44.) As

American feminism absorbed the French feminism of Hélène Cixous's unruly, laughing Medusa and the hysteric/sorceress of *The Newly Born Woman* (Cixous and Catherine Clément, 1979), Carol F. Karlsen in *The Devil in the Shape of a Woman* (1987) and others argued that the "witches" of New England were "unruly" tongued women dissatisfied with their roles.

By the late 1960s, second wave feminism's view of Salem as a battle of the sexes led, however indirectly, to three horror blockbusters. In the films *Rosemary's Baby* (1968), *The Exorcist* (1972), and *Carrie* (1976), female biology—specifically pregnancy and childbirth, female puberty, and menstruation—was imbued with the terror and power associated with possession and witchcraft. Protagonists Rosemary, Regan, and Carrie are demon-possessed in some sense, or literally carry the devil's spawn. They are also victims and, ultimately, heroines of a profoundly ambivalent sort. As Stephen King has admitted, his 1974 novel *Carrie* was "about how women find their own channels of power, and what men fear about women and women's sexuality.... [W]riting the book in 1973..., I was fully aware of what Women's Liberation implied for me and others of my sex" (170). The film, like the book, intimated that women inculcated under Judeo-Christian monotheism and patriarchal misogyny (however handed down by their mothers, for example *Carrie*'s fanatically religious Mrs. White) in turn became avenging witches.

Finally, as the female action film emerged in the 1980s and 1990s, with the *Alien* films (1979–1997), *The Silence of the Lambs* (1991) and *Terminator 2* (1991), the witch evolved from the second-wave-feminist victim-monster-heroine to the unqualified heroine and the outspoken pro-woman woman—the bitch. Celebrating Halloween, *Ms. Magazine* editor Marcia Gillespie announced in October 1999, "I want to affirm the witch in me," and criticized past stereotypes:

> A woman was denounced as a witch if she didn't mind her mouth, her dress, her attitude.... Witches were said to ... kill babies, enjoy sex too much or too little, steal men's potency and their power. They were spoilers, troublemakers—unnatural.... No need for pointed hats or brooms or black cats. All you need ... do is be a feminist.

Affirming the witch meant reenvisioning the crone as an image of female power and creativity and the third aspect of the nature goddess, a primary icon in feminist spirituality and ecofeminism.

Once signifying a Satanic conspiracy, in popular film and television of the 1990s the coven bond, Wiccan circle, and the craft became metaphors for feminist sisterhood, lesbian feminism, and separatism. The title characters of *The Witches of Eastwick* (1987) effectively contain the devil (Jack Nicholson) and establish a matriarchy. In *Carrie 2: The Rage* (1998), Rachel is in love with her best friend, and her telepathic powers emerge as lesbian feminist rage over her friend's date rape and suicide. A goth turned riot grrrl, she emerges as a Cixousian hysteric/sorceress who avenges what men have done to women. Young witches discovered and perfected their crafts on primetime television, in *Sabrina, Charmed*, and *Buffy the Vampire Slayer*. In the latter show's fourth season, Willow, Buffy's brainy best friend and the cyberwitch of the team of slayers, explored her powers through a sexual relationship with Tara that culminated in orgasmic, object-moving spells and declarations of love. Despite occasional dates and boyfriends, even Sabrina's aunts were configured as lesbian parents (Projansky and Vande Berg 4).

If it was hip to be an outsider, it was cooler to be a witch. Hollywood films such as *The Witches of Eastwick, Practical Magic* (1996), and *The Craft* (1996) featured A-list actresses such as Michelle Pfeiffer, Susan Sarandon, Nicole Kidman, Sandra Bullock, and Neve Campbell as witches. In the Harry Potter mythos, which has been assimilated by American culture, the "craft" taught at the Hogwarts School for Witchcraft and Wizardry is genderless; boys and girls alike carry wands and ride broomsticks. As in *Buffy the Vampire Slayer*, the witch became another version of "the chosen one," the child burdened and blessed with special powers against evil. Thus integrated into the canon by way of feminism, as Purkiss concludes her study of *The Witch in History*, the witch was "no longer" frightening: she was "clean, pretty, an herbalist with a . . . career in midwifery, a feminist, sexy but nothing too kinky" (282). She had become the postfeminist, the witch contained, domesticated, and almost universally white. *Buffy* comments on this fact in "Hush," a February 2000 episode in which Willow complains that her campus Wiccan group is "Talk, all talk. Blah, blah, Gaia. Blah, blah, moon.

Susan Sarandon as Jane Spofford, Cher as Alexandra Medford, and Michelle Pfeiffer as Sukie Ridgemont in *The Witches of Eastwick*, 1987. Courtesy of Photofest.

Menstrual life-force thingy. . . . Bunch of wanna blessed be's. Nowadays every girl with a henna tattoo and a spice rack thinks she's a sister with the dark ones."

The "good" (white, liberal, Wiccan) witch, however, frightened those on the religious right, to whom she (and, increasingly, he) represented a growing threat to monotheistic orthodoxy and the patriarchal family. Besides breaking sales records and thrilling reading teachers, the Harry Potter books alarmed fundamentalist Christians. A Web site devoted to *Exposing Satanism* called the Potter books "Satan's way to undermine the family" and a move to infiltrate schools and indoctrinate children, "the oldest marketing scheme there is" ("Harry Potter").

Such "spiritual"—or sectarian, political, or gender-related—anxieties, that found a focus in witch-themed popular culture, were played on by the indie horror blockbuster *The Blair Witch Project* (1999). Oddly enough, and however briefly, at the height of the "enlightened" Buffy, Sabrina, and Harry Potter era, the Blair Witch marked the surprise return of the "evil" witch. Besides unexpectedly filling theaters and provoking literal nausea in audiences, the experimental pseudo-documentary "fragment," together with its bewildering layers of mock-documentation and Internet discussion, caused hundreds of teenagers to invade the town of Burkettsville, Maryland (population 214), in search of the film's titular character.

The Blair witch was a version of the Salem witch in another sense as well, as the victim who haunts a community and avenges her persecution over succeeding generations. In the Sci-Fi Channel mockumentary *Curse of the Blair Witch* (1999), the Salem witch trials were dramatized in a clip in which Puritan women shout at one Elizabeth Sewell, "Burn the witch!" The Project itself centered on the local legends surrounding Elly Kedward, an old woman accused in 1785 of using pins to bleed children and subsequently tried, convicted, and banished to the forest, where she is presumed to have died. The following winter, all her accusers and more than half the town's children disappear, and the township of Blair vanishes. In subsequent incidents, recurring in fifty-year cycles, an "old woman" is responsible for the deaths of numerous children and men. This legend of the hag who devours men and makes children disappear is repeated, moreover, in the feature story of protagonist Heather Donohue's ill-fated film project. Finally, there is an unstated connection between feminism, through women who use technology, and witchcraft that the film draws on for character delineation and gender-based conflict. Thus *Village Voice*'s J. Hoberman notes the movie leaves "the sly suggestion that the project's real witch might be the driven director, Heather" (see also Badley).

In *The Blair Witch Project*, the evil witch stereotype that feminists had long viewed as a patriarchal plot seemed to win the power struggle. Might not her return have signaled a backlash, a reversion to monotheism and repression of the feminine? In 1999, with its spate of supernatural thrillers (*The Haunting, The Sixth Sense, Stigmata, Stir of Echoes*) such a conclusion seemed more than plausible. Even so, Harry Potter ruled among the preteen crowd, and on teen-targeted television, *Sabrina*, *Charmed*, and *Buffy* still held sway. Indeed, by *Buffy*'s sixth and final seasons (2002–2003), most of the Scooby Gang and all of *Buffy*'s demonic antagonists practiced some sort of witchcraft or otherwise wielded special powers. In that season, the self-proclaimed magic "junkie" Willow abstained—until her lover Tara was killed in an episode entitled "Seeing Red"; then Willow's vengeance very nearly ended the world, until all was saved, however temporarily, by love, camaraderie, and a final episode in which individual power was given over to all the "chosen"—for example, the show's fans.

Presently, well into the twenty-first century and engulfed by conservatism—a conservatism that the TV series–to-movie remake *du jour*, *Bewitched* (2005), only confirms—the millennial hysteria seems to have abated. After their 2003 season, *Sabrina* and *Buffy* retired—amid warnings, however, from Christian media personality Steve Wohlberg that "Wicca Witchcraft is one of the fastest-growing religions with teenagers in America" ("Hour of the Witch"). As for the next witch craze, it should only be a matter of time. The sinister spirits of Salem lie within contemporary American Puritanism, and the "wicked" witch will return.

WORKS CITED AND RECOMMENDED

Badley, Linda C. "Spiritual Warfare: Postfeminism and the Cultural Politics of the *Blair Witch* Craze." *Intensities: A Journal of Cult Media* 3 (Spring 2003) <http://www.cult-media.com>. Portions of the entry "Witch" were first published in this article, and appear here with the kind permission of the editor of *Intensities: A Journal of Cult Media*.

Clément, Catherine, and Hélène Cixous. *The Newly Born Woman*. Trans. Betsy Wing. Minneapolis: U of Minnesota P, 1986.

Gillespie, Marcia Ann. "I Feel Witchy." Editorial. *Ms. Magazine* 9.16 (Oct.–Nov. 1999): 1.

Guiley, Rosemary Ellen. *The Encyclopedia of Witches and Witchcraft*. 2nd ed. New York: Checkmark Books, 1999.

"Harry Potter: A New Twist to Witchcraft!" *Exposing Satanism* 1 July 2000. 2 June 2005 <http://www.exposingsatanism.org/harrypotter.htm>.

Hawthorne, Nathaniel. "The Custom-House." *The Scarlet Letter*. Ed. Seymour Gross et al. 3rd ed. New York: Norton, 1988. 4–34.

Hoberman, J. "Creaming & Kicking." Rev. of *The Blair Witch Project*. *The Village Voice* 14–20 July 1999. 19 Mar. 2005 <http://www.villagevoice.com/issues/9928/hoberman.shtml>.

"Hour of the Witch to Precede the Next Potter." *Prudent Press Agency: Media Megaphone for the Little Guy*. 10 June 2005 <https://www.Prudentpress agency.Com/CENTER/articlePreview.Php?Article-id=2141>.

Karlsen, Carol F. *Devil in the Shape of a Woman: Witchcraft in Colonial New England*. New York: W. W. Norton, 1987.

King, Stephen. *Danse Macabre*. New York: Everest, 1981.

Miller, Perry. *The New England Mind: From Colony to Province*. 1953. Boston: Beacon, 1966.

Projansky, Sarah, and Leah R. Vande Berg. "Sabrina, the Teenage . . . ? Girls, Witches, Mortals, and the Limitations of Prime-Time Feminism." *Fantasy Girls: Gender in the New Universe of Science Fiction and Fantasy Television*. Ed. Elyce Rae Helford. New York: Rowman & Littlefield, 2000. 13–40.

Purkiss, Diane. *The Witch in History: Early Modern and Twentieth-Century Representations*. New York: Routledge, 1996.

Reis, Elizabeth. "Introduction." *Spellbound: Women and Witchcraft in America*. Ed. Elizabeth Reis. Wilmington, DE: Scholarly Resources, 1998.

Rosenthal, Bernard. *Salem Story*. Cambridge: Cambridge UP, 1995.

Showalter, Elaine. *Sister's Choice: Tradition and Change in American Women's Writing*. Oxford: Clarendon, 1991.

Upham, Charles W. "Witchcraft at Salem." From Part 3 of *Salem Witchcraft*. Boston, 1867. Rpt. in *The Salem Witch Trials Reader*. Ed. Frances Hill. New York: Da Capo, 2000. 227–28.

Tiger Woods

Michael K. Schoenecke

On Sunday afternoons at professional golf tournaments, Eldrick Tont "Tiger" Woods, dressed in his lucky colors—black pants and a red Nike shirt, a lucky color in Thai culture—and a baseball cap, seems hypnotized as he walks purposefully to the first tee. His cold-steel eyes indicate that he is on a mission: win the golf tournament. Woods's focus is so intent that he rarely acknowledges the cheering fans until he is introduced; bodyguard and caddy Steve Williams's eyes suggest that he will pinch off the head of anyone who approaches or attempts to touch Tiger. Once on the tee and after his introduction, Woods flashes his trademark smile and mechanically prepares to hit his first shot of the day. Even when his swing was more blocked than a Stetson, crowds roared approval and admiration for Woods's soaring drives, while competitors feared them. Since he turned pro in 1997, Woods has symbolized the historical changes that have been influencing golf since the 1930s; his appearance on the Professional Golf Association (PGA) Tour has had a major wallop on the game of golf as well as gained him international acclaim. His megacelebrity is earned. Tiger Woods, however, is an enigmatic icon, shaped for success and also contradiction by his father and the media.

Eldrick Woods seemed destined for greatness from birth; he was born on December 30, 1975, in Orange County, California, to Earl and Tida Woods. His mother created the name Eldrick by using letters from his parents' first names. That same year Lee Elder became the first black golfer to play in the Masters in Augusta, Georgia. His father selected the unusual nickname "Tiger" to distinguish his son from everyone else; later, this moniker has come to suggest a golfer who prowls the world's fairways and greens using his clubs like claws, and pounces on his prey, a trophy, at tournament's end. Tiger was also named after Colonel Phong, a Vietnamese officer with whom Earl served, called "Tiger" because he was a relentless and decorated soldier.

Earl and Tida Woods early introduced their son to golf and to the media. When Tiger was two, his mother called Jim Hill, a local California television sportscaster, and invited him to watch Tiger play golf. Tiger endeared himself to Hill and audiences; in his tiny voice and childish speech he explained that he was good at golf because of "pwactice." In 1978 Tiger appeared on the syndicated *Mike Douglas Show* along with Bob Hope and James Stewart. Following his introduction, Tiger, toting a little golf bag made by his mother, trotted onto the stage and drove a ball into the back of the studio. After Douglas suggested that Tiger and Hope have a putting contest, Hope strode next to Tiger and asked, "You got any money?" The audience's and guests' laughter increased when Tiger picked up his own ball and moved it closer to the hole.

A few years later, Tiger appeared on ABC's *That's Incredible*, co-hosted by Fran Tarkenton; after demonstrating his golfing prowess, Tiger sidled up to Tarkenton and declared: "When I get big I'm going to beat Jack Nicklaus and Tom Watson." Again, his voice and his smile endeared him to audiences. Unbeknownst to the television audience, however, Tiger concisely and precisely identified his golfing goals, and they have not changed: to win more major tournaments—the Masters, U.S. Open, Open Championship (British), and Professional Golf Association Championship—than Nicklaus. As of June 2005, Nicklaus' record stands at eighteen and Woods has won nine.

When Tiger was 6, his father doggedly began to make him more competitive and to hone him for tournament golf. Tiger listened to audiotapes that contained subliminal messages such as "My Will Moves Mountains!" To prepare him for potential course distractions, Earl Woods abruptly dropped golf bags and played loud music when Tiger was swinging. Like his hero Jack Nicklaus, Tiger became a mature, focused, and serious-minded golfer; and both enjoyed early success in junior golf. Woods won the Optimist International Junior World championship's under-10 category when he was 8; he won again at ages 9, 12, and 13. Winning his first tournament, he has recounted, is still his most memorable golfing moment because he earned his first taste of victory.

Success on golf courses, as with life itself, comes from hard work and its rewards, which breed confidence. As a junior golfer, Woods won the U.S. Junior Amateur Championship in 1991, 1992, and 1993. After the 1992 championship, he acknowledged the extreme stress of the tournament; the 16-year-old, who had already experienced death threats because of his ethnicity, burst into tears: "You can't believe just how much tension there is out there," he said. "I'm so glad that it's over" ("You Can't Believe the Pressure"). In the final round of the Phoenix Open in February 1999, a man who had been aggressively heckling Tiger was wrestled to the ground by security, who discovered that he was carrying a gun; the man was arrested and later released. By not discussing his personal life or the death threats with the media, Woods kept his attention on his job, playing golf. His father hired Dr. Brunza, a psychologist, to train him to eliminate all distractions—on and off course—and enter into a trance-like state when on the golf course. As a result, when Woods plays in a tournament, he passes through crowds of people, including his mother, without apparently realizing their presence. This unique ability to focus on and visualize each shot and then to execute the shot has provided Woods with the confidence to perform at a superior level. Woods's mental strength was intentionally crafted to imitate that of Jack Nicklaus and Ben Hogan.

In 1994, 1995, and 1996, Woods stunned the amateur golfing ranks by winning the U.S. Amateur Championships. This young golf phenom hid his

face as he wept in 1994. He had joined the ranks of Bobby Jones, Arnold Palmer, and Jack Nicklaus; he broke Nicklaus's record by being the youngest player to win the Havemeyer Trophy; more importantly to some, including his father, he was the first person of color to win. He received congratulatory letters from President Clinton and Philip H. Knight, founder of Nike, who would later sign Tiger to lucrative endorsement contracts. Having won all the major amateur championships, Tiger turned professional; however, he quit Stanford University without winning a

Tiger Woods, 1999. Courtesy of Photofest.

NCAA team championship. His teammates heard on the news that Tiger, always shy and never close to anyone but his father, would not return to Stanford.

When Tiger turned pro on August 27, 1996, he played the Milwaukee Open. Before he hit a shot as a professional, his endorsement offers and contracts paled his future golf winnings. Titleist signed Tiger for $20 million to play its golf balls and clubs, wear its gloves, and carry its bag; Nike, Inc., known for their clever marketing and signing of appealing sports stars such as Michael Jordan, offered Woods $40 million to wear and endorse their clothing and shoes. Prior to Tiger's contracts, Greg Norman had the richest golf contract at $2.5 million a year with Reebok. Although some sports businesses thought that Nike had paid too much to sign Tiger, he helped double their sales by 1997 when he won the Masters and established a record of 270 for the tournament. International Management Group (IMG), known for creating the model of marketing sports stars such as Arnold Palmer and Jack Nicklaus, courted Woods for years. As early as July 31, 1996, IMG purchased a $475,000 house in Isleworth, Florida; this gated community provides Woods with easy access to Mark O'Meara, a close friend, as well as solitude and a sense of normality. In 2001 Woods built a $2.5 million home in Isleworth and gave his first home to his father. By moving to Florida, Tiger escaped California's high state income tax and still had a location with a good golfing climate. Woods is the highest-paid sports figure in the world. In 2004, he earned better than $90 million from prize money and endorsements.

Tiger Woods, with the possible exceptions of Muhammad Ali and Michael Jordan, is the most recognizable sports figure in the world. Unlike previously adored and canonized golf heroes such as Bobby Jones, Byron Nelson, Ben Hogan, Arnold Palmer, and Jack Nicklaus, Tiger's ethnic background includes Chinese, Caucasian, Thai, and African. This racial palette became significant in Woods's career because the media and businesses marketed him as a racial everyman. Most golfers, commentators, and fans have enthusiastically embraced and welcomed Woods to the professional game, where few people of color are generally seen among the galleries. Although Arnie's Army's roar was aurally distinct, Woods' raucous fans celebrate his "un-WASP-like" approach to the game. His famous fist-pumping when he holes a putt visually suggests showmanship and aggressiveness, particularly when it is directed at a fellow competitor; the fist-pumping also diminishes golf's "gentlemanly" tradition. Nevertheless, Woods has played himself into the hearts and minds of young, middle-class white males as well as women who relish Woods' on-course brashness.

A tiger conjures up images of strength and daring; Tiger plays golf that way. Although he generally swings a club at 125–135 miles per hour, at the 1997 Masters, he swung his driver at 180 miles per hour on the first tee; the average golfer swings between 75–90 miles per hour, and the average professional male golfer between 110–125 miles per hour. In 2005, Tiger's drives average better than 305 yards, which are 20 yards longer than the average tour player's. Possessing the short game of a locksmith, along with imagination and the skill to execute shots from what seem to be impossible lies and locations, Tiger saves par and thrills his galleries.

Long, towering drives combined with an expert marksmanship from his short irons make Woods an exciting, dominating, and intimidating figure on the golf course—but not a predictable one. At times, Tiger crushes his opponents—competitors and the golf course. In June 2000, the 100th U.S. Open was held at Pebble Beach Golf Links, a course Tiger considers the best American golf course. The world saw Tiger at his best at Pebble—and his worst. He demolished the field; he had a ten-stroke lead at the end of three rounds and won by fifteen strokes, the largest margin of victory in the history of the majors. He did not miss a putt under six feet; he excelled with his short game. However, even though his father and Dr. Brunza had trained Tiger to maintain focus on the golf course, he can be as foulmouthed and as petulant as a child. On Saturday at the eighteenth tee, Woods hit his ball into the Pacific and called himself a "fucking prick." The microphones on the tee broadcast the words live to the television public, while the camera captured an angry, tantrum-driven Woods slamming his driver into the ground in frustration. Although some critics claimed that he was merely demonstrating that he cares about his game, others argued that Woods lacked the class of Jack Nicklaus as well as professionalism and respect for the game.

Woods's bad temper has created instances where he violates the codes and traditions of the game he loves. At the ninth hole of the 2005 U.S. Open at Pinehurst number 2, Woods three-putted when he missed a nine-foot par putt; reacting in anger and frustration, he raked the green with his putter and created a swathe of approximately three feet; even Johnny Miller, NBC's golf color commentator, was dismayed by Woods' behavior. By intentionally damaging and not repairing the green, Woods clearly showed disrespect for the game and his fellow competitors. If they have a similar putt, they cannot repair the "raised grass." Whereas Woods' supporters are attracted to his passion for the game, sometimes his fervor and behavior become destructive to it. Still, he is distinctive because the fans do not know how he will respond to bad luck. The media, too, capture and heighten the drama of Tiger the entertainer's improbable recovery shots and his spontaneous excitement.

Woods's approach has influenced the golf world in a big way. Since Woods turned professional, he has unleashed a tidal wave of more than $1.5 billion washing over the golf world. Ticket sales shot up, TV ratings jumped, interest in the game increased, and the spirits of tournament directors soared as they anticipated a spillover boom to events in which Woods does not play. People who don't play golf are paying attention to the sport. At the 1997 PGA Championship, a college-age spectator wearing a Columbia University shirt asked: "I'm in a pool. Can you tell me the names of four players beside Tiger I should pick?" Golf galleries have changed; when Tiger plays in televised tournaments, ratings go up significantly. Dede Patterson, tournament director of the Buick Classic in suburban New York, where advance sales are sometimes up as much as 35 percent when Tiger plays, said, "Tiger introduced golf to a new audience." Many of the young people who want to be like Tiger, however, have been and remain unable to pay green fees or purchase golf equipment.

Prior to Woods' arrival on the PGA tour, many critics complained that the golfers were indistinguishable either by their dress or their play. The game needed someone exciting. Woods's attire reflects his personality, and he ranks among the most fashionable tour players, along with Sergio Garcia, Jesper Parnevik, and Ian Poulter. Although he has not distanced himself sartorially as much as he has on the scorecard, he has turned the fairways into runways. His hand-sewn pants have knife-edge creases; a snow white, neatly folded golf glove hangs from his rear pocket. He wears black Nike golf shoes with the Nike swoosh on the outside of each heel. His mock turtlenecks are reminiscent of the restrained, elegant, gentlemanly pursuit golf was back in the 1920s and 1930s when male golfers wore knickers, dress shirts, and ties. In fact, country clubs, municipal and resort courses, which required collars on all shirts, now allow golfers to play in mock turtle necks; business professionals often slip on these same turtlenecks rather than the traditional shirt and tie when going to work or to church. Woods plays the game sublimely in his work uniform, and he looks every part the winner at the end of a tournament.

Just as his name, clothing, and tiger club-head cover are distinctive, so are his sense of style and his physique. Golf does not demand athleticism, but Tiger, at six feet two inches and 190 pounds, is an athlete of classical proportions. His upper body is V-shaped; lifting weights and swinging clubs have built his arms to Popeye-like proportions. Even in high school he would get up around 5:00 A.M. to work out at the gym for one hour before going to the practice tee and green and then to school. As a professional, Woods cuts a fine, distinctive figure that differentiates him from and intimidates his PGA competitors; prior to his arrival on the tour, the majority of golfers did not lift weights or hone stonelike bodies. However, once they noticed he had been developing, shaping, and strengthening his physique, the PGA professionals started visiting the tour's training facilities or jogging before or after a round of golf. Physical conditioning has also caught on with public school and collegiate golf programs.

Because Woods has been followed by the media like a star athlete, his personal life has provided fans with glamor, romance, and also suspense. Although Woods had several woman companions in high school and college, golf and his father did not allow him to develop potential marital relationships. In 2001 Jesper Parnevik and his wife and their children traveled on the PGA tour; the family brought an entourage of eight helpers that included a 21-year-old nanny named Elin Nordegren. She had previously worked as a model—once she posed for swimwear photographs—and spoke perfect English. Tiger and Elin met at the Open Championship at Royal Lytham and St. Annes. When he asked her for a date, she did not accept immediately. Later, they lived together for several years, and in 2005 they married. Golfers such as Jack Nicklaus claim that marriage can detract from one's performance on the course, because the golfers prefer to be at home with their families rather than pounding balls on practice ranges thousands of miles away. As a result, while home fires and desires burn brightly, competitive fires slowly become glowing coals.

Tiger Woods's golfing achievements are remarkable and unparalleled. In 1999 he founded the Tiger Woods Foundation, with World Challenge as one of the principal fundraisers. A small field of tour players attends, plays a tournament, and conducts clinics. The foundation and tournament present Woods as a philanthropist; when he turned professional he said he would help the young and the disadvantaged. Woods gives about twenty to twenty-five days a year of his time to his foundation, but very little of his own money. He does donate his potential winnings from the World Challenge; if he wins, he would give approximately $600,000, which is approximately 5 percent of his total income.

Woods's insistence on his individuality has distanced him from minority politics. In his appearance on *The Oprah Winfrey Show* in 1997, after he had won the Masters and gained celebrity status, Oprah asked him if it bothered him to be called African American, and he replied that it did. He indicated that as a child he coined the term "Cablinasian," which combines the words Caucasian, black, and Asian. Woods angered many black viewers when he thus deemphasized their ethnic heritage. Fairly or not, Woods's disinterest in minority identification has been blamed for his failure to encourage more active minority participation in golf. Although he has expanded interest in it, the game is expensive; and no program has afforded poor children the means and equipment to play. Moreover, as a minority role model, Woods is questionable. There are fewer black players on tour now than in the 1970s when Lee Elder, Charlie Sifford, and Calvin Peete played. In fact, because Woods says he is not black, there are none.

Woods is exciting and invigorating as a golfer. He seldom speaks to his fans, and certainly, with good reason, does not like to be touched by them. With his fame, money, good looks, media attention, and beautiful wife, Woods seems to have achieved the American Dream. He did it, too, with hard work; he has earned his riches. If the ancient Greeks had played golf rather than wrestling and running, the classical athlete in stone statues might resemble Woods. When he arrives at the first tee, he is picture-perfect. When he hits the ball, the gallery hears the loud crack and can watch the ball sail for better than 300 yards; he then gives his driver to Steve Williams, and they walk down the fairway. Thousands of fans stumble along to catch a glimpse of him or to overhear him talk with Williams. As they do, they are caught up in curiosity and suspense about the man whose talent, style, and personality have not only triumphed in a tradition-laden game but also cast its future into uncertainty. For the "racial everyman" success story with which Woods and the media gave democratic popularity to golf has its contradiction in Woods's aloof individualism and lack of social outreach. Although Woods formed his strategies on models of earlier golfers, he also broke conventions they upheld of restraint and respect; so the game's balance of sociability and competition has a doubtful future. Much depends upon Woods himself, in possibilities suggesting the power of an enigmatic, complex icon.

WORKS CITED AND RECOMMENDED

Callahan, Tom. *In Search of Tiger*. New York: Crown, 2003.

Collins, David R. *Tiger Woods: Golfing Champion*. Gretna, LA: Pelican, 1999.

Edwards, Nicholas. *Tiger Woods: An American Master*. New York: Scholastic, 2001.

Feinstein, John. *The First Coming/Tiger Woods: Master or Martyr*. New York: Library of Contemporary Thought, 1998.

Kramer, S. A. *Tiger Woods: Golfing to Greatness*. New York: Random House, 1997.

Rosaforte, Tim. *Raising the Bar: The Championship Years of Tiger Woods*. New York: Thomas Dunne/St. Martin's, 2000.

Strege, John. *Tiger: A Biography of Tiger Woods*. London: Piatkus, 1998.

Woods, Earl, and the Tiger Woods Foundation, with Shari Lesser Wenk. *Start Something*. New York: Simon & Schuster, 2000.

"You Can't Believe the Pressure." *USA Today* 13 Aug. 1992: C4.

Wright Brothers

Roger B. Rollin

It is the single most famous photograph of the twentieth century and arguably the most important. It shows two brothers, Wilbur and Orville Wright, bicycle builders from Dayton, Ohio, and their new flying machine. Orville is at the controls of the Wright Flyer, lying prone on the biplane's lower wing, a man in a dark suit, his feet towards us, his head not visible. Just a few paces from the machine's right wingtips, also wearing a dark suit as well as a billed cap, is Wilbur, his legs apart, his arms akimbo, as if in wonderment at what he is witnessing. This delicate and beautiful machine made of spruce and ash, covered with muslin, held together with piano wire, and powered by a hand-made twelve-horsepower gasoline engine, is *flying!* Flying under its own power. Flying under human control. *This has never happened before in the history of the world.* The date is December 17, 1903. The place is the wind-swept sand dunes of Kill Devil Hills, Kitty Hawk, North Carolina. The time is approximately 10:37 A.M. And the world has been forever changed.

The quality of the photograph is amazingly good for 1903 or for any time, and this in itself is a small miracle that complements the great one. With superior clarity and fidelity it shows a sizable flying machine, with a more than 40-foot wingspan and 21-foot fuselage, three or so feet off the ground, airborne more than a yard before reaching the end of the launching track that has guided its takeoff.

The excellent quality of the photograph is extraordinary because the Wright Brothers, superb technical types though they were, were not professional photographers. The camera's shutter was actually tripped by an amateur, a member of the Kill Devil Hills lifesaving station, one John Daniels. Mr. Daniels did very well indeed. He had, after all, only one chance. In his excitement he might have taken the photograph too soon, while the Flyer was still on its trolley, careening down the launching track. Or he might have taken it too late, when the aeroplane had flown out of the frame. The total timespan of the flight was only twelve seconds, but Daniels caught the aircraft one to two seconds into that flight. Perfect! The camera probably belonged to the brothers and had been positioned by them: over the course of the years they had spent experimenting with flight they exercised firm control over everything. But professional lifesaver John Daniels is chiefly responsible for *the* iconic photograph of the twentieth century.

It is iconic, first of all, because of its timing. The twentieth century was only in its fourth year. Wireless telegraphy, the automobile, the electric light, the telephone, the motion picture, and the phonograph had already been invented, though, except for the telegraph, they were not yet in widespread use. In themselves these marvelous inventions did not lend themselves to visual representation. The horseless carriage would not really become an American icon until the advent of Mr. Ford's Model T. Motion pictures create icons (Charlie Chaplin, Marilyn Monroe), but a motion picture camera or screen is not in itself iconic. (The great movie palaces of cinema's Golden Age, the twenties and thirties, would eventually become themselves iconic, but by then the century was well advanced.) We have no special image of the electric light, the telephone, or the phonograph that is etched in the collective sensibility of the twentieth century. (The image of the terrier listening to a Victrola and hearing "His master's voice" is an advertiser's contrivance that would eventually become iconic, like more than a few Madison Avenue creations later on in the century.)

Secondly, the first flight photo is iconic because of its historicity. It is the first-ever photograph to capture a profoundly world-changing event in real time and space, as that event is actually happening. Thanks to John Daniels we are, so to speak, present at creation. True, this single photograph is not proof positive that manned, controlled, powered flight had actually taken place: the Wright Flyer might have ignominiously nosed over in the next second. But we know from eyewitness accounts of the three flights that followed, each of longer duration and greater distance than the last that, by early afternoon on December 17, 1903, the bold aviators from Dayton, Ohio had accomplished what none of their many predecessors—most of them more distinguished and better financed—had been able to accomplish: human flight by means of a viable, self-propelled, controllable machine.

Thirdly, the photograph is iconic because of its aesthetic quality. Its sheer beauty is partly due to someone's prescient positioning and focusing of the camera as well as the serendipitous timing of John Daniels. But what artist could have imagined the slightly low left wing of the Flyer, indicating a less-than-perfect takeoff? The aircraft's instability—like bicycles, flying machines are inherently unstable and must be controlled—is emphasized by the line of the horizon, which bisects the photograph with eye-pleasing, realistic unevenness. The Atlantic Ocean may be the most distant part of that horizon line—it is difficult to tell—but whether it is or not, the grey December sky is there, the Flyer lifting into it, suggesting an infinity of possibilities.

Moreover, subsequent artists would not find it easy to effectively capture in oils or watercolors, pen or ink, the thrilling whirl of an airplane propeller. But the photograph gets just right the blur of those two slender spruce props, scientifically designed and hand-made by the brothers. The engine, handmade by another meagerly educated Dayton boy, Charlie Taylor, the Wrights' assistant, is barely visible, but the whirling chains and pulleys linking that twelve-horsepower marvel to those beautiful wooden propellers, convey the sense that, yes, there is here sufficient controlled power to lift a skinny, middle-aged man into the air and carry him 120 feet. By the fourth and final flight of that day the craft would cover an incredible 852 feet.

There is also a kind of artlessness about the photograph that, for all its beauty and its magic, grounds it in reality. Note the crude wooden bench in the foreground. It looks handmade. Beneath the seat is what appears to be a large metal clamp. But why is it sitting there, occupying almost the dead center of the foreground? Perhaps it was used to steady the lower right wing against the powerful gusts coming off the

Wright Brothers airplane in flight, 1910. Courtesy of the Library of Congress.

ocean. But if that were the case one would think it would be located up at the head of the launching track, which here is out of the frame. Finally, adding to the photograph's verisimilitude is the still life in the right foreground: a shovel; a tin can (of oil?) with a handle sticking out of it; a curlicue of wire which may or may not be attached to a mysterious small box with what looks like a large u-bolt protruding from it; a carelessly dropped piece of board. These objects tell the careful viewer: "All this is real." Thus, an almost metaphysical moment is grounded in real space, real time. Only since the invention of photography in the nineteenth century could icons, which are in essence religious, be captured in the here and now.

As wonderful as the machine upon which the photograph is focused are the brothers themselves, even though they may initially appear to be mere supporting players in this historic tableau. Soon they would recognize that for reasons of safety, comfort, and more precise control both airman and passenger needed to be seated in the airplane. But here, as in their earlier man-carrying gliders, the pilot is prone. Orville's body is fully extended, almost as if he were a part of the wing's curvature, head down, "streamlined." Which is how thirty-three years later Siegel and Schuster would imagine their Man of Steel arcing his way through the air.

And Wilbur! His stance is dancer-like, feet apart, arms slightly outspread, his jacket billowing. Has he positioned himself there, at the end of the launch track (which the supporting dolly has already reached, ahead of the airplane) so as to get the best view when the Flyer takes to the air—if the Flyer takes to the air? Or, as is more likely, given their previous practice, has he been running alongside the aircraft, steadying the lower right wing tip with his left hand, until he feels the machine lifting off, at which moment he pulls up and is caught in the dynamic posture depicted in the photograph? There seems to be more apprehension than triumph in his body language. After all, in their first attempt earlier that morning he had crashed, slightly damaging the aircraft. As the recruited photographer, John Daniels, later recalled, before Orville's attempt, the brothers "shook hands and we couldn't help notice how they held on to each others' hand ... like two folks parting who weren't sure they'd ever see each other again" (Grant 26).

(In 2003, the year of the centennial of flight, the Jet Engine Division of General Electric would create a masterpiece of the genre of the television commercial. In grainy black and white, December 17, 1903, is recreated. We view a group of spectators, including a non-historical female figure, present to observe the First Flight. Suddenly a mighty wind sends hats and umbrellas flying and causes a horse to rear up in panic. The reason is that, atop the Wright Flyer sits, anachronistically, a mighty GE jet engine. It sends the fragile biplane roaring off into the sky as a small boy tosses his cap into the air in celebration. The contrast between that jubilant boy-actor and the apprehensive Wilbur Wright of the 1903 photograph could not be more pointed: in hindsight the success of December 17, 1903 was assured; on December 17, 1903 it was not.)

Finally, the photograph of the First Flight is iconic for its multiple levels and its multiple significances. At its most fundamental level it is of course a historical document, one of the earlier photographic records of man's efforts to fly. Though not the earliest: we have, for example, snapshots of some of the Wright Brothers' own experiments with

The Wright Brothers at the International Aviation Tournament, Belmont Park, Long Island, NY, October 1910. Courtesy of the Library of Congress.

man-carrying gliders as well as photographic records of such ill-fated attempts at powered, controlled flight as that of the distinguished Samuel
Langley's "Aerodrome."

At another level the photograph is symbolic, for it requires no stretch of the
imagination, only a sense of history, to see how it can represent an array of
powerful human themes. Most obviously it incarnates mankind's ancient
dream of conquering the air. Moreover, as the Industrial Revolution is
coming to a close, the photograph is a triumphant validation of science and
technology. In retrospect it represents the crowning achievement of the Age of
Progress that will end in the horrors of the Great War. And it signals the true
dawning of a new century and a new world. Not the least symbolic value of
this photograph is its significance as a victory of the human spirit, a tribute to
mankind's potential for vision, daring, and courage. At the sociocultural level
the depiction of the two brothers demonstrates the uncommonness of the
Common Man. Even the theme patriotic is implicit here: The United States of
America beats the world into the air!

Few of these themes found expression in the mass media of the new century, which for the most part ignored or distorted or discounted the
achievement of December 17, 1903. But as the century rumbled on, the
significance of what had happened that winter day at Kill Devil Hills gradually dawned on the collective consciousness, and thus an understanding of
and appreciation for the Wright Brothers' achievement grew.

Wilbur and Orville themselves, however, achieved the status of icons first
in France, not in their own country. It was partly their own fault. Raised in a
strict Protestant household that practiced Christian humility, they were also
by nature modest men of few words. Self-celebration, even when justifiable,
was alien to them. Consequently they were reluctant to give interviews and
they were less than assiduous about correcting the distortions and downright
fictions that the newspapers and magazines of the day perpetrated about them
and their craft. Being stiffly upright and rigorously honest themselves, they
were quite naturally offended by the doubts expressed by some journalists
that they had actually accomplished powered, controlled flight.

Moreover, although the Wrights were shrewd and fairly successful businessmen, they were still small businessmen from a small town in Ohio. They
soon became obsessive about safeguarding the patents to the Flyer, which by
1905 had been improved to the point where it was no longer an experimental
but a practical aircraft. They even refused to give aerial demonstrations
without orders for their flying machine. Finally, however, they had to succumb
to the pressure of the reported achievements of French aviators like Alberto
Santos-Dumont and the Voisin brothers. Thus it was that on August 8, 1908,
Wilbur demonstrated the superiority of the Wright Brothers' new Type A
aircraft in a flight near Le Mans, France, a flight so technologically advanced
compared to those of his Continental competitors that it made him the toast of
Europe. Soon he and Orville were not only world famous but found themselves surrounded by, in Wilbur's words, "Princes & millionaires...as thick

as fleas" (Grant 33). Every newspaper and popular periodical featured photographs of the two American inventor-aviators.

But these first true iconic figures of the new century did not look much like heroes. They were slender, ascetic-looking men, invariably dressed in sober dark suits, and wearing homburgs, or on some occasions, in Wilbur's case, a workman's flat cap. Both the brothers had strong noses and chins and generally regular features. Wilbur was clean-shaven while Orville sported a rather fashionable mustache. Wilbur's male-pattern balding was more advanced than his younger brother's. While not unattractive men, neither would have been likely to have been asked to pose for the popular Arrow Collar advertisements of the era, nor is there any record of the new moving picture industry clamoring for them to star in some fictionalized aerial film adventure.

But their eyes! In twin portraits made just two years after their first flights Wilbur and Orville Wright look out at the camera, unsmiling but clear-eyed, their native intelligence manifest in their gaze. Now, more than one hundred years after their historic, heroic achievement, we understand that these taciturn midwesterners were not merely lucky—they were certifiable geniuses. Though neither ever attended college, they were careful researchers, learned scholars in the new field of aeronautics, insightful theorists, and brilliant, methodical experimenters. They were also highly skilled craftsmen and self-taught engineers. The simple fact is that they succeeded brilliantly where better educated, more sophisticated, better financed inventors had totally failed.

Nor were these American icons intellectual heroes only. They were fit, strong men, dogged and almost tireless. They were abstemious in their conduct and athletic in their physical coordination. Most importantly, Wilbur and Orville Wright were, to put it most simply, incredibly brave. Though never foolhardy, they literally risked life and limb when they went up in, first, their man-carrying gliders, and then in the Flyer. They were adventurers. They were the first human beings to experience first-hand the perils of continuous powered locomotion through three dimensions in a heavier-than-air craft. In 1908, while demonstrating the Wright Military Flyer to the U.S. Army, an equipment failure caused Orville to crash, leaving him with broken ribs, a fractured thigh, and severe lacerations of the scalp; his passenger, Lt. Thomas Selfridge, died, the first person to perish in a powered flying machine. We now have a phrase for what the Wright Brothers possessed in abundance— the right stuff. In the third decade of the new century, another aviator, Charles Augustus Lindbergh, would also demonstrate that he had the Right Stuff. It would make him too an American icon.

AFTERWORD

On December 17, 2003, 15,000 people gathered in the Wright Brothers National Memorial Park, as did millions more around the world via radio and television, to commemorate the one hundredth anniversary of powered, controlled flight and to do homage to that event's icons—the brothers Wright and their amazing flying machine. By that date Wilbur had been dead for ninety-one years, Orville fifty-five years, and the original Wright Flyer, heavily restored, was established in a place of honor in the National Air and Space Museum in Washington, D.C. The centerpiece of the celebration was a meticulously accurate flying replica of the brothers' fabled aircraft. At approximately 8:45 A.M. the rains came, with a vengeance. Within an hour most of the aviation enthusiasts present were soaked to the skin, but they didn't appear to mind. When the precise historical moment, 10:37 A.M., arrived, the rains had become torrential and the Flyer replica had to remain in its display hanger. But its engine was started up and the crowd cheered. They cheered again when, in the early afternoon, an attempt was made to fly the replica. However the winds were insufficient and the Flyer failed to get airborne. Still the crowd cheered—not only for the valiant attempt by these spiritual descendants of the Wright Brothers, but for those two magnificent men and their flying machine that had so profoundly changed the world a hundred years earlier.

WORKS CITED AND RECOMMENDED

Crouch, Tom D. *The Bishop's Boys: A Life of Wilbur and Orville Wright.* Rev. ed. New York: Knopf, 1998.

Grant, R. G. *Flight: 100 Years of Aviation.* New York: D. K. Publishing, 2002.

Moolman, Valerie, and the editors of Time-Life Books. *The Road to Kitty Hawk.* Alexandria, VA: Time-Life Books, 1980.

Tobin, James. *To Conquer the Air: The Wright Brothers and the Great Race for Flight.* New York: Free P, 2003.

Zipper

Robert Friedel

The zipper was invented, in its first, primitive form, in the early 1890s, in the United States. It was promoted primarily as a shoe fastener, replacing laces or buckles. This early slide fastener (to use its technical name) worked very poorly indeed, and sold even less well. From this inauspicious beginning, the zipper, over the course of the next century, was to become one of the most ubiquitous mechanical technologies of modern life. In so doing, it also took on a host of meanings and associations, many of which had iconic value, as the common-place little fastener came to stand for a host of fundamental relationships—separations and joinings, opening and closings, and, above all, sex.

Toward the end of one of the great satirical novels of the twentieth century, Aldous Huxley's 1932 *Brave New World,* Mustapha Mond, one of the world's "controllers," confronts the savage, John, and tries to explain why Shakespeare and the Bible and other classics must be kept locked away in this world 600 years into the future:

> "God isn't compatible with machinery and scientific medicine and universal happiness. You must make your choice. Our civilization has chosen machinery and medicine and happiness. That's why I have to keep these books locked up in the safe. They're smut. People would be shocked if..."
>
> The Savage interrupted him. "But isn't it *natural* to feel there's a God?"
>
> "You might as well ask if it's natural to do up one's trousers with zippers," said the Controller sarcastically. (159)

In fact, to Huxley, there was nothing at all natural about zippers—they still were not widely available in ordinary garments in the early 1930s—and that is just why they are such a powerful, yet subtle, symbol throughout his novel. The great irony, of course, is that in the years since *Brave New World* was published, the zipper has become such a universal part of daily life that it does seem almost natural. The symbolism loses much of its power by the ubiquity of the symbol—how many of today's readers really notice Huxley's zippers?

To Huxley, zippers bring together two essential ingredients of his nightmare world of the future—sex and machines. In this future, human beings are condemned to lives of meaningless contentment, kept that way by artificial pleasures such as "feelies," (the next logical step after "movies") and "soma," a drug that effectively and universally banishes anxiety and concern. An essential part of this mechanization of life is divorcing procreation from sex. The former is now the province of factories, in which human beings are created in test tubes. The latter is thus converted into yet another tool of enforced contentment, and garments are supplied with zippers to enhance the message that sex is easy and uncomplicated (Hazlitt 215–16). Throughout the novel are references to zipping and unzipping and to garments that seem particularly characterized by their zippers ("zippicamiknicks" and "zippyjamas"). This satire is perhaps the earliest iconic use of zippers in English, certainly in a work by a distinguished writer. The combined themes that moved Huxley to this usage—sex and machinery—became central to much of the use of zipper imagery in the remainder of the twentieth century.

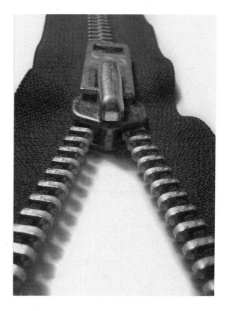

Your classic zipper. Courtesy of Shutterstock.

The literary uses of the zipper in this connection did not, of course, cease with Huxley. Particularly striking was the persistence of the combination of sexuality with machinery that was so central to the zipper's place in *Brave New World*. The best modern example is probably the following scene in Tom Robbins's 1984 satire *Jitterbug Perfume*, in which the somewhat randy and loony Wiggs Dannyboy is seducing the (relatively) innocent Priscilla:

Ahh, I do love zippers. Zippers remind me o' crocodiles, lobsters, and Aztec serpents. I wish me tweeds had more than the single fly. . . . Zippers are primal and modern at the very same time. On the one hand, your zipper is primitive and reptilian, on the other, mechanical and slick. A zipper is where the Industrial Revolution meets the Cobra Cult, don't you think? Ahh. Little alligators of ecstasy, that's what zippers are. Sexy, too. Now your button, a button is prim and persnickety. There's somethin' Victorian about a row o' buttons. But a zipper, why a zipper is the very snake at the gate of Eden, waitin' to escort a true believer into the Garden.

At the same time that Dannyboy is waxing so poetic, he is struggling with Priscilla's dress, "to part the teeth of the Talon that ran down the length of her green knit back." It doesn't budge, however, until Priscilla finally loosens it herself: "And with one smooth stroke, she separated the interlocking tracks, the 'gator yawned, and, lo, there she sat in her underwear." Even in such a scene of seduction, the zipper's mechanical nature—here represented by its resistance to working—is never far away (272–75).

The zipper has remained a tool and symbol of seduction, not only in literature but in other cultural expressions, such as cartoons, motion pictures, and song. One early and notable example of the latter appeared in the Richard Rodgers and Lorenz Hart musical *Pal Joey*, in 1940. Here, seasoned newspaper reporter Melba Snyder interviews the scrapping and somewhat phony crooner Joey Evans, and she describes with gusto one of her more successful past interviews, with the great stripper Gypsy Rose Lee, while pantomiming a striptease herself, singing a song punctuated with the word "zip." With remarkable speed, the zipper established itself as the instrument for allure and seduction, whether private or public.

As with so much else in American culture, perhaps the most powerful and evocative venue for the use of the zipper as sexual sign was in motion pictures. By the 1940s, Hollywood had recognized the dramatic uses of the novel fastener, which was particularly important in an age when the explicit depiction of the bare body or of sexual contact was censored. *Gilda*, a 1946 film starring George Macready, Glen Ford, and Rita Hayworth, is a prime example. In one scene of this somewhat convoluted movie set in Argentina, Hayworth repeats her complaint to her new husband, Macready (who is a Nazi agent) that zippers are always giving her trouble, and she asks for help getting undressed. In this simple act, the movie exploits both the mechanical nature of the zipper (with its occasional difficulties, especially for the non-mechanical female) and the potential that even a balky zipper always presents of a quick and complete disrobing. Later in *Gilda*, Hayworth begins the motions of a striptease in Macready's club, to the dismay of Ford, who is now her protector. The last straw in her performance, before Ford intervenes, is the moment she again asks for help with her zipper. The zipper is an instrument both of seduction and subjugation. With its ease of opening and its relatively public accessibility, it offers opportunities for attracting sexual advances, but at the same time its mechanical nature makes the zipper a masculine intrusion—even weapon—in the intimate environment of a woman's clothing. The women who wrote and produced *Gilda*, like the woman who starred in it, probably had some sense of how their use of the zipper, still novel enough to titillate their audience, conveyed these mixed messages (Michaels 244–52).

So tightly bound was the zipper's sexual image that it became one of the most readily understood and powerful metaphors for sexuality, especially for an uninhibited and promiscuous sexuality. Perhaps the ultimate expression of that power, and one of the most memorable evocations of zippers in modern fiction, was in Erica Jong's 1974 novel *Fear of Flying*. Unquestionably the image that stuck in reader's minds, even many years after encountering the book, was that of the "zipless fuck." In a book that claimed to break new ground in giving free expression to women's feelings about sex, this fantasy of "ziplessness" was the one that seemed to speak to universal desires. Jong's heroine Isadora explains, "It was a platonic ideal. Zipless because when you came together zippers fell away like rose petals, underwear blew off in one breath like dandelion fluff." This ideal was sex without guilt, without consequences, without games of power or love: "The zipless fuck is the purest thing there is. And it is rarer than the unicorn." "Ziplessness" had nothing to do literally with zippers; it was rather a symbol of dispensing with the barriers and complications that men and women set up between themselves. Jong represents the zipper itself as a complication, rather than an invitation or simplification of sex. In so doing, she in a sense turns the zipper's usual literary role on its head, but by doing so, she is able to suggest how truly extraordinary "ziplessness" would be if it were ever achieved. Jong also provided a much more enduring symbol than she could have with "buttonless," "snapless," or any alternative (11, 14).

In the second half of the twentieth century, a man who might earlier have been accused of "chasing skirts," was instead said to have a "fast zipper." The zipper became a visual metaphor as well, with cartoonists making ready and early use of it to suggest sexual opportunity. One of the most notorious record album covers of the 1960s was designed by Andy Warhol for the Rolling Stones' *Sticky Fingers*, on which a real zipper opened to reveal Mick Jagger's underwear. When *Time* magazine (July 11, 1969) featured a story on the "Sexual Revolution," a zipper was the prominent symbol on its cover. The visual message was often a direct one, when uninhibited fashion designers made zippers prominent, frontal elements of a woman's dress. Elsa Schiaparelli's 1935 gowns, initiating this trend, were festooned with brightly colored plastic zippers. This was to a degree a logical step for a flamboyant designer already famous for putting outrageous buttons in the oddest places, but the large, showy (and typically superfluous) zippers still caused a great stir. Any modern reader will be familiar with any number of other means in which the zipper is used to speak about or signal sexual possibilities or activity.

The mechanical character of the zipper is the other fundamental aspect of its image, and of the uses to which it is put in literature and art. To one degree, its technology is even more intrinsic to the device than its sexuality, for the slide fastener was, after all, designed from the first to be a mechanical closure. The zipper is the first machine that any of us encounters on a regular basis in our daily lives, and this familiarity carries with it messages both good and ill. On the positive side, it is the machinery of the zipper that is at the heart of its utility. All of the promotions of the fastener rest eventually on the convenience and ease of opening and closing with a mechanism, rather than by hand manipulation of buttons or ties. In this sense, the zipper is very much part of that great trend in Western civilization in which, to use the term of the Swiss architectural critic Siegfried Giedion, "mechanization takes command." With its meshing scoops, pulled together by a (hopefully) smoothly running guide, the zipper fits comfortably into the most general image of the machine, that of meshing gears. The zipper is thus, to borrow another phrase from another notable technological critic, Lewis Mumford, a perfect representative of "paleotechnic" culture—the phase in material development characterized by metals and mechanisms.

The negative messages conveyed by the zipper's mechanical nature are more complex and ambiguous. On one level, the intrusion of a machine, however small and harmless, into the intimate realms of dressing and undressing, is to some, like Aldous Huxley, an unwelcome event. It can be seen to represent the greater threat posed by the intrusion of modern technology in all realms of human life, from daily routine to lovemaking, to government. The capacity of the zipper to convey this kind of image has diminished since the 1930s, for its ubiquity necessarily dulls whatever threat it may seem to imply. And yet, a closer reading of later allusions to the zipper, in high literature and low, suggests another aspect of the sometimes tortured relationship between human beings and their machines: the ever-present threat of failure.

The earlier depictions of the zipper spoke of the ease of its working, the cleverness of its mechanism, and the convenience it afforded; but once the device had become commonplace, attention was more likely to be drawn to its unreliability. An important aspect of the threat that machines pose to human beings lies in their treachery. By refusing to work as they promise and are designed to do, machines become demons that betray human trust. The scene described above from *Jitterbug Perfume* is an excellent example of this demonic side of the zipper, when Dannyboy "couldn't budge the damn thing." Such scenes and characterizations of zippers can be found in a great range of post–World War literary settings. The popular critic and essayist Cleveland Amory, writing in one of his last *Saturday Review* columns, provided a good example:

> Toward the zipper we harbor—and harboring is one of the things we do best—nothing but ill will. The fact is that, over a lifetime of trying to make the damn things work, we have at last reached the inescapable conclusion, which should have been obvious from the first, that they don't.

From the 1930s, the zipper was seen as one of the defining elements of modernity. When the readers of London's *Daily Express* late in the decade were asked to name the inventions that seemed most distinctive of the twentieth century, the zipper was named by more respondents than anything else. This perception was reflected also in cartoons of the period: the appearance of a zipper on a mummy or a churchman's gown seemed the height of unlikely anachronism, an intrusion of the most obviously modern into the ancient or traditional. In the years after World War II, the zipper naturally lost some of its power to convey this idea of the up-to-date, but it acquired other meanings in specific contexts, demonstrating powerfully the plasticity of the messages that an artifact can be used to convey.

One of the more curious, yet widely recognized, messages that zippers came to be used to deliver in the postwar years was that of generational and cultural rebellion. While the zippered jacket had been introduced as early as the late 1920s, as a relatively expensive article of sports clothing, in the 1930s it was wedded to an old American tradition of leather jackets. This style was further influenced by military usage, especially for pilots and parachutists during the war years, so that by the late 1940s the zippered leather jacket was readily available, and was associated with sporting and other outdoors activities that exposed the wearer to wind and weather. One of these activities was motorcycling, and when Hollywood celebrated the anti-establishment nature of this alternative form of transportation—noisy, powerful, exposed to the elements and thus the province of uninhibited young men (and their "molls")—in the 1953 movie *The Wild One*, the "biker jacket" became one of the decade's most evocative symbols of youthful rebellion. Marlon Brando's jacket did not simply use zippers to fasten, but long, prominent zippers in the sleeves emphasized the vulgar, brash, alienated culture that he (and his motorcycle) represented. The prominent metallic gleam of the zippers (and the accenting metal studs) reinforced the message of brash, unrestrained machinery (and sexuality) in the service of rebellion.

More broadly, the zipper came with increasing frequency to be used as a general sign of opening and closing, of joining and separating. Its message could be conveyed verbally or visually. A noisy young child told to "zip it up" understood the demand to keep his mouth shut. A sandwich bag with a "Ziploc" seal was one that could be opened and closed with ease. Cartoonists used zippers to play with the idea of firm closure, quick closure, and even unlikely closure. The zipper became an icon, in the sense of being a distinctive image that could be conjured up in a wide variety of forms to convey its message. A classic puzzle in which square pieces are moved around in a frame can use the zipper as its basic image, for everyone knows and appreciates what it should look like in its proper form. Jewelry in the form of necklaces, earrings, and tie clasps can feature the slide of a zipper as central pieces, for it possesses an elegant symmetry in metal, which is appreciated only by taking it out of its functional context. Instructions to tear an envelope open will often be accompanied—or completely conveyed—by zipper imagery, for it is international and wordless. By the last quarter of the twentieth century, the zipper had become as universally understood and used a sign as industrialized culture had yet generated. If the meanings of this icon seemed to shift and turn, that was perhaps simply the ultimate indication that the device itself had achieved some kind of significant transcendence over its normally mundane utility.

WORKS CITED AND RECOMMENDED

Amory, Cleveland. "Curmudgeon-at-Large." *SR/World* 23 Oct. 1973: 53.

Friedel, Robert. *Zipper: An Exploration in Novelty.* New York: W. W. Norton, 1994.

Giedion, Siegfried. *Mechanization Takes Command.* New York: Oxford UP, 1948.

Hartmann, Helmuth. *Open-Shut: A Book around and about Zip-Fasteners.* Trans. Alan Braley. N.p.: by the author, 1980.

Hazlitt, Henry. "What's Wrong with Utopia." *The Nation* 17 Feb. 1932: 204+. Rpt. in *Aldous Huxley, the Critical Heritage.* Ed. Donald Watt. London: Routledge & Kegan Paul, 1975. 215–17.

Huxley, Aldous. *Brave New World.* 1932. New York: Bantam Books, 1968.

Jong, Erica. *Fear of Flying.* New York: New American Library, 1974.

Mays, John Bentley. "Deciphering the Zip Code." *Toronto Globe and Mail* 27 Feb. 1991.

Michaels, Leonard. "The Zipper." *The Best American Essays, 1992.* Ed. Susan Sontag. New York: Ticknor & Fields, 1992. 244–52.

Mumford, Lewis. *Technics and Civilization.* New York: Harcourt, Brace, 1934.

Robbins, Tom. *Jitterbug Perfume.* New York: Bantam Books, 1984.

Schoeffler, O. E., and William Gale. *Esquire's Encyclopedia of Twentieth Century Men's Fashions.* New York: McGraw-Hill, 1973.

Selected Bibliography

Arnheim, Rudolf. *Visual Thinking*. Berkeley: U of California P, 1969.

Bal, Mieke. "Seeing Signs: The Use of Semiotics for the Understanding of Visual Art." *The Subjects of Art History: Historical Objects in Contemporary Perspective*. Ed. Mark A. Cheetham, Michael Ann Holly, and Keith Moxey. New York: Cambridge UP, 1998. 74–93.

Barbas, Samantha. *Movie Crazy: Fans, Stars, and the Cult of Celebrity*. New York: Palgrave, 2001.

Barker, P. *Michel Foucault: An Introduction*. Edinburgh: Edinburgh UP, 1998.

Barthes, Roland. *Camera Lucida: Reflections on Photography*. 1980. London: Vintage, 1993.

———. *Mythologies*. Trans. Annette Lavers. New York: Hill and Wang, 1972.

Baudrillard, Jean. *Selected Writings*. Ed. Mark Poster. Stanford, CA: Stanford UP, 1988.

Benjamin, David, ed. *The Home: Words, Interpretations, Meanings, and Environments*. Brookfield, VT: Avery, 1995.

Berger, Arthur Asa. *The Comic-Stripped American: What Dick Tracy, Blondie, Daddy Warbucks, and Charlie Brown Tell Us About Ourselves*. New York: Walker, 1973.

———. *Media Analysis Techniques*. Beverly Hills, CA: Sage, 1982.

———. *Seeing Is Believing: An Introduction to Visual Communication*. 2nd ed. Mountain View, CA: Mayfield, 1998.

Berger, John. *Ways of Seeing*. New York: Penguin, 1972.

Biederman, Hans. *Dictionary of Symbolism: Cultural Icons and the Meanings Behind Them*. Trans. James Hulbert. New York: Penguin, 1994.

Bigsby, C.W.E., ed. *Approaches to Popular Culture*. London: Edward Arnold, 1976.

Blonsky, Marshall. *American Mythologies*. New York: Oxford UP, 1992.

———, ed. *On Signs*. Baltimore, MD: Johns Hopkins UP, 1985.

Boime, Albert. *The Unveiling of the National Icons*. Cambridge: Cambridge UP, 1998.

Boorstin, Daniel. *The Image: A Guide to Pseudo Events in America*. 1962. New York: Vintage, 1992.

Bordo, Susan. *Twilight Zones: The Hidden Life of Cultural Images from Plato to O.J.* Berkeley: U of California P, 1998.

Braudy, Leo. *The Frenzy of Renown: Fame and Its History*. 1986. New York: Vintage, 1997.

Browne, Ray B., and Pat Browne, eds. *The Guide to United States Popular Culture*. Bowling Green, OH: Popular P, 2001.

Browne, Ray B., and Marshall Fishwick, eds. *Icons of America*. Bowling Green, OH: Popular P, 1978.

Cawelti, John. *Adventure, Mystery, and Romance: Formula Stories as Art and Popular Culture*. Chicago: U of Chicago P, 1976.

Chevalier, Jean, and Alain Gheerbrant. *The Penguin Dictionary of Symbols*. Trans. John Buchanan-Brown. New York: Penguin, 1996.

Crary, Jonathan. *Suspension of Perception: Attention, Spectacle and Modern Culture*. Cambridge, MA: MIT P, 2000.

Cross, Mary, ed. *A Century of American Icons: 100 Products and Slogans from 20th-Century Consumer Culture*. Westport, CT: Greenwood, 2002.

Csikszentmihalyi, Mihaly, and Eugene Rochberg-Halton. *The Meaning of Things: Domestic Symbols and the Self*. New York: Cambridge UP, 1981.

Dickstein, Morris. *Gates of Eden: American Culture in the Sixties*. 1977. Cambridge, MA: Harvard UP, 1997.

Dunne, Michael. "The Study of Popular Culture." *The Greenwood Guide to American Popular Culture*. Ed. M. Thomas Inge and Dennis Hall. Westport, CT: Greenwood, 2002. Vol. 1, xxvii–liii.

Dyer, Richard. *Heavenly Bodies: Film Stars and Society*. New York: St. Martin's, 1987.

———. *Stars*. London: British Film Institute, 1998.

Eco, Umberto. *Travels in Hyperreality: Essays*. Trans. William Weaver. New York: Harcourt, 1986.

Edgar, Andrew, and Peter Sedgwick, eds. *Critical Theory: The Key Concepts*. New York: Routledge, 1999.

Evans, Jessica, and Stuart Hall, eds. *Visual Culture: The Reader*. Thousand Oaks, CA: Sage, 2001.

Ewen, Stuart, and Elizabeth Ewen. *Channels of Desire: Mass Images and the Shaping of American Consciousness*. Minneapolis: U of Minnesota P, 1992.

Featherstone, Mike. *Consumer Culture and Postmodernism*. London: Sage, 1991.

Fiedler, Leslie A. *What Was Literature? Class, Culture, and Mass Society*. New York: Simon and Schuster, 1982.

Fiske, John, ed. *Reading Popular Culture*. New York: Routledge, 1991.

———. *Reading the Popular*. Boston: Unwin Hyman, 1989.

———. *Television Culture*. New York: Routledge, 1987.

Gamson, Joshua. *Claims to Fame: Celebrity in Contemporary America*. Berkeley: U of California P, 1994.

Gans, Herbert J. *Popular Culture and High Culture: An Analysis and Evaluation of Taste*. New York: Basic Books, 1974.

Gledhill, Christine, ed. *Stardom: Industry of Desire*. London: Routledge, 1991.

Gregory, Thomas. *How to Design Logos, Symbols, and Icons*. Cincinnati, OH: How Design, 2003.

Groden, Michael, and Martin Kreiswirth, eds. *The Johns Hopkins Guide to Literary Theory and Criticism*. Baltimore: Johns Hopkins UP, 1994.

Harvey, David. *The Condition of Postmodernity*. Cambridge, MA: Basil Blackwell, 1990.

Hayword, Susan. *Key Concepts in Cinema Studies*. New York: Routledge, 1996.

Hebdige, Dick. *Hiding in the Light: On Images and Things*. New York: Routledge, 1988.

———. *Subculture: The Meaning of Style*. London: Methuen, 1979.

Heywood, Ian, and Barry Sandywell, eds. *Interpreting Visual Culture: Explorations in the Hermeneutics of the Vision*. New York: Routledge, 1998.

Hill, Charles A., and Marguerite Helmers, eds. *Defining Visual Rhetorics*. Mahwah, NJ: Lawrence Erlbaum, 2003.

Holt, Douglas B. *How Brands Become Icons: The Principles of Cultural Branding*. Boston: Harvard Business School P, 2004.

Horkheimer, Max. "Art and Mass Culture." *Critical Theory: Selected Essays*. New York: Continuum, 1986.

Inge, M. Thomas. *Comics as Culture*. Jackson: U of Mississippi P, 1990.

———. *Concise Histories of American Popular Culture*. Westport, CT: Greenwood, 1982.

Inge, M. Thomas, and Dennis Hall, eds. *The Greenwood Guide to American Popular Culture*. 4 vols. Westport, CT: Greenwood, 2002.

Jaffe, Aaron. *Modernism and the Culture of Celebrity*. Cambridge: Cambridge UP, 2005.

Jameson, Frederic. *Postmodernism, or The Cultural Logic of Late Capitalism*. Durham, NC: Duke UP, 1991.

Jenks, Chris, ed. *Visual Culture*. New York: Routledge, 1995.

Journal of Visual Literacy [Official Journal of the International Visual Literacy Association]. 12 Dec. 2005 <http://www.cameron.edu/jvl/>.

Kasson, Joy. *Buffalo Bill's Wild West: Celebrity, Memory, and Popular History*. New York: Hill and Wang, 2000.

Kottak, Conrad Phillip. *Researching American Culture*. Ann Arbor: U of Michigan P, 1982.

Kress, Gunther, and Theo Van Leeuwen. *Reading Images: The Grammar of Visual Design*. New York: Routledge, 1996.

Lewis, David L., and Laurence Goldstein, eds. *The Automobile and American Culture*. Ann Arbor: U of Michigan P, 1983.

Loss, Archie. *Pop Dreams: Music, Movies, and the Media in the 1960s*. Fort Worth, TX: Harcourt Brace, 1999.

Lowenthal, Leo. *Literature, Popular Culture, and Society*. Englewood Cliffs, NJ: Prentice-Hall, 1961.

Maltin, Leonard. *Of Mice and Magic: A History of American Animated Cartoons*. New York: Plume, 1987.

Marshall, P. David. *Celebrity and Power: Fame in Contemporary Culture*. Minneapolis: U of Minnesota P, 1997.

———, ed. "Fame": A Special Issue of *M/C: A Journal of Media and Culture*. Nov. 2004. 12 Dec. 2005 <http://journal.media-culture.org.au/journal/past_vol_7.php>.

McLuhan, Marshall. *Understanding Media*. London: Routledge and Kegan Paul, 1964.

McMann, Jean. *Altars and Icons: Sacred Spaces in Everyday Life*. San Francisco: Chronicle Books, 1998.

McRobbie, Angela. *Postmodernism and Popular Culture*. New York: Routledge, 1994.

Melly, George. *Revolt into Style: The Pop Arts in Britain*. London: Allen Lane, 1970.

Mirzoeff, Nicholas. *An Introduction to Visual Culture*. New York: Routledge, 1999.

Mitchell, W.J.T. *Iconology: Text, Image, Ideology*. Chicago: U of Chicago P, 1986.

Moran, Joe. *Star Authors: Literary Celebrity in America*. London: Pluto P, 2000.

Mukerji, Chandra, and Michael Schudson, eds. *Rethinking Popular Culture*. Berkeley: U of California P, 1991.

Mulvey, Laura. "Visual Pleasure and Narrative Cinema." *Screen* 16.3 (1975): 6–18.

Norton, Anne. *Republic of Signs: Liberal Theory and American Popular Culture*. Chicago: U of Chicago P, 1993.

Robbins, Derek. *Pierre Bourdieu*. Thousand Oaks, CA: Sage, 2000.

Rybczynski, Witold. *Home: A Short History of an Idea*. New York: Penguin, 1986.

Sanford, Charles L., ed. *The Automobile in American Life*. Troy, NY: Rensselaer Polytechnic Institute, 1977.

Schickel, Richard. *Intimate Strangers: The Culture of Celebrity*. Garden City, NY: Doubleday & Company, 1985.

Seldes, Gilbert. *The 7 Lively Arts*. Rev. ed. New York: Harper, 1957.

Smith, Henry Nash. *Virgin Land: The American West as Symbol and Myth*. Cambridge, MA: Harvard UP, 1950.

Sontag, Susan. *Against Interpretation and Other Essays*. New York: Farrar, Straus, and Giroux, 1966.

———. *On Photography*. New York: Anchor, 1977.

Stafford, Barbara Maria. *Good Looking: Essays on the Virtue of Images*. Cambridge, MA: MIT P, 1996.

Stefik, Mark. *Internet Dreams: Archetypes, Myths, and Metaphors*. Cambridge, MA: MIT P, 1996.

Strinati, Dominic. *An Introduction to Theories of Popular Culture*. New York: Routledge, 1995.

Sturken, Marita, and Lisa Cartwright. *Practices of Looking: An Introduction to Visual Culture*. New York: Oxford UP, 2001.

Turner, Graeme. *Understanding Celebrity*. Thousand Oaks, CA: Sage, 2004.

Index

Note: Page numbers in **bold** indicate main entries.

About the Contributors

MICHAEL C. C. ADAMS was Regents Professor and Director of the Military History Program at Northern Kentucky University, before his resignation in 2003 to pursue creative writing. His publications include *Our Masters the Rebels: Union Military Failure in the East 1861–1865* (Harvard University Press, 1978), winner of the Jefferson Davis book prize, and reissued by the University of Nebraska Press in 1992 as *Fighting for Defeat*; also *The Great Adventure: Male Desire and the Coming of World War One* (Indiana University Press, 1990); *The Best War Ever: America and World War Two* (Johns Hopkins University Press, 1994); and *Echoes of War: A Thousand Years of Military History in Popular Culture* (University Press of Kentucky, 2002). Adams pursues his thoughts on Custer as a cultural symbol further in chapter five of *Echoes*.

JUDITH A. ADAMS-VOLPE is Director, University and External Relations, in the University Libraries, University of Buffalo. She is the author of several books, including *The American Amusement Park Industry: A History of Technology and Thrills*. She has also published numerous articles on technology and popular culture in America. She continues to escape to amusement parks for "research" and fun, while beginning to settle for vicarious experiencing of thrill rides.

PAULINE ADEMA's research considers food discourses in contemporary American culture. She is interested not so much in what we eat but the conversations we as a society have about food. Her recent work explores place-based food festivals, food television, and celebrity chefs—past and present, real and fictitious. She has taught at Indiana University (Bloomington) and the Culinary Institute of America (Hyde Park, New York). When she is not writing or watching food television (strictly for research purposes!), she enjoys wining and dining with friends.

RANDAL ALLRED is Associate Professor of English at Brigham Young University Hawaii and Director of the University Honors Program. Specializing in

American literature and culture, he has regularly presented at conferences on literary and Civil War topics, and has published articles on Civil War battle reenacting as cultural text, Stephen Crane, and Living History. He has also written a number of articles for the *Encyclopedia of War and American Popular Culture* and for the *Encyclopedia of American War Literature*. He is completing a book on Civil War battle reenactment for Praeger/Greenwood this year.

JACK ASHWORTH has taught music history and directed the Early Music Ensemble at the University of Louisville since 1977. Primarily a harpsi-chordist and player of early strings, he also has a passion for popular and traditional music of Appalachia and the South. Jack plays fiddle with the Kentucky Knob Hoppers, a local string band. He does not play the banjo, but he knows people who do.

KAREN AUBREY, Associate Professor of English, teaches English Literature and Humanities at Augusta State University in Augusta, Georgia. She has published in the fields of literature, satire, and popular culture, including creating an original short film, *Bug Stories*. She is also an outdoors enthusiast who loves adventure, music, and gourmet restaurants, and who refuses to grow up.

LINDA BADLEY is Professor of English at Middle Tennessee State University, where she codirects the film series for the biennial Women and Power Conference. With R. Barton Palmer, she serves as General Editor of the Traditions in World Cinema series at Edinburgh University Press. She has written widely on popular culture, television, and film, and is the author or editor of *Film, Horror, and the Body Fantastic* (Greenwood), *Writing Horror and the Body: The Fiction of Stephen King, Clive Barker, and Anne Rice* (Greenwood), and *Traditions in World Cinema* (Edinburgh). Current projects include *Indiewood: Contemporary American Commercial/Independent Film* (with R. Barton Palmer) and a book on Lars von Trier.

WILLIAM J. BADLEY is Director of General Education and Assistant Vice Provost for Academic Affairs at Middle Tennessee State University. He has presented papers frequently at meetings of the Popular Culture Association and the Popular Culture Association of the South. He is cobuilder and owner of a log cabin in Bouchette, Quebec, Canada, and wishes to dedicate his entry to Linda and the Baltimore and Cheverly Cornetts.

ROBERT BARSHAY has a Ph.D. in American Studies from the University of Maryland and a J.D. from the University of Baltimore. He serves as Dean of Liberal Arts at Prince George's Community College, and on the Executive Board of the Association of Departments of English. He is the author of *Philip Wylie: The Man and His Work* (University Press of America, 1979), and essays on popular culture including "The Cartoon of Modern Sensibility" (*Journal of Popular Culture*, 1974) and "Ethnic Stereotypes in Flash Gordon" (*Journal of Popular Film*, 1974).

MAURINE H. BEASLEY is a professor of journalism at the Philip Merrill College of Journalism, University of Maryland, College Park. She is the author of *Eleanor Roosevelt and the Media: A Public Quest for Self-Fulfillment* (University of Illinois Press, 1987).

BETSY BEAULIEU is an assistant professor in the Department of Interdisciplinary Studies at Appalachian State University where she teaches courses in food studies and the literature of oppressed peoples. She is the author of *Black Women Writers and the American Neo-Slave Narrative: Femininity Unfettered* (1999) and the editor of *The Toni Morrison Encyclopedia* (2003) and *The Feminist Encyclopedia of African American Literature* (forthcoming). After giving birth to her son Sebastian, she immediately requested a McDonald's filet o'fish sandwich, fries, and a chocolate shake, but she doesn't eat much fast food anymore. Sebastian, however, being an all-American kid, has never met a Happy Meal he didn't like.

MICHAEL BERTZ is a Senior Research Analyst covering semiconductors, specializing in consumer electronics applications. He began his career doing research at Georgia Tech and was a structural engineer in Irvine, California, and his background includes degrees in architecture and physics from Miami University as well as a Master's and Doctorate in Structural Engineering from Georgia Tech. In his spare time, his passions include playing and coaching volleyball, music, cooking, and Civil War history.

THOMAS S. BREMER is Assistant Professor of Religious Studies at Rhodes College in Memphis, Tennessee. He teaches classes on Religion in America, American Sacred Space, and Religion and Tourism, among others. His book *Blessed with Tourists: The Borderlands of Religion and Tourism in San Antonio* (University of North Carolina Press) appeared in 2004.

RAY B. BROWNE, Distinguished Professor of Popular Culture, Emeritus, at Bowling Green State University, is the author of some seventy-five books and of numerous articles. He founded and edited until 2002 the *Journal of Popular Culture* and the *Journal of American Culture*. He cofounded the Popular Culture Association and the American Culture Association, and with his wife, Pat, the Popular Press.

PATRICIA PRANDINI BUCKLER has been studying scrapbooks for more than fifteen years. Her most recent publication is *Scrapbooks in American Life*, coedited with Katherine Ott and Susan Tucker (Temple University Press, 2006). She is Associate Professor of English and Director of Composition at

Purdue University North Central in Westville, Indiana. She graduated from Bennington College and the University of Louisville, where she earned a Ph.D. in Rhetoric and Composition.

THOMAS B. BYERS is Professor of English and Director of the Commonwealth Center for the Humanities and Society at the University of Louisville, where he teaches contemporary U.S. literature and film studies. His essays on Hollywood movies have been published in *Modern Fiction Studies, Cultural Critique, Science-Fiction Studies, Arizona Quarterly, zeitgeschichste* (Austria), and other venues. He loves the movies.

DIANE CALHOUN-FRENCH is the Provost of Jefferson Community and Technical College in Louisville, Kentucky. She is a former president of the National Association for Women in Education and a former editor of its quarterly publication, *Initiatives*. Since 1987 she has served as the Executive Secretary of the Popular Culture Association in the South. Her research interests include mystery fiction, soap operas, and romance novels. She lives with five cats, an African frog named Tad, and two Siamese fighting fish.

MARY CAROTHERS is a socially integrated artist exploring alternative venues for display and public interaction. Interested in issues of American mobility, she has shown her work in the back of rental trucks, on signposts, at campgrounds, and at home improvement centers. She has also exhibited her work more formally at CEPA (Center for Exploratory and Perceptual Art), Buffalo, and Pittsburgh Filmmakers. Recently funded by the Atlanta College of Art, Carothers created a traveling exhibit that included the employment of a bomb technician to blow up her most beloved car. She currently lives in Louisville, Kentucky, where she teaches Fine Art at University of Louisville and is trying to resolve how to freeze the car in her garage into a block of ice for the winter.

EDWARD P. COMENTALE is Associate Professor of Literature at Indiana University. His teaching and research focus on modernism, the avant-garde, and twentieth-century popular culture. He is the author of *Modernism, Cultural Production, and the British Avant-Garde* (Cambridge, 2004) and the coeditor of *Ian Fleming and James Bond: The Cultural Politics of 007* (Indiana University Press, 2005) and *T. E. Hulme and the Question of Modernism* (Ashgate Press, 2006). His favorite Dylan album is *John Wesley Harding*, and he's willing to argue about it: ecomenta@indiana.edu.

PATRICIA A. CUNNINGHAM teaches the history of fashion at The Ohio State University, Columbus, Ohio. Her publications include *Twentieth-Century American Fashion*, edited with Linda Welters (Berg, 2005); *Reforming Women's Fashion: 1850–1920: Politics, Health, and Art* (Kent State University, 2003); *Dress in American Culture*, edited with Susan Lab (Popular

Press, 1993); *Dress and Popular Culture*, edited with Susan Lab (Popular Press, 1991). She sometimes wears Polartec when figure skating, skiing, and playing tennis.

DON CUSIC is the author of fourteen books, including *Man in Black and White: The Lyrics of Johnny Cash*. He is a major scholar of American country music and is currently Professor of Music Business at Belmont University, in Nashville.

RICHARD DANIELS, a medievalist and Associate Professor Emeritus, Oregon State University, has published articles on Chaucer, medieval drama, and the Frankfurt School, as well as poems and short stories. He is working on a series of essays on dialectical thinking in the works of C.L.R. James, Walter Benjamin, Theodor Adorno, and Peter Dale Scott.

PHILIP C. DOLCE is Professor of History and Chair of the Social and Behavioral Science Department at Bergen Community College. He created and hosted the award-winning radio series *Suburbia: The American Dream and Dilemma* and created many television series for the three major networks, including the CBS series *Suburbia: The Promised Land*. He has edited or coedited a number of books including *Cities in Transition* and *Suburbia: The American Dream and Dilemma*. He has received the National Education Association's national award for teaching; the Blackburn Award for Leadership from the American Association of University Administrators; a Garden State Black Journalist Award; a finalist award from the International Film and Television Festival; and a nomination for cable television's highest honor, the ACE Award.

MICHAEL DUNNE, Professor of English at Middle Tennessee State University, is the author of *Metapop: Self-Referentiality in Contemporary American Popular Culture, Hawthorne's Narrative Strategies, Intertextual Encounters in American Fiction, Film, and Popular Culture*, and *American Film Musical Themes and Forms*, as well as of numerous critical articles, including "Fred Astaire as Cultural Allusion" in *Studies in Popular Culture* 16.2 (1994).

SARA LEWIS DUNNE is a professor in the English Department of Middle Tennessee State University. She, with her husband Michael Dunne, is coeditor of *Studies in Popular Culture*. She teaches a broad range of film courses, a class in American Humor, and a class in the Comic Tradition. She has written and published several articles on food in literature and popular culture, most recently on food in *The Sopranos* in *This Thing of Ours: Investigating the Sopranos* and on food as a major element in *Seinfeld* for a collection of essays, which she coedited with David Lavery, titled *Master of Its Domain: Revisiting Seinfeld, TV's Greatest Show*, forthcoming from

Continuum Press. She is presently at work on a book about food and hostility in popular culture.

KATHLEEN L. ENDRES is Distinguished Professor of Communication at the University of Akron. She has written extensively on women, the media, and history. Her books include *Akron Women* (2005), *Rosie the Rubber Worker* (2000), and three edited works.

JOHN P. FERRÉ is a Professor of Communication at the University of Louisville, where he teaches courses on historical, religious, and ethical dimensions of mass media. A past president of the American Journalism Historians Association, he is the author of numerous reviews and articles as well as several books, including *A Social Gospel for Millions: The Religious Bestsellers of Charles Sheldon, Charles Gordon, and Harold Bell Wright* and *Channels of Belief: Religion and American Commercial Television.*

IVÁN FIGUEROA is a graduate of Oklahoma State University with an Ed.D. in Adult Education. His interests are Adult Learning, Multicultural Studies, and Second Language learning. He enjoys music and movies.

DAVID FILLINGIM teaches Religion and Philosophy at Shorter College in Rome, Georgia. He is the author of *Redneck Liberation: Country Music as Theology* (Mercer University Press, 2003) and *Extreme Virtues: Living on the Prophetic Edge* (Herald Press, 2003), and coeditor, with Michael Graves, of *More Than Precious Memories: The Rhetoric of Southern Gospel Music* (Mercer University Press, 2004).

RICHARD R. FLORES is Associate Dean in the College of Liberal Arts and C. B. Smith, Sr., Centennial Chair in U.S.-Mexico Relations at the University of Texas at Austin. He works in the areas of critical theory, performance studies, semiotics, and historical anthropology. He is a native of San Antonio, Texas, and received his B.A. from the University of Notre Dame and Ph.D. from the University of Texas at Austin in 1989. He is the author of *Remembering the Alamo: Memory, Modernity, and the Master Symbol* (University of Texas Press, 2002), *Los Pastores: History and Performance in the Mexican Shepherd's Play of South Texas* (Smithsonian Institution Press, 1995), and editor of Adina De Zavala's, *History and Legends of the Alamo* (Arte Publico Press, 1996). He is married, has three daughters, and even finds time for the garden now and then.

SYLVESTER FRAZIER, JR., is currently a doctoral candidate at the University of Texas-Arlington. He completed an M.A. in English at Lamar University in Beaumont, Texas, with a mixed content thesis of poetry, short stories, and critical analysis, entitled "Songs for People Who Don't Sing." He has presented several conference papers in Sports Literature, including

"Football: The Unofficial Religion of Texas," "I Can Say We: Sports Stadiums as Public Space," and "Tailgating and the Making of Men." His education also includes a B.S. in Business Administration from Florida A&M University and a B.A. in English with a minor in philosophy from Lamar University.

ROBERT FRIEDEL is a professor of history at the University of Maryland, College Park, where he has taught the history of technology and science since 1984. Prior to this he was a historian at the Smithsonian Institution's National Museum of American History and at the Institute of Electrical and Electronics Engineers in New York City. Most of his writings have focused on invention and novelty, including monographs on the development of plastics, the electric light bulb, and the zipper, as well as articles on subjects ranging from aluminum to Teflon. He currently lives in a glass house in the woods outside of Washington, D.C.

ANNA FROULA is a doctoral candidate in the English department at the University of Kentucky in Lexington, Kentucky. When she is not attempting to master the art of homemade pasta, she is writing a dissertation on masculinity and nationalism in American war films. Anna would like to thank Sean Morris for his loving assaults on her tangled prose.

THOMAS A. GREENFIELD is Professor of English and American Studies as well as Lecturer in the School of Performing Arts at SUNY-Geneseo. He is the author of *Work and the Work Ethic in American Drama 1920–1970* and *Radio: A Reference Guide* as well as numerous articles and reviews on mass media, theater and drama, and cultural studies. Periodically he leads student overseas study groups in England and Ireland. In the 1980s he served as Vice Chair of the Federation of State Humanities Councils in Washington, D.C., and Chair of the Kentucky Humanities Council.

SYLVIA GRIDER is Associate Professor of Anthropology at Texas A&M University. She holds a Ph.D. in Folklore from Indiana University. She has published widely on topics ranging from Coke bottles to children's ghost stories to spontaneous shrines to Texas women writers. She raises box turtles, loves basketball, and prefers Bugs Bunny to Mickey Mouse.

JOY HAENLEIN has been the editorial page editor of *The Advocate*, a daily newspaper in Stamford, Connecticut, since 1995. An award-winning editorial and arts writer, she caught the music bug in high school during the mid-1970s while working in a record store that was located just below *Creem* magazine's office in Detroit. She's written record and concert reviews for a number of publications.

ANGELA HAGUE is Professor of English at Middle Tennessee State University, where she teaches courses in modern British literature, popular culture, and mythology. The author of *Iris Murdoch's Comic Vision* and *Fiction, Intuition, and Creativity: Studies in Bronte, James, Woolf, and Lessing*, she co-edited *Deny All Knowledge: Reading the X-Files* and *Teleparody: Predicting/Preventing the Television Discourse of the Future*. She is completing a book on alien abduction.

ANN C. HALL is Professor of English at Ohio Dominican University. She recently served as president of the Midwest Modern Language Association and edited the convention journal on Performance which will appear in the Fall of 2005. She has published widely on drama, film, feminism, and modern literature.

DENNIS HALL is Professor of English at the University of Louisville, where he teaches expository writing, British Literature, and the odd course in popular culture. He is a regular participant in the annual meetings of the Kentucky Philological Association, NCTE's Conference on College Composition and Communication, the Popular and American Culture Associations, and the Popular and American Culture Associations in the South. He is a former editor of *Studies in Popular Culture* and is a regular writer of journal articles, principally on popular culture subjects. He is coeditor (with M. Thomas Inge) of *The Greenwood Guide to American Popular Culture*.

ELIZABETH ARMSTRONG HALL is a writer and popular culture historian specializing in the "odd corners" of U.S. history. She coauthored *The Great American Medicine Show* with David Armstrong (Prentice-Hall, 1991), and has written for general interest and children's magazines. Her work appears in *St. Louis* magazine, *American History*, *National Geographic World*, *Pennsylvania Heritage*, *Cobblestone*, and *AppleSeeds*, and in the *Dictionary of American History* (3rd ed.). She lives in Prince William County, Virginia.

R. MARK HALL is Assistant Professor of Rhetoric, Composition, and Literary Studies at California State University, Chico. He teaches writing, directs the University Writing Center, and writes about composition, literacy, and writing center theory and practice. His essay "The 'Oprahfication' of Literacy: Reading Oprah's Book Club" was published in *College English* 65.6 (July 2003).

SUSAN GROVE HALL has a doctorate in English, has taught creative and expository writing and literature at several universities, and is now an independent scholar. Her publications include poetry, fiction, literary and popular culture criticism, and a history: *Appalachian Ohio and the Civil War, 1862–1863* (McFarland, 2000). Her current research involves poetry by nineteenth-century American women. In her leisure she pursues Americana by quilting, shape-note singing, and playing banjo, harmonica, and knee cymbals in her one-woman street-corner band on election mornings.

GARY HARMON is Professor Emeritus of English and Chair of the Department of World Languages at the University of North Florida in Jacksonville, Florida. His work includes several books and over a hundred papers and articles on American culture and film. He is one of the founders of the Popular and American Culture Associations of the South and has been at various times an officer and board member of both the American Culture Association and the Popular Culture Association. His work on film will result in two forthcoming books: "Film and Gender: Myth, Power, and Change" and "Mythic Film Stars and American Culture."

KARELISA V. HARTIGAN is Professor of Classics at the University of Florida. Her research interests lie in Greek drama, and in the relevance of the ancient world to the modern. Beyond the classroom she is an improv actress with the Arts-in-Medicine program at UF's hospital, and gives port destination lectures for cruise lines.

JUDITH HATCHETT is Professor of English at Midway College, Kentucky's only college for women. She teaches a variety of subjects including women's literature and adolescent literature. Recent research projects have included Pentecostalism in the fiction of Silas House and female Episcopal priests in detective fiction. Other projects have examined women's humor, the challenges of biography, and the fiction of Bobbie Ann Mason, Robert Penn Warren, and Henry James. She is a book reviewer for the *Lexington Herald Leader*.

CHARLES HATFIELD, Assistant Professor of English at California State University, Northridge, specializes in comics, word/image studies, and children's literature. The author of *Alternative Comics: An Emerging Literature* (UP of Mississippi, 2005), he has published widely in comics theory and criticism. Charles is now coediting a collection of essays on American underground comix, and serves on the editorial boards of both the *International Journal of Comic Art* and the online *ImageText: Interdisciplinary Comics Studies*. In addition, he serves on the Executive Committee for the annual International Comic Arts Festival.

DAWN HEINECKEN is Assistant Professor of Women's and Gender Studies at the University of Louisville and is the author of *The Warrior Women of Television: A Feminist Cultural Analysis of the New Female Body in Popular Media* (Peter Lang, 2004). Along with Vickie Rutledge Shields, she has coauthored *Measuring Up: How Advertising Affects Self-Image* (U of Pennsylvania P, 2002), which received the 2004 National Communication Association's Excellence in Visual Communication Research Award. She has published articles on such topics as Christian garage bands, professional wrestling, as well as TV shows like *Buffy the Vampire Slayer* and *La Femme Nikita*. She received her Ph.D. in American Culture Studies from Bowling

Green State University; and her teaching includes courses in Women, Media and Culture; Gender and Children's Literature; and The Body in Popular Media.

MARGOT A. HENRIKSEN is an associate professor in the Department of History at the University of Hawaii at Manoa in Honolulu. Her research and teaching interests focus on the cultural history of post–World War II America. She explored the revolutionary cultural impact of the atomic bomb in *Dr. Strangelove's America: Society and Culture in the Atomic Age* (Berkeley, 1997), and she is currently at work on a history of the 1950s for Rowman & Littlefield's American Thought and Culture Series; the volume is tentatively titled "Fear and Loathing in the Fifties." She teaches undergraduate courses such as American Television History and Viva Las Vegas! and graduate seminars organized around the themes of murder and cultural mayhem, which relate to her ongoing book project on "lethal women."

MICKEY HESS earned his Ph.D. in rhetoric and composition at the University of Louisville, writing a dissertation on hip hop's rhetoric of realness. His articles and stories have been published in *Popular Music and Society, Computers and Composition, Composition Studies*, and *Created in Darkness by Troubled Americans: Best of McSweeney's Humor Category*. He teaches writing at Indiana University Southeast.

TOM HOLM is Professor of American Indian Studies and a founder of that program at the University of Arizona in Tuscon. His *Strong Hearts, Wounded Souls: The Native American Veterans of the Vietnam War* (1996) was a finalist for the Victor Turner Prize in ethnographic writing, and his *The Great Confusion in Indian Affairs: Native American and White in the Progressive Era* was published by the University of Texas Press in 2005. A Cherokee-Muskogee Creek from Oklahoma, Professor Holm has served on numerous Native American boards, panels, and working groups. He is a Marine Corps veteran of the Vietnam War and active in veterans' affairs.

ROBERT HOLTZCLAW is Professor of English and advisor for the Film Studies minor at Middle Tennessee State University. He has published articles and essays on film history, adaptations (including *Tom Jones* and *Fanny Hill*) and other film topics as well as presenting many papers at regional and national conferences.

J. BLAINE HUDSON is Professor of Pan-African Studies and dean of Arts and Sciences at the University of Louisville. He has published numerous articles and *Fugitive Slaves and the Underground Railroad in the Kentucky Borderland* (2002). He was Consulting Editor of the *Encyclopedia of Louisville* (2001) and his *Encyclopedia of Fugitive Slaves and the Underground Railroad* is scheduled for publication in 2006. He has served as chair of the Kentucky African American Heritage Commission since 1999 and was appointed chair of the Kentucky State Advisory Committee to the U.S. Commission on Civil Rights in 2005.

BARBARA S. HUGENBERG is an assistant professor in the Department of Communication Studies at Kent State University. She has made numerous presentations during recent conventions of the Popular Culture Association based on her observations at NASCAR races. She is coauthor of a forthcoming article on NASCAR fans in the *Journal of Popular Culture*. Her doctoral dissertation was an ethnographic study of Cleveland Browns' fans upon the return of the team to the National Football League in 1999. Her research interests include organizational cultural studies, critical studies, and popular culture.

LAWRENCE W. HUGENBERG is Professor of Communication Studies in the Department of Communication and Theater at Youngstown State University. He has given numerous presentations during recent conventions of the Popular Culture Association on NASCAR fans, James Bond movies, the Extreme Football League (XFL), and the World Wrestling Organization. He is coauthor of a forthcoming article on NASCAR fans in the *Journal of Popular Culture*.

M. THOMAS INGE is the Blackwell Professor of Humanities at Randolph-Macon College in Ashland, Virginia, where he teaches and writes about American culture, humor, film, animation, and Southern literature. His publications on comic art include *Comics as Culture* (1990) and *Charles M. Schulz: Conversations* (2001). He coedited with Dennis Hall the four-volume reference work *The Greenwood Guide to American Popular Culture* (2002), and he is editor of the journal *Studies in American Humor*. As much as he enjoys teaching, he still regrets not having become a comic strip artist.

MARY JOHNSON has been covering the U.S. disability rights movement since the 1980s, as editor of *The Disability Rag* magazine and now *Ragged Edge Magazine Online*. She is the author of the book *Make Them Go Away: Clint Eastwood, Christopher Reeve and the Case Against Disability Rights* (Advocado Press, 2003).

RICKY L. JONES is Associate Professor and Chair of the Pan-African Studies Department at the University of Louisville. He is a graduate of Morehouse College, the alma mater of Martin Luther King, Jr. In addition to his lifelong addiction to American political and historical studies, he is still a hopeless sci-fi fanatic living by the mantra of Paul Maud' Dib from Frank Herbert's *Dune* series, "Long live the fighters!"

DANIEL S. KERR, in a kind of Thoreauvian experiment in simple living, lives in the much manicured nature of a Kansas state park, snug inside a small fifth-wheel travel trailer. He has written as a journalist in communities across the United States and abroad. Currently he works as a lecturer in English while pursuing a doctoral degree in American Studies, with a concentration in Great Plains culture and environment, at the University of Kansas at Lawrence.

ELAINE A. KING is Professor of the History of Art and Theory at Carnegie Mellon University. She is the former Executive Director and Curator of the Contemporary Art Center in Cincinnati, as well as the Carnegie Mellon Art Gallery. In 2000 she was a Senior Research Fellow at the Smithsonian Institution working at the National Gallery of American Art, doing a research project titled Portraiture in the USA: 1965–2000. In 2001 she was awarded an IREX grant to examine contemporary art and culture in Prague, as well as a Short-Term Research fellowship at the national Portrait Gallery. In 2003 she was American Curator for the Master of Graphic Arts Biennial, in Gyor, Hungary. Currently, she is coauthoring *Ethics in the Visual Arts* with Gail Levin, and writing a book titled *Facing America: Portraits 1960– Now!*

JASON R. KIRBY is an instructor in the History Department at the University of South Carolina at Aiken. His M.A. thesis at the University of South Carolina was "General William C. Westmoreland and African American Troops: A Varied Legacy in Race Relations," which he is preparing for publication. He plans to begin Ph.D. studies in history in 2005. He also referees basketball and umpires baseball games in their seasons about twenty hours a week.

WILLIAM R. KLINK is Professor of English at the College of Southern Maryland, La Plata, Maryland, where he has taught for more than three decades. He is the author or presenter of more than 100 articles on literature, history, and popular culture. He is the current President of the Popular Culture Association in the South. And he has been known to take a drink in a sports bar, strictly for research purposes.

BENNETT KRAVITZ teaches American studies and popular culture in the Department of English Language and Literature at the University of Haifa. He is currently working on a book-length manuscript that examines the connections between culture and disease in popular culture and literary settings, and has published a number of relevant articles. He also has a great interest in and regularly teaches courses on African American literature, which is especially popular among minority student groups at his university.

DAVID LAVERY is Professor of English at Middle Tennessee State University and the author of over ninety published essays and reviews and author/ editor/coeditor of eleven books, including *Full of Secrets: Critical Approaches to* Twin Peaks and *Reading* The Sopranos: *Hit TV from HBO.* He coedits the e-journal *Slayage: The Online International Journal of* Buffy *Studies* and is one of the founding editors of the new journal *Critical Studies in Television: Scholarly Studies of Small Screen Fictions.*

DAVID MAGILL is Assistant Professor of English at the University of Pittsburgh at Johnstown, where he teaches courses in American and African American literature and culture. He is currently completing his manuscript "Modern Masculinities: Modernist Nostalgia and Jazz Age White Manhood," which examines the production of white masculinities in the 1920s United States. He has presented several papers on race and masculinity at such conferences as the Modernist Studies Association, American Studies Association, Modern Language Association, and American Culture Association. He is an avid New York Mets fan and cinema devotee.

REGINALD MARTIN is Professor of Composition and Coordinator of African American Literature Programs at the University of Memphis. His publications include *Erotique Noire* (1991), *Dark Eros* (1997), and the blues novel *Everybody Knows What Time It Is* (2001). He is editor of *A Deeper Shade of Sex: The Best in Black Erotic Writing* (Blue Moon, 2006). He plays blues guitar for his own benefit late at night.

RICHARD N. MASTELLER has a Ph.D. in American Studies from the University of Minnesota, and is a professor of English at Whitman College. In addition to teaching history of photography in the Department of Art History and Visual Culture Studies, he has organized exhibitions of photography and of graphic art, including *Auto As Icon, Seeing Through Photography*, and *We the People? Satiric Prints of the 1930s.* His other publications include a bibliographical essay on photography as popular culture and essays related to various aspects of visual culture, including western stereographs, the modernism of Constantin Brancusi, the satiric vision of Reginald Marsh and John Dos Passos, and the "Masters of American Photography" stamp series published by the U.S. Postal Service.

KEN S. McALLISTER codirects the Learning Games Initiative, an interinstitutional, interdisciplinary research collective that studies, teaches with, and builds computer games. His book *Game Work: Language, Power, and Computer Game Culture* was recently published by the University of Alabama Press.

RANDY D. McBEE is Associate Professor of History at Texas Tech University, where he teaches courses in U.S. immigration and urban history and recent U.S. history. He is currently working on a history of motorcyclists and bikers since the end of World War II. He lives with his wife and two children in Lubbock, Texas.

PATRICK McGREEVY is Professor and Chair of the Department of An-thropology, Geography and Earth Science at Clarion University. He is the author of *Imagining Niagara: Meaning and the Making of Niagara Falls* (1994) and numerous articles on American and Canadian identity, the Erie Canal, and cultural geography. He served as Fulbright Chair of American Studies at the University of Debrecen, Hungary, in 1999–2000. He enjoys getting lost, especially in cities, and playing the accordion.

NICHOLAS MERIWETHER was educated at Princeton and Cambridge, where his doctoral work focused on the idea of bohemianism in U.S. history and in the Haight-Ashbury in the 1960s. He has written scholarly articles on South Carolina history as well as published several short stories, although he is probably proudest of the lyrics he has had recorded by two rock bands. The editor of two volumes of academic essays on the Grateful Dead, he has written widely on rock music history and served as the researcher for Dennis McNally's authorized history of the Grateful Dead.

THOMAS J. MICKEY since 1989 has been Professor of Communication Studies at Bridgewater State College in Bridgewater, Massachusetts, where he teaches public relations and public relations writing. He has written two books and presents regularly at conferences. He is a Master Gardener for the state of New Hampshire, and writes the garden column for two New England newspapers. In his spare time he is working on a Graduate Certificate in Landscape Design from Harvard. He is a member of the Garden Writers Association and the Association for Professional Landscape Designers.

ARTHUR H. MILLER is Archivist and Librarian for Special Collections, Donnelley and Lee Library, Lake Forest College, and a director of the Board of the Center for Railroad Photography and Art. The Lake Forest library's railroad collection serves as the archive of the Center, and it hosts the Cen-ter's annual photography conference in March. Miller has a Ph.D. in English (American Literature) from Northwestern University and is the author of the article on "Trains and Railroading" for *The Greenwood Guide to American Popular Culure* (1988 and later editions).

P. ANDREW MILLER is an assistant professor at Northern Kentucky Uni-versity. He has published articles on the X-Men and *Buffy the Vampire Slayer*. He is also a fiction writer and a poet, with works appearing in the *MacGuffin, Sword and Sorceress* numbers 13 and 19, and many others. His current research interests include looking at the portrayal of gays and lesbians in superhero comics—in other words, a queer eye on the caped guy.

R. H. MILLER is Emeritus Professor of English at the University of Louis-ville, where he continues to teach while he pursues his interests in reading, writing, fly fishing, and bird hunting. His most recent book is a memoir of growing up with deaf parents, *Deaf Hearing Boy* (Gallaudet University Press, 2004).

LAWRENCE E. MINTZ is Associate Professor of American Studies and the director of the Art Gliner Center for Humor Studies at the University of Maryland. His publications include *Humor in America* (Greenwood Press, 1988) and numerous articles, book chapters, reviews, and conference papers, nearly all of which deal with humor or popular culture. Most recently he has been working on tourism and themed environments.

WENDY MOON is a Lecturer for the Engineering Writing Program at the University of Southern California Viterbi School of Engineering. She holds an M.A. in Theology from Franciscan University of Steubenville and an M.A. in Professional Writing from USC. She is a regular contributor to *Motorcycle Consumer News* where she specializes in investigative reports. Moon is also a comanaging editor of the *International Journal of Motorcycle Studies* and presents work on motorcycle issues across the country. She is the screenwriter for the forthcoming film *She-Devils on Wheels* and a first and second round judge for the prestigious Nicholl Screenwriting Fellowship through the Academy of Motion Picture Arts.

ANTHONY O'KEEFFE is a distinguished Irishman and Professor of English at Bellarmine University, Louisville, Kentucky. His central academic interest is autobiography, particularly autobiographies written by scientists.

DAVID RAY PAPKE earned his J.D. from the Yale Law School and his Ph.D. in American Studies from the University of Michigan. He is currently Professor of Law at Marquette University, where he teaches Property Law, Family Law, American Legal History, and a range of seminars exploring the interrelationships of law and the humanities. His two most recent books are *Heretics in the Temple: Americans Who Reject the Nation's Legal Faith* (1998) and *The Pullman Case: The Clash of Labor and Capital in Industrial America* (1999), and he has a continuing scholarly interest in the role of law in American culture.

DIANE PECKNOLD is a Postdoctoral Teaching Scholar at the Commonwealth Center for the Humanities at the University of Louisville, where she teaches courses in women's and gender studies and popular music. She is coeditor of *A Boy Named Sue: Gender and Country Music*, and is at work on a book about the Nashville Sound, as well as a reader of primary sources on popular music in the twentieth century.

SUSANA PEREA-FOX is a graduate of the University of Oklahoma with a Ph.D. in Hispanic-American literature, with a minor in Anthropology and a Certificate in Latin-American Studies. She has published poetry and short stories. She is currently working on a short novel, and doing research on the legends and myths of the Mapuche Indians of Neuquen, Argentina.

THOMAS PIONTEK is Visiting Assistant Professor of English at Otterbein College in Westerville, Ohio. His scholarly interests include gender and sexuality studies, film, and American literature. He has written articles and book chapters on American culture, representations of AIDS, and pedagogy which have been published in such journals as *Discourse, Concerns*, and the *Journal of Homosexuality*, as well as in several recent anthologies. His book *Queering Gay and Lesbian Studies* (University of Illinois Press, 2006) contains a chapter that extends the analysis of Stonewall presented in this volume.

GEORGE PLASKETES is Professor of Radio-Television-Film in the Department of Communication and Journalism at Auburn University in Alabama. He is author of *Images of Elvis Presley in American Culture 1977–1997: The Mystery Terrain* (The Haworth Press, 1997), *True Disbelievers: The Elvis Contagion* (with R. Serge Denisoff, Transaction Press 1995), and numerous journal articles on popular culture, music, television, and film. He is an editorial board member and discography editor for *Popular Music and Society*. He is currently considering seeking a writing therapist to treat his alliteration addiction. His wife Julie, daughter Anais, and son Rivers treat him like a king, though they aren't too crazy about Elvis.

MICHAEL PROKOPOW holds a Ph.D. in American history from Harvard University. Currently he is a professor of history at Ryerson University in Toronto where he teaches courses in North American material culture and in design history and theory. He is also the curator at the Design Exchange, Canada's only design center and musuem of post-1945 design. He is (slowly) working on a book on the meanings of domestic style in North America in the period between 1945 and 1970. He has never met a thrift store he did not like.

ROBERT T. RHODE was raised on a farm in northwest Indiana. He holds a Ph.D. in English from Indiana University and has taught for twenty-five years at Northern Kentucky University. His specialties include William Dean Howells, Edgar Allan Poe, Walt Whitman, the cultures of small towns and rural areas, and the steam-power era in literature and history. He is the author of *The Harvest Story: Recollections of Old-Time Threshermen* (Purdue University Press, 2001) and *Classic American Steamrollers* (with Judge Raymond L. Drake) (Iconografix, 2001). The former book was nominated for the Theodore Saloutos prize, given for the best new book in agricultural history. The latter won the Silver Jubilee Certificate presented by the international Road Roller Association. He has contributed an invited chapter to *Black Earth and Ivory Tower*, an anthology of essays by academic authors having backgrounds in farming. He has also published seventeen refereed articles; twenty articles in edited journals; ninety-three articles in magazines covering the subject of agricultural history and literature; and over twenty poems in refereed journals. He is the owner of a steam traction engine built by the J. I. Case Threshing Machine Company in 1923, which he runs at shows devoted to the display of vintage agricultural machines.

BRENDAN RILEY teaches Composition and New Media Studies in the English Department at Columbia College Chicago. His research explores writing, cinema, the Internet, and electracy (the emerging digital age). In his spare time, Brendan reads lots of novels and comics, watches too much TV, and hangs out with Jenny, his favorite person and, conveniently, his wife; bucking demographic trends, they watch *Murder, She Wrote* avidly.

LUCY ROLLIN is Professor Emeritus of English at Clemson University, where she taught Children's and Adolescent Literature. She has written on various popular culture topics, including nursery rhymes, fairy tales, Pinocchio, and Mickey Mouse. She published *Twentieth Century Teen Culture, by the Decades* (Greenwood 1999) and coedited with Charles H. Frey *Classics of Young Adult Literature* (Prentice-Hall 2004). Since her early teens, she has longed (unsuccessfully) to look like Audrey Hepburn.

ROGER B. ROLLIN is William James Lemon Professor of Literature Emeritus, Clemson University. During his thirty-six-year academic career his special interests were seventeenth-century British Literature and Popular Culture Studies. His most recent article was on humor in the poetry of John Milton. In 2006 an aviation article of his will be published in the British magazine, *Aeroplane*.

JUDD ETHAN RUGGILL codirects the Learning Games Initiative, an interinstitutional, interdisciplinary research collective that studies, teaches with, and builds computer games. His dissertation, "Licensed to Shill: How Video and Computer Games Tarnished the Silver Screen," is currently being revised for publication.

KENNETH M. SANDERSON and his wife LAURA KENNEDY are partners in Kennedy & Sanderson Editorial Services in Oakland, California. Laura is a writer and editor who has worked in the fields of publishing and psychotherapy over the last twenty years. Ken is retired after a career at the Mark Twain Project at the University of California, Berkeley. He is assistant editor or coeditor of *Mark Twain: The Critical Heritage* (1971), *Mark Twain's Fables of Man* (1972), *Mark Twain's Notebooks and Journals, Vol. 1, 1855–1873* (1975), and *Mark Twain's Letters, Vol. 1, 1853–1866* (1988), and is a contributing editor to other volumes in the Project's two series, *The Mark Twain Papers* and *The Works of Mark Twain*. He enjoys walking in cities, on beaches, and across bridges. It would comfort his very liver to know what Mark Twain and Robert Louis Stevenson chatted about while sitting together on a bench in Washington Square, New York City, one sunny afternoon in April 1888, but no one knows. Laura gardens enthusiastically, and is, believe it or not, learning to read hands. They are lucky enough to be able to see a tiny bit of the Golden Gate Bridge from their bedroom window.

RICHARD SANZENBACHER is Professor of Humanities at Embry-Riddle University. He has written a textbook, *Connecting the Pieces: The ART of Composing*. He has made many presentations at professional meetings on various aspects of animal culture and is currently working on a monograph on the dog in popular culture.

MICHAEL K. SCHOENECKE teaches film studies at Texas Tech University. He also serves as Executive Director for the Popular Culture Association and the American Culture Association. He has published on such diverse topics as Jack London, architecture, popular music, sports, and film. After shooting back-to-back 78s in a USGA Amateur Qualifier, he decided to spend more time researching the game's rich history.

SHARON SCOTT combines visual art with political research to examine systems of power. Funded by a grant from the Kentucky Foundation for Women, she has been collaborating with Zapatista dollmakers in Chiapas, Mexico. Her continued interest in rebel communities has recently spawned an art installation project for Belfast, Ireland. Exhibiting internationally in museums and nontraditional venues, Scott persistently challenges social, aesthetic, and geographic borders. She has curated at the Woodruff Art Center, written for *Atlanta Magazine*, and researched for ABC Discovery News. She is pursuing a Ph.D. at the University of Louisville and plans to have the spaceship ready by June.

BARRETT SHAW has a Ph.D. in English and American literature from the University of Louisville and has worked in newspapers, magazines, and book publishing and as a freelancer in all aspects of print publication from writing and editing to design and production. During her stint as editor of a national magazine for thoroughbred trainers, a story she assigned and edited won the Eclipse Award for best magazine article on racing. Though horse-crazed since childhood, she wasn't able to get her first till she was past 40 and has been with her current equine partner, Bogi, for eleven years. She's working on a memoir of sorts of her experiences with horses, tentatively titled "How to Fall Off a Horse."

LINDA MARIE SMALL is affiliated with Stepping Stones: Research and Alternative Worker Organization, Tucson, Arizona, and has more than thirty years' experience in rehabilitative medicine working with a variety of populations, etiologies, diagnoses, cultural orientations, and environments. She has completed research in various areas and published results in peer-reviewed journals as well as in more popular venues. She has advanced degrees in medical anthropology and her passionate interests are in rehabilitation, human occupation, quality of life enhancement, marketing, popular culture, and the anthropology of work/well-being.

CLAUDE J. SMITH, long-term member of Popular Culture Association in the South, has presented over twenty papers at its annual conventions and has published several articles, primarily about films and one about the radio show *Car Talk*. Just retired from Florida Community College, where he made numerous television productions, he has made twenty-five trips to London for theater exploration, sings with the Jacksonville Symphony Chorus, and appeared in John Sayles' *Sunshine State*. A current passion is collecting CDs by lesser known but worthy classical composers and improving his taste in fine wine.

JIMMY DEAN SMITH has published articles about World War I poets, habitually lying academics, and the musical tastes of George W. Bush. He lives in Barbourville, Kentucky, with Sharee St. Louis Smith and two of their sons, Brendan and Cullen. His favorite room, which now has nothing but a comfy chair and reading lamp in it, used to belong to his other son, Rion, who has gone off to graduate school. He is happy with what he has got. He teaches English and Communication at Union College in Barbourville, Kentucky.

MICHAEL SMITH teaches in the Writing and Rhetoric program at James Madison University. He holds a B.A. in English from Knox College and an M.F.A. in creative writing from Penn State. As a newspaper reporter, he covered everything from Civil War reenactments to *Fargo*-esque drug kidnappings for the *Gettysburg Times*. He is a regular contributor to the *Antiques Roadshow Insider*, with articles on the Cult of Elvis, Hemingway, Lincoln, Hitchcock, and Mark Twain (in conjunction with Ken Burns' PBS documentary).

RICHARD TAYLOR is Professor of English at Kentucky State University in Frankfort, Kentucky, where he and his wife own Poor Richard's Books. A former Kentucky Poet Laureate (1999–2001), he has published five collections of poetry, a novel (*Girty*), and several books relating to frontier history. He has just completed a novel about Sue Mundy, Kentucky's most notorious guerilla during the Civil War.

HEINZ TSCHACHLER, Associate Professor of English and American Studies at the University of Klagenfurt, Austria, has always been interested in relations between representations and ideologies in American culture. His books in this area include *Ökologie und Arkadien*, a study of ideological uses of "nature," *Lewis Mumford's Reception in German Translation and Criticism*, *Prisoners of the Nominal*, an essay on the disciplinary unconscious of international American Studies, and *Ursula K. Le Guin*, a monograph. He has also edited three books on cultural studies, *Dialog der Texte*, *Experiencing a Foreign Culture*, and *The EmBodyment of American Culture*. More recently, his focus has shifted to discursive constructions of national identity, through the Lewis and Clark expedition and through the U.S. national currency. Whenever his academic pursuits (and duties) leave any time, he works-plays as a track and field coach, runs marathons, rides his mountainbike, or, like every good inhabitant of mountainous (and wintry) areas, freerides his skis. Additionally, he has followed his wife into various of her art projects, such as, most recently, www.granatapfel.com.

THOMAS A. VAN is English Professor Emeritus at the University of Louisville. During his first year of retirement he is teaching English to the Latino workers at Churchill Downs and continuing his work on the Irish in nineteenth-century Britain, with trips to Liverpool, Preston, and Oxford. He will be in a Spanish immersion program in Morelia, Mexico, in January of 2006. His enthusiasms in ranked order are Chopin, the Mediterranean languages, and the plays of Brian Friel.

SCOTT VANDER PLOEG is Professor of Humanities at Madisonville Community College in western Kentucky. When not competing in Magic or Gathering card tournaments, or leading tai chi training sessions, he teaches writing and literature classes and researches English Renaissance poetry, contemporary novels, and popular culture. He has written extensively on science fiction and fantasy literature, and various phenomena of the popular culture: tattoos, role-playing games, cinema. He is the Executive Director of the Kentucky Philological Association.

DAVID L. WEAVER-ZERCHER is Associate Professor of American Religious History and Chair of the Department of Biblical and Religious Studies at Messiah College in Grantham, Pennsylvania. He is author of *The Amish in the American Imagination* (Johns Hopkins University Press, 2001) and editor of *Writing the Amish: The Worlds of John A. Hostetler* (Pennsylvania Sate University Press, 2005).

GEOFFREY WEISS is an assistant professor in the Department of Language and Literature at Mt. Olive College. He has written on Clint Eastwood and visited the birthplaces, homes, or graves of such iconic Americans as Elvis Presley (Memphis), Vincent Price (St. Louis), Randolph Scott (Charlotte, North Carolina), D. W. Griffith (Crestwood, Kentucky), Virgil I. "Gus" Grissom (Mitchell, Indiana), and Frank Lloyd Wright (Oak Park, Illinois). Currently he is working on a book about single screen neighborhood movie theaters and a musical version of Faust. He believes that, be it ever so humble, there's no place like Louisville.

IRA WELLS grew up in Lethbridge, Alberta, Canada, and completed his undergraduate work at the University of Calgary in 2003. He is currently a doctoral student in the Department of English at the University of Toronto. His academic interests focus on representations of masculinity in nineteenth- and twentieth-century American texts, and particularly in the works of Melville, Faulkner, and Cormac McCarthy. He is also an accomplished squash player.

RHONDA WILCOX is Professor of English at Gordon College in Barnesville, Georgia. She has written numerous articles and book chapters on good television, including the chapter on television in the *Greenwood Guide to American Popular Culture* and the "Unreal TV" chapter in *Thinking Outside the Box: A Contemporary Television Genre Reader* (University Press of Kentucky, forthcoming). She is the author of *Why Buffy Matters: The Art of* Buffy the Vampire Slayer (Tauris 2005). With David Lavery, she is the coeditor of *Fighting the Forces: What's at Stake in* Buffy the Vampire Slayer and of *Slayage: The Online International Journal of Buffy Studies* (www.slayage.tv), a refereed quarterly in its fifth year of publication. Her mother, June Lee Tugman Wilcox, has red hair.

CLYDE V. WILLIAMS retired in 2004 from the English faculty at Mississippi State University, where he taught for thirty-six years. During his checkered career he worked on the administrative staff of the National Endowment for the Humanities, from 1974 to 1976; and he worked his way to the B.A. degree at Millsaps College by pounding an Underwood manual as a sports writer for a Jackson, Mississippi, daily.

J. PETER WILLIAMS got his three degrees in English literature from Yale, Columbia, and the University of Michigan. He spent six years at the University of Delaware without publishing, but after he moved to County College of Morris in New Jersey, where he still works, he published numerous poems and several essays and reviews, plus three books on sports journalism, baseball history, and myth in sport. He currently lives in Caldwell, New Jersey, one town away from Tony Soprano.

MARK A. WILSON is the Lewis M. and Marian Senter Nixon Professor of Natural Sciences at the College of Wooster in Ohio. He earned a Ph.D. in paleontology from the University of California, Berkeley, in 1982. He teaches courses in evolution, paleontology, and the history of life, and he has an extensive professional publication record in paleontology and geology. He is also active in the ongoing struggle to keep evolution in the curriculum of American schools.

ROBERT WOLOSIN is Adjunct Associate Professor of Anthropology at the University of Notre Dame, and Research Product Manager at Press Ganey Associates, Inc., of South Bend, Indiana. From 1981 until 2002, he taught in the Family Practice Residency Program at Memorial Hospital of South Bend. Trained as a social psychologist, he has published articles in scholarly works, trade journals, and popular venues. He enjoys biking and is an avid amateur potter.